Oxford Revise

AQA GCSE

FRENCH

Higher

COMPLETE REVISION AND PRACTICE

Sheena Newland

OXFORD
UNIVERSITY PRESS

Contents

Shade in each level of the circle as you feel more confident and ready for your exam.

This book uses a three-step approach to revision: **Knowledge**, **Retrieval** and **Practice**.
It is important that you do all three; they work together to make your revision effective.

⚙ Knowledge

Knowledge comes first. Each chapter starts with a **Knowledge Organiser**. These are clear, easy-to-understand, concise summaries of the content that you need to know for your exam. The vocabulary, grammar and sounds content is organised to cover all the themes in the specification in a logical order so you can see how everything fits together.

Sample answers and guidance on tackling different questions are also provided where appropriate to help you understand what makes a good answer.

⚙ Knowledge GRAMMAR

Adverbs

Forming and using adverbs

- Adverbs are often used with verbs to describe **how** an action is being done, for example 'slowly', 'quickly' or 'easily'. They follow the verb in a sentence:
  Il court lentement. He runs slowly.
- Regular adverbs are usually formed by adding *-ment* to the feminine, singular form of an adjective:
  - *complètement* = completely
  - *parfaitement* = perfectly
  - *régulièrement* = regularly
- Some adverbs are formed by dropping the *-ant(e)* or *-ent(e)* ending from an adjective and adding *-amment* or *-emment* instead. For example:
  - *récent* = recent → *récemment* = recently
  - *suffisant* = sufficient → *suffisamment* = sufficiently
- Some adverbs are completely irregular. These do not have a *-ment* ending and may look quite different to their adjectives. For example: *bien* (well), *mal* (badly) and *vite* (quickly / fast).

Adverbs of time, frequency and place

- Adverbs are also used to describe **where** things happen, as well as **when** and **how often**.
- Adverbs of place include words like *dehors* (outside), *loin* (far) and *près* (near). They usually follow the verb in a sentence.
  Vous habitez ici? Do you live here?
  Regardez là-bas! Look over there!
  Ils sont partout. They are everywhere.
- Adverbs of time and frequency often follow the verb:
  On chante souvent dans un groupe. We often sing in a group.

  However, the following adverbs usually come at the start of a sentence:
  parfois (sometimes), *normalement* (normally), *récemment* (recently), *généralement* (generally).

REMEMBER ❗
The prefixes *in-* and *im-* can also be used with adverbs: *insuffisamment* (insufficiently), *impatiemment* (impatiently).

REVISION TIP 📝
Memorise common adverbial phrases like *l'année dernière* (last year) and *l'année prochaine* (next year) to use in your speaking and writing.

LINK 🔗
See pages 7–8 for more adverbs of time and frequency.

Tu prends toujours le petit-déjeuner? *Do you always have breakfast?*

Généralement, je prends mon petit-déjeuner **assez tôt chaque jour**. Je préfère manger **lentement**. **Avant**, je prenais **souvent** du lait mais **maintenant** je bois **tout le temps** du café. **Parfois**, je dois partir **vite** le matin, mais je peux **toujours** acheter quelque chose **plus tard**.

Generally, I have my breakfast quite early every day. I prefer to eat slowly. Before, I often used to have milk but now I drink coffee all the time. Sometimes, I have to leave quickly in the mornings, but I can always buy something later.

EXAM TIP ✅
Try to include a range of different adverbs in your own speaking and writing to add variety and complexity.

120 Adverbs

REMEMBER ❗
The **Remember** box offers helpful reminders and highlights things to watch out for.

REVISION TIP 📝
Revision tips offer you useful advice and guidance to aid your revision. They help with preparing for each of the four exam papers and with memorising key content.

⚙ Knowledge VOCABULARY

2.2 Customs, festivals and celebrations

Religious customs, festivals and events

Les fêtes religieuses	Religious festivals
À l'Aïd, j'adore donner et recevoir des cadeaux.	At Eid, I love giving and receiving presents.
À Pâques, on va à l'église pour prier Dieu.	At Easter, we go to church to pray to God.
Aller à la synagogue est une tradition familiale.	Going to the synagogue is a family tradition.
Nous allons ensemble à la mosquée.	We go to the mosque together.
Des millions de personnes célèbrent la fête des Lumières.	Millions of people celebrate the Festival of Lights.
Les jours de fête, ma famille va au temple.	My family goes to the temple on festival days.

Les festivals et les événements Festivals and events

On va voir le feu d'artifice.	We are going to see the firework display.
Nous allons assister à **cet événement** français.	We're going to attend this French event.
Cette année, nous regarderons le Tour de France.	This year, we will watch the Tour de France.
Ces gâteaux sont pour la fête des Rois.	These cakes are for the festival of Kings / Twelfth Night.
Ce festival a lieu le 6 janvier.	This festival takes place on 6 January.
Cet été, je vais participer à la Fête de la Musique.	I'm going to take part in the Music Festival this summer.
Pour la fête nationale, il y a toujours des défilés.	There are always parades for Bastille Day.
Je m'intéresse à **ce festival** de cuisine, Goût de France.	I'm interested in this cooking festival, Taste of France.

La fête nationale à Paris Bastille Day in Paris

J'allais à Paris pour la fête nationale quand j'ai rencontré mon ami dans le train. **Nous parlions** encore quand le train est arrivé donc nous sommes allés en ville ensemble. **Tout le monde attendait** le défilé militaire quand nous avons trouvé un bon endroit pour nous arrêter. **Je regardais** les soldats quand le feu d'artifice a commencé. **C'était** formidable!

I was going to Paris for Bastille Day when I met my friend on the train. We were still talking when the train arrived so we went into town together. Everyone was waiting for the military parade when we found a good place to stop. I was watching the soldiers when the firework display started. It was terrific!

GRAMMAR TIP ⭐
To say 'this' or 'these' in French, use the **demonstrative adjectives** *ce* (before a masculine, singular noun), *cette* (before a feminine, singular noun) or *ces* (before a plural noun). *Cet* is used before a masculine noun beginning with a vowel or a silent 'h'.

SOUNDS TIP 🎤
When the letter 'c' is followed by an 'i' or an 'e' in French, it always makes a soft 's' sound rather than a hard 'k' sound. Remember that a 'ç' (with a cedilla accent) also makes an 's' sound. Try saying: *ce, cette, ces, français, leçon, reçois*.

GRAMMAR TIP ⭐
The imperfect tense can be used to describe what you **were** doing or what **was** happening when other events took place. See page 152.

LINK 🔗
The **Link** box directs you to relevant pages to help you make connections between topics.

GRAMMAR TIP ⭐
Grammar tips remind you of key grammatical knowledge and often provide a page reference to the grammar section for more details.

SOUNDS TIP 🎤
Sounds tips support your understanding of how to pronounce different words and sounds in the target language.

Retrieval

The **Retrieval questions** help you learn and quickly recall the information you've acquired. These are short questions and answers about the content in the Knowledge Organiser you have just reviewed. Cover up the answers with some paper and write down as many answers as you can from memory. Refer back to the Knowledge Organiser for any you got wrong, then cover the answers and attempt all the questions again until you can answer *all* the questions correctly.

Make sure you revisit the Retrieval questions on different days to help them stick in your memory. You need to write down the answers each time, or say them out loud, otherwise it won't work.

Previous questions

Most Retrieval pages also have some **Retrieval questions** from **previous topics**. Answer these to see if you can remember the content from the earlier sections. If you get the answers wrong, go back and do the Retrieval questions for the earlier topics again.

Retrieval — VOCABULARY

Answer the questions below. Cover the answers column with a piece of paper and write down as many answers as you can. Check and repeat.

Questions	Answers
1. Answer this question in French: *Quelle est ton émission préférée?*	*Mon émission préférée s'appelle…*
2. List five things you could watch on TV in French.	Possible answers: *un film d'action; la télé-réalité; les pubs; une série; la météo*
3. What do the direct object pronouns *le, la* and *les* mean?	It / him; it / her; them
4. Translate this sentence into English: *Quand j'étais petit(e), je regardais la télé chaque matin.*	When I was little, I used to watch TV every morning
5. What is the name of the tense used to say what you and other people used to do?	The imperfect tense
6. Which verb is the odd one out and why? *diffuser, enregistrer, rire*	*Rire* (to laugh) as *diffuser* (to broadcast) and *enregistrer* (to record) are both things you can do with a programme
7. Translate these phrases into French: for me, with him, without us.	*Pour moi; avec lui; sans nous*
8. Where is *chez eux*?	At their place / house
9. List three words related to clothing in French.	Possible answers: *un manteau / un vêtement / un chapeau / une poche*
10. Translate this question into French: Do you want to go shopping?	Possible answer: *Est-ce que tu veux faire du shopping?*
11. List as many adverbs of frequency as you can in French.	Possible answers: *souvent; toutes les semaines; toujours; normalement; parfois; de temps en temps*
12. Answer this question in French: *Où fais-tu du shopping?*	Possible answer: *Je fais du shopping au centre commercial avec mes amis*

Previous questions

Use these questions to check your knowledge of previous topics.

Questions	Answers
1. Give one advantage and one disadvantage of learning Maths.	Possible answer: *L'avantage, c'est que c'est intéressant mais l'inconvénient, c'est que c'est difficile*
2. What ending do you add to the infinitive of regular *-er* verbs to make the *je* form of the conditional?	*-ais*
3. List five places where you could do sport in French.	Possible answers: *au centre sportif / au stade, à la piscine / sur la plage / au parc / au terrain de jeux*

64 Retrieval

Practice

Once you are confident with the Knowledge Organisers and Retrieval questions, you can move on to the final stage: **Practice**.

Each chapter has **exam-style questions** to help you apply all the knowledge you have learned.

EXAM TIP

Exam tips help you understand different question types, provide guidance on how to answer them, and give advice on how to secure as many marks as possible.

Audio

You can scan the audio QR codes to access the audio for listening and speaking exam-style questions.

Answers and Glossary

You can scan the QR codes to access sample answers and mark schemes, a vocabulary glossary, and further revision support. You can also go to go.oup.com/OR/GCSE/A/MFL/French/H

Practice — EXAM

Theme 1 Listening practice

Section A: Listening comprehension

Relationships

You hear some French exchange students talking about relationships.

What is the opinion of the students on the following aspects?

Write **P** for a **positive** opinion.

   N for a **negative** opinion.

   P+N for a **positive** and **negative** opinion.

EXAM TIP
Listen carefully for positive and negative adjectives and adverbs to help you decide on your answer.

1. Parents [ ] [1 mark]
2. Friends [ ] [1 mark]
3. Partner [ ] [1 mark]
4. Teachers [ ] [1 mark]

A French YouTuber

You hear this online documentary about Maxime, a French YouTuber.

Choose the correct answer and write the letter in each box.

EXAM TIP
You may hear all these options mentioned but only one will be true of Maxime.

Answer both parts of question 5.

5.1 Maxime is a… [1 mark]

A	writer.
B	lawyer.
C	student.	[ ]

5.2 He shared his school resources to… [1 mark]

A	help his friends.
B	support year 12 students.
C	make some money.	[ ]

Answer both parts of question 6.

6.1 Maxime's website… [1 mark]

A	was immediately successful.
B	includes memory games.
C	made him well-known internationally.	[ ]

6.2 Maxime's book… [1 mark]

A	will be written soon.
B	includes well-being advice.
C	is for year 11 students.	[ ]

7. Recently, Maxime announced that he… [1 mark]

A	has left university.
B	is going to travel for a year.
C	will work on a government education project.	[ ]

Practice 49

v

Basics

Numbers

Les chiffres de 1 à 19 / *Numbers from 1 to 19*

Les chiffres de 1 à 19	*Numbers from 1 to 19*
J'ai un frère et une sœur.	*I have one brother and one sister.*
Ça coûte deux / trois euros.	*That costs two / three euros.*
Il y a quatre / cinq personnes ici.	*There are four / five people here.*
Nous avons six / sept / huit semaines de vacances.	*We have six / seven / eight weeks' holiday.*
Mon frère a neuf / dix / onze ans.	*My brother is nine / ten / eleven years old.*
J'ai douze / treize euros.	*I have 12 / 13 euros.*
J'ai quatorze / quinze / seize ans.	*I'm 14 / 15 / 16 years old.*
Ma sœur a dix-sept / dix-huit / dix-neuf ans.	*My sister is 17 / 18 / 19 years old.*

Les chiffres plus grands / *Bigger numbers*

Les chiffres plus grands	*Bigger numbers*
Il y a **vingt-et-un** élèves.	*There are 21 students.*
Je gagne **trente-trois** euros de l'heure.	*I earn 33 euros an hour.*
Nous avons **quarante-cinq** professeurs.	*We have 45 teachers.*
Ma mère a cinquante ans.	*My mother is 50 years old.*
Soixante-quatre euros?	*64 euros?*
Nous avons **soixante-dix** salles de classe.	*We have 70 classrooms.*
Il y a entre **quatre-vingts** et **quatre-vingt-dix** personnes.	*There are between 80 and 90 people.*
Nous sommes cent.	*There are 100 of us.*

SOUNDS TIP 🎤

Get your pronunciation of numbers right to help you say other words which contain the same sound.

*tr**oi**s   m**oi**   f**oi**s*

REMEMBER ❗

Remember to add *-et-un* for 21, 31, 41, 51 and 61. In front of feminine nouns, *un* changes to *une*.

For other numbers in the twenties and thirties, add *-deux*, *-trois*, and so on.

REMEMBER ❗

Numbers in the 70s and 90s work differently. You have to add the French words for 11 to 19 to *soixante* and *quatre-vingts*.

71   *soixante-et-onze*

99   *quatre-vingt-dix-neuf*

Parle-moi de ton collège. *Tell me about your school.*

Mon collège est très grand, avec environ mille cinq cents élèves et **une centaine** de professeurs. Il y a **une dizaine** de bâtiments. Dans chaque classe, il y a entre vingt et trente-deux élèves. Pour ma classe, le premier cours de la journée est toujours dans la même salle. C'est la salle numéro soixante-dix.

My school is very big, with about 1500 pupils and around 100 teachers. There are about 10 buildings. In every class, there are between 20 and 32 pupils. For my class, the first lesson of the day is always in the same room. It's classroom number 70.

REVISION TIP ☑

Try remembering bigger French numbers using a literal English translation or a calculation:

88   *quatre-vingt-huit* 'four twenties eight' (4 × 20 + 8)

GRAMMAR TIP ⭐

Une centaine means 'about 100' and *une dizaine* means 'about 10'.

Times and days of the week

Les heures

Il est une heure.

De deux heures à trois heures dix.

À quatre heures et quart.

À cinq heures vingt-cinq.

Jusqu'à six heures et demie.

Jusqu'à sept heures moins vingt.

À neuf heures moins le quart.

À midi.

À (environ) minuit.

Times

It's one o'clock.

From two o'clock to ten past three.

At quarter past four.

At five twenty-five.

Until half past six.

Until twenty to seven.

At quarter to nine.

At midday.

At (about) midnight.

Les jours de la semaine

On est quel jour de la semaine?

Aujourd'hui, on est lundi / mardi.

À mercredi!

Je vais au cinéma jeudi / vendredi.

Je joue au foot le samedi matin.

Je vais en ville le dimanche après-midi / soir.

Days of the week

Which day of the week is it?

Today it's Monday / Tuesday.

See you on Wednesday!

I'm going to the cinema on Thursday / Friday.

I play football on Saturday mornings.

I go into town on Sunday afternoons / evenings.

> **REMEMBER** !
>
> In France, they use the 24-hour clock.
>
> *Il est vingt-deux heures.* It's 10:00pm.

> **GRAMMAR TIP** ⭐
>
> Use *le* in front of any day of the week when something happens regularly on that day.

Qu'est-ce que tu fais le week-end? *What do you do at (the) weekends?*

Le samedi matin, je joue au foot pendant deux heures. À midi, on mange. **L'après-midi**, je vais toujours en ville et puis, **le soir**, nous sortons de vingt heures jusqu'à environ minuit. Le lendemain, je dors souvent jusqu'à onze heures.

On Saturday mornings, I play football for two hours. At midday, we eat. In the afternoon, I always go into town and then, in the evening, we go out from 8:00pm to about midnight. The next day, I often sleep until 11:00am.

> **GRAMMAR TIP** ⭐
>
> You don't need to add a French word for 'on' or 'in' before the words in bold.

Basics

Months, seasons and time phrases

Les mois de l'année et les saisons	The months of the year and the seasons
Mon anniversaire, c'est le quinze janvier.	*My birthday is on the fifteenth of January.*
Mon mois préféré, c'est février / mars.	*My favourite month is February / March.*
Avril est au printemps.	*April is in spring.*
C'est en mai / juin.	*It's in May / June.*
J'adore l'été, surtout juillet / août.	*I love summer, especially July / August.*
Il va au collège en septembre.	*He's going to secondary school in September.*
L'anniversaire de mon frère, c'est le premier octobre.	*My brother's birthday is on the first of October.*
Novembre est en automne.	*November is in autumn.*
Je fais ça en décembre.	*I do that in December.*
Ma saison préférée, c'est l'hiver.	*My favourite season is winter.*

Quand?	When?
tous les jours	*every day*
chaque soir	*each evening*
toutes les semaines	*every week*
toute la journée / soirée / nuit	*the whole day / evening / night*
une / deux fois par mois / an	*once / twice a month / year*
le week-end dernier	*last weekend*
la semaine dernière	*last week*
l'année prochaine	*next year*

Quel est ton mois préféré? *What is your favourite month?*

Mon mois préféré, c'est le mois de mai parce que j'adore le printemps. En mai, je joue au foot tous les jours, souvent pendant toute la soirée. En plus, le quatorze mai, c'est mon anniversaire. L'année **dernière**, j'ai invité tous mes amis à une fête et l'année **prochaine**, nous allons aller au cinéma ensemble.

My favourite month is the month of May because I love spring. In May, I play football every day, often for the whole evening. Also, 14 May is my birthday. Last year, I invited all my friends to a party, and next year, we are going to go to the cinema together.

REMEMBER ❗

Don't use capital letters for months of the year and days of the week in French.

To say the date in French, use *le* + the number + the month.

For the first of the month, use *le premier* + the month.

REVISION TIP ☑

Practise answering questions on different topics about what you **did** last weekend, last week and last year as well as what you **are going to do** next weekend, next week and next year.

SOUNDS TIP 🎤

The words for 'last' (*dernier / dernière*) and 'next' (*prochain / prochaine*) sound different in their masculine and feminine forms. Practise saying them out loud.

Vocabulary learning

Learn this vocabulary and then use the 'look, cover, write, check' technique to make sure you really know it. Cover the English first and then the French.

Numbers and times

French	✓	English	✓
cent		one hundred	
une centaine		about a hundred	
cinq		five	
cinquante		fifty	
demi(e)		half	
deux		two	
dix		ten	
une dizaine		approximately ten	
douze		twelve	
heure		hour, time	
huit		eight	
midi		midday	
minuit		midnight	
mille		one thousand	
neuf		nine	
onze		eleven	
premier / première		first	
le quart		quarter	
quarante		forty	
quatorze		fourteen	
quatre		four	
quinze		fifteen	
seize		sixteen	
sept		seven	
six		six	
soixante		sixty	
treize		thirteen	
trente		thirty	
trois		three	
un		one	

Other useful words

French	✓	English	✓
vingt		twenty	
avec		with	
avoir		to have	
le bâtiment		building	
le chiffre		figure, number	
la classe		class	
le collège		secondary school	
le cours		lesson	
coûter		to cost	
l'élève (m. / f.)		pupil, student	
entre		between	
environ		about	
l'euro (m.)		euro	
être		to be	
le frère		brother	
gagner		to earn, win	
grand(e)		big, tall, large	
il y a		there is / are	
jusque, jusqu'à		until, to, up to	
même		same, even	
la mère		mother	
le numéro		number	
parler		to speak, talk	
la personne		person	
le professeur		teacher	
la salle		room	
la sœur		sister	
toujours		always	
très		very	
les vacances (f.pl.)		holiday	

Basics

Vocabulary learning

Learn this vocabulary and then use the 'look, cover, write, check' technique to make sure you really know it. Cover the English first and then the French.

Days, months and seasons

French	✓	English	✓
l'an (m.) / l'année (f.)		*year*	
août		*August*	
l'automne (m.)		*autumn*	
avril		*April*	
décembre		*December*	
dimanche		*Sunday*	
l'été (m.)		*summer*	
février		*February*	
l'hiver (m.)		*winter*	
janvier		*January*	
jeudi		*Thursday*	
le jour / la journée		*day*	
juillet		*July*	
juin		*June*	
lundi		*Monday*	
mai		*May*	
mardi		*Tuesday*	
mars		*March*	
mercredi		*Wednesday*	
le mois		*month*	
novembre		*November*	
octobre		*October*	
le printemps		*spring*	
la saison		*season*	
samedi		*Saturday*	
la semaine		*week*	
septembre		*September*	
vendredi		*Friday*	

Other useful vocabulary

French	✓	English	✓
aller		*to go*	
l'ami(e) (m. / f.)		*friend*	
l'anniversaire		*birthday*	
l'après-midi (m.)		*afternoon*	
aujourd'hui		*today*	
chaque		*each, every*	
dernier / dernière		*last*	
dormir		*to sleep*	
en plus		*in addition, also*	
ensemble		*together*	
la fête		*party*	
la fois (une fois)		*time (once)*	
le foot		*football*	
inviter		*to invite*	
jouer		*to play*	
le lendemain		*next day*	
manger		*to eat*	
le matin		*(in the) morning*	
la nuit		*(at) night*	
par		*by, per*	
parce que		*because*	
pendant		*during*	
préféré(e)		*favourite*	
prochain / prochaine		*next*	
puis		*then*	
le soir / la soirée		*evening*	
sortir		*to go out*	
souvent		*often*	
surtout		*especially*	
tout / toute		*all, the whole*	
la ville		*town*	
le week-end		*(at the) weekend*	

> **REVISION TIP** ☑
> Practise using some of the vocabulary above by making up some French sentences about what you normally do and when.

Retrieval

Answer the questions below. Cover the answers column with a piece of paper and write down as many answers as you can. Check and repeat.

Questions

Answers

1 Count out loud from 1 to 30 in French.

Un, deux, trois, quatre, cinq, six… See numbers on page 9 to check your answers

2 How do you say the following numbers in French? 40, 50, 60, 70, 80, 90, 100

Quarante; cinquante; soixante; soixante-dix; quatre-vingts; quatre-vingt-dix; cent

3 How many is *une dizaine*?

About ten

4 What time is this: *Il est midi moins le quart*?

11:45am

5 Write down the days of the week in French.

Lundi; mardi; mercredi; jeudi; vendredi; samedi; dimanche

6 How do you say in French 'morning, afternoon, evening, night'?

Le matin; l'après-midi; le soir; la nuit

7 Say the months of the year in French.

Janvier; février; mars; avril; mai; juin; juillet; août; septembre; octobre; novembre; décembre

8 Which is the odd one out and why? *en hiver / en été / en août*

En août (in August) as the other two are seasons (in winter / in summer)

9 Translate into French: once a month; twice a year.

Une fois par mois; deux fois par an

10 What do *tous les jours* and *toute la journée* mean?

Every day and the whole day

11 How do you say in French 'last weekend, today and next year'?

Le week-end dernier, aujourd'hui et l'année prochaine

12 When is *le mois prochain*?

Next month

Put paper here *Put paper here* *Put paper here* *Put paper here*

REVISION TIP

After testing yourself using retrieval questions, think about which questions you found easy or difficult and why. Make sure you revisit anything you need to learn more thoroughly.

⚙ Knowledge

Basics

Asking questions

Les questions

Est-ce que tu aimes le français?	*Do you like French?*
Pourquoi? Pourquoi pas?	*Why? Why not?*
Quand vas-tu au cinéma?	*When do you go to the cinema?*
Qui est ton / ta meilleur(e) ami(e)?	*Who is your best friend?*
Que fais-tu le week-end?	*What do you do at (the) weekends?*
Où est ta sœur?	*Where is your sister?*
Quelle est ta couleur préférée?	*Which is your favourite colour?*
Tu as combien de frères?	*How many brothers do you have?*
Comment vas-tu au collège?	*How do you get to school?*
C'est quoi?	*What is it?*

J'ai une question pour toi

I have a question for you

Que fais-tu pendant ton temps libre?	*What do you do in your free time?*
Quel est ton passe-temps préféré?	*Which is your favourite hobby?*
Qu'est-ce que tu fais?	*What are you doing?*
Aimes-tu le collège?	*Do you like school?*
Combien de temps passes-tu en ligne par jour?	*How long do you spend online per day?*
Où vas-tu en vacances?	*Where do you go on holiday?*
Comment préfères-tu regarder des films?	*How do you prefer to watch films?*

Quelques questions *Some questions*

Je voudrais te poser **qu**el**qu**es **qu**estions. **Qu**elle est ton opinion sur le cinéma et **qu**'est-ce **qu**e tu penses des stars? **Qu**and est-ce **qu**e tu regardes des films et avec **qu**i?

I would like to ask you some questions. What is your opinion of the cinema and what do you think of stars? When do you watch films and with whom?

GRAMMAR TIP ★

You can use *est-ce que / qu'…* in front of any statement to turn it into a question. You can also add a question word at the start:

Pourquoi est-ce que tu aimes le français? Why do you like French?

GRAMMAR TIP ★

You can also form questions using the structure: **Question word + verb + subject.**

REMEMBER ❗

Quel / quelle / quels / quelles (which) needs to agree with the noun that follows it. Other question words do not change.

GRAMMAR TIP ★

You can also use the upwards intonation of your voice to make any sentence into a question.

Tu aimes le foot? Do you like football?

SOUNDS TIP 🎤

The *qu* sound in French is a hard sound a bit like an English 'k'. Practise reading the text on the left aloud.

Giving opinions

Les opinions et les raisons

J'adore les plantes.

J'aime beaucoup le beau paysage.

Je n'aime pas (du tout) le foot.

Je déteste ça car c'est affreux.

Je préfère le mercredi puisqu'on a un cours de français.

Je ne supporte pas le racisme.

Je trouve ça (assez) intéressant.

Je pense que c'est (très) embêtant.

Je crois que le problème, c'est le coût.

À mon avis, c'est (extrêmement) joli.

Pour moi, c'est (vraiment) étonnant.

À mon avis, c'est un peu inquiétant.

Cela me semble génial.

Opinions and reasons

I love plants.

I like the beautiful scenery a lot.

I don't like football (at all).

I hate that because it's awful.

I prefer Wednesdays as we have a French lesson.

I don't put up with racism.

I find that (quite) interesting.

I think that it is (very) annoying.

I believe that the problem is the cost.

In my opinion, it's (extremely) pretty.

For me, it's (really) amazing / surprising.

In my opinion, it's a bit worrying.

It seems brilliant to me.

Quels sont les avantages / inconvénients?

L'avantage, c'est les vacances.

L'inconvénient, c'est l'heure.

Le mieux, c'est que c'est facile.

Le pire, c'est que c'est cher.

Je suis pour / contre les changements.

What are the advantages / disadvantages?

The advantage is the holidays.

The disadvantage is the time.

The best thing is that it's easy.

The worst thing is that it's expensive.

I am for / against the changes.

GRAMMAR TIP ⭐

When giving opinions of things, remember to use *le / la / les* before the French noun, even when this isn't needed in English.

REVISION TIP 🗓

Using a range of structures to give opinions is a good way to show variety in your language.

Que penses-tu du sport? *What do you think of sport?*

Je déteste le sport parce que je pense que c'est nul. Je n'aime pas du tout le foot au collège. Je crois que le problème, c'est l'équipe. **Je trouve les cours très embêtants** et je préfère les passe-temps en ligne.

I hate sport because I think that it's rubbish. I don't like football at school at all. I think that the problem is the team. I find the lessons very annoying and I prefer hobbies online.

REMEMBER ❗

If you use the structure **Je trouve + noun + adjective**, then the adjective must agree with the noun.

Basics

Useful verbs in different time frames

Décris-moi...	***Describe to me...***
C'était passionnant.	*It was exciting.*
C'est très ennuyeux.	*It's very boring.*
Ça va être difficile.	*It's going to be difficult.*
Ce sera facile.	*It will be easy.*
Ce serait génial.	*It would be great.*
Il y avait beaucoup d'élèves.	*There were a lot of pupils.*
Il y a des avantages.	*There are advantages.*
Il y aura des cadeaux.	*There will be presents.*
Il y aurait un jardin.	*There would be a garden.*

> **GRAMMAR TIP** ★
> Always use the masculine singular form of the adjective after *c'était, c'est, ça va être, ce sera* and *ce serait*.

Dix verbes utiles au présent — ***Ten useful verbs in the present tense***

J'ai un nouveau vélo.	*I have a new bike.*
Je suis content(e).	*I am pleased / happy.*
Je joue au foot.	*I play football.*
J'écoute de la musique.	*I listen to music.*
Je regarde un film.	*I watch a film.*
Je fais du vélo.	*I do cycling. / I ride a bike.*
Je vais au collège.	*I go to school.*
Je mange un peu de tout.	*I eat a bit of everything.*
Je bois du café.	*I drink coffee.*
J'achète un cadeau.	*I buy / I'm buying a present.*

> **GRAMMAR TIP** ★
> Make sure you can use all the different forms of the verb, not just the *je* forms. See pages 144–149 to revise present tense verbs.

Que fais-tu chez toi le soir?　*What do you do at home in the evenings?*

Normalement, en hiver, j'écoute de la musique en ligne ou je regarde un film avec mon frère. Cependant, c'est un peu ennuyeux. En été, je fais du vélo chaque soir avec mon meilleur ami et c'est génial. Je suis content parce que j'ai un nouveau vélo.

Normally, in the winter, I listen to music online or I watch a film with my brother. However, it's a bit boring. In the summer, I go cycling every evening with my best friend and it's great. I'm happy because I have a new bike.

> **REVISION TIP** ☑
> When talking about any activity, develop your answers by adding **who** you do it with, **when**, **where** and **why**.

Dix verbes utiles au passé composé

Ten useful verbs in the perfect tense

J'ai eu un problème.	*I had a problem.*
Je suis allé à Londres.	*I have been to London.*
J'ai joué au tennis.	*I played tennis.*
J'ai écouté la radio.	*I listened to the radio.*
J'ai regardé un bon film.	*I watched a good film.*
J'ai fait des efforts.	*I made an effort.*
Je suis allé(e) en ville.	*I went to town.*
J'ai mangé une pizza.	*I ate a pizza.*
J'ai bu un café.	*I drank a coffee.*
J'ai acheté une plante.	*I bought a plant.*

GRAMMAR TIP ⭐

See pages 150–151 to revise perfect tense verbs. Remember that *je suis allé(e)* (I went) is the odd one out in this list as it doesn't start with *j'ai*.

Dix verbes utiles au futur proche

Ten useful verbs in the near future tense

Je vais avoir du temps libre.	*I'm going to have some free time.*
Je vais être célèbre.	*I'm going to be famous.*
Je vais jouer pour l'Angleterre.	*I'm going to play for England.*
Je vais écouter ma mère.	*I'm going to listen to my mother.*
Je vais regarder le match.	*I'm going to watch the match.*
Je vais faire ça samedi.	*I'm going to do that on Saturday.*
Je vais aller au cinéma.	*I'm going to go to the cinema.*
Je vais manger en ville.	*I'm going to eat in town.*
Je vais boire du lait.	*I'm going to drink some milk.*
Je vais acheter un livre.	*I'm going to buy a book.*

GRAMMAR TIP ⭐

The near future tense is easy to form, with *je vais* **+ infinitive**. You can also use the simple future tense, for example: *Je mangerai* (I will eat). See page 154 to revise verbs in both future tenses.

Mes activités en ville *My activities in town*

Hier, je suis allé en ville et j'ai acheté un livre. Ensuite, j'ai bu un café avec ma mère, ce qui était sympa. Demain, je vais aller au cinéma avec mes amis et je pense que ce sera génial. **Je voudrais manger** dans un café mais c'est souvent trop cher.

Yesterday, I went into town and I bought a book. Next, I drank a coffee with my mum, which was nice. Tomorrow, I'm going to go to the cinema with my friends and I think that it will be great. I would like to eat in a café but it is often too expensive.

GRAMMAR TIP ⭐

You can use *je voudrais* + **infinitive** to say what you **would like** to do.

Learn this vocabulary and then use the 'look, cover, write, check' technique to make sure you really know it. Cover the English first and then the French.

Question words

French	✓	English	✓
combien		*how many / much*	
comment		*how*	
où		*where*	
pourquoi (pas)		*why (not)*	
quand		*when*	
que		*what*	
quel(le)		*which*	
qui		*who*	
quoi		*what*	
acheter		*to buy*	
adorer		*to love*	
aimer		*to like, love*	

> **REVISION TIP**
>
> Practise forming some questions in French using the question words above. For more support, you could adapt some of the questions on page 12.

Useful verbs

French	✓	English	✓
aller		*to go*	
avoir		*to have*	
boire		*to drink*	
croire		*to believe*	
détester		*to hate*	
écouter		*to listen (to)*	
être		*to be*	
faire		*to do / make*	
jouer		*to play*	
manger		*to eat*	
penser		*to think*	
préférer		*to prefer*	
regarder		*to watch, look at*	
sembler		*to seem*	
supporter		*to tolerate, bear, put up with*	
trouver		*to find*	

More opinions and reasons

French	✓	English	✓
l'avantage (m.)		*advantage*	
l'avis (m.)		*opinion*	
beaucoup		*a lot*	
car		*because, for*	
contre		*against*	
l'inconvénient (m.)		*disadvantage*	
le mieux		*the best (thing)*	
l'opinion (f.)		*opinion*	
le pire		*the worst (thing)*	
pour		*for*	
le problème		*problem*	
puisque		*as, because*	
la raison		*reason*	

Descriptions in different time frames

French	✓	English	✓
c'est		*it is*	
c'était		*it was*	
ce sera		*it will be*	
ce serait		*it would be*	
ça va être		*it's going to be*	
demain		*tomorrow*	
ensuite		*next*	
hier		*yesterday*	
il y a		*there is / are*	
il y aura		*there will be*	
il y aurait		*there would be*	
il y avait		*there was / were*	
normalement		*normally*	

Vocabulary learning

Useful adjectives and qualifiers / intensifiers

French	✓	English	✓
affreux / affreuse		awful	
assez		quite	
beau / belle		beautiful	
bon(ne)		good	
célèbre		famous	
cher / chère		expensive	
content(e)		glad, pleased	
difficile		difficult	
embêtant(e)		annoying	
ennuyeux / ennuyeuse		boring	
étonnant(e)		surprising, amazing	
extrêmement		extremely	
facile		easy	
génial(e)		great	
inquiétant(e)		worrying	
intéressant(e)		interesting	
joli(e)		pretty	
nouveau / nouvelle		new	
passionnant(e)		exciting	
sympa / sympathique		nice, kind	
trop		too, too much, too many	
un peu		a bit, a little	
vraiment		really	
l'Angleterre (f.)		England	
le cadeau		present	

Other useful words

French	✓	English	✓
le café		café, coffee	
le changement		change	
la couleur		colour	
le coût		cost	
décrire		to describe	
l'effort (m.)		effort	
en ligne		online	
l'équipe (f.)		team	
le film		film	
le français		French	
le jardin		garden	
le lait		milk	
libre		free	
le livre		book	
Londres		London	
meilleur(e)		best, better	
la musique		music	
passer		to spend	
le passe-temps		hobby	
le paysage		scenery	
la plante		plant	
poser		to ask, put	
quelque		some	
la question		question	
le racisme		racism	
la star		star	
le temps		time	
le vélo		bike	
je voudrais		I would like to	

REVISION TIP

Practise describing things in different time frames. Make sure you have a bank of positive and negative adjectives that you can use across different topics.

Answer the questions below. Cover the answers column with a piece of paper and write down as many answers as you can. Check and repeat.

Questions	Answers
1 Say the French question words for 'what', 'where', 'when', 'who' and 'why'.	*Que / Quoi / Qu'est-ce que*; *où*; *quand*; *qui*; *pourquoi*
2 What do you need to remember to do with the question word *quel*?	Make sure it agrees with the noun that follows it (*quel / quelle / quels / quelles*)
3 Give three ways to introduce your opinion in French (e.g. in my opinion, I think that, for me).	*À mon avis*; *je pense que*; *pour moi*
4 How do you say 'the best thing' and 'the worst thing' in French?	*Le mieux* – the best thing; *le pire* – the worst thing
5 Give three positive and three negative adjectives in French.	Possible answers: *facile*; *génial*; *sympa / cher*; *difficile*; *ennuyeux*
6 Translate into French: it was, it is, it will be.	*C'était, c'est, ce sera*
7 Which tense are these verbs in? *J'ai joué / je suis allé(e) / j'ai fait*	The perfect tense (a past tense) – I played / I went / I did
8 How do you say in French: I have, I am, I do, I go?	*J'ai; je suis; je fais; je vais*
9 How do you form the near future tense in the 'I' form?	*Je vais* + infinitive
10 Give the *je* forms of the verb *boire* in three time frames.	*J'ai bu; je bois; je vais boire* (I drank; I drink; I'm going to drink)
11 Translate this sentence into French: I would like to watch a film.	*Je voudrais regarder un film*
12 Give one advantage and one disadvantage of learning Maths.	Possible answer: *L'avantage, c'est que c'est intéressant mais l'inconvénient, c'est que c'est difficile*

(Put paper here)

Previous questions

Use the questions below to check your knowledge from previous chapters.

Questions	Answers
1 How do you say in French 'morning, afternoon, evening, night'?	*Le matin; l'après-midi; le soir; la nuit*
2 Translate into French: once a month; twice a year.	*Une fois par mois; deux fois par an*
3 How do you say in French 'last weekend, today and next year'?	*Le week-end dernier, aujourd'hui et l'année prochaine*

(Put paper here)

1.1 Identity and relationships with others

Introducing yourself and your friends

Mes amis et moi	My friends and I
Je m'appelle … et j'ai … ans.	My name is … and I'm … years old.
Je suis gay / lesbienne / queer / hétéro.	I am gay / lesbian / queer / straight.
Je suis bi / bisexuel(le).	I am bi(sexual).
Je suis non-binaire.	I am non-binary.
Je suis transgenre.	I am trans.
Je suis handicapé(e).	I am disabled.
Mon meilleur ami / Ma meilleure amie s'appelle…	My best friend is called…
Il / Elle a … ans.	He / She is … years old.
Il / Elle est bouddhiste.	He / She is a Buddhist.
Il / Elle est chrétien(ne).	He / She is Christian.
Il / Elle est juif / juive.	He / She is Jewish.
Il / Elle est musulman(e).	He / She is a Muslim.

Les nationalités et les langues	Nationalities and languages
Je suis britannique et je parle anglais.	I am British and I speak English.
Mon ami(e) est marocain(e) et francophone.	My friend is Moroccan and French-speaking.
Je parle arabe et français.	I speak Arabic and French.
Ma copine parle plusieurs langues africaines.	My girlfriend speaks several African languages.

> **REMEMBER** ❗
> In French, use the verb *avoir* (to have) to give ages.

> **GRAMMAR TIP** ★
> Make sure you know all parts of the key verbs *avoir* (to have) and *être* (to be). See page 146.

> **GRAMMAR TIP** ★
> If you want non-binary alternatives to *il / elle* and *ils / elles*, you can use *iel* and *iels*.

Parle-moi de toi et de tes amis.
Tell me about yourself and about your friends.

Je m'appelle Mohamed et j'ai quinze an**s**. Je sui**s** anglai**s** et musulman. Me**s** copain**s** et moi, nou**s** somme**s** de foi**s** diverse**s** et nou**s** avon**s** des origine**s** différente**s**. Ma copine, qui s'appelle Céline, est chrétienne et d'origine chinoise. Elle parle plusieur**s** langue**s**. Nou**s** avon**s** beaucoup de respect pour notre diversité.

I'm called Mohamed and I'm 15 years old. I am English and Muslim. My friends and I are of diverse faiths and we have different origins. My friend, who is called Céline, is Christian and of Chinese origin. She speaks several languages. We have lots of respect for our diversity.

> **SOUNDS TIP** 🎤
> If a French word ends in an 's', this is not usually pronounced. However, where a final 's' is followed by a word which starts with a vowel or silent 'h', the 's' **is** pronounced.

1.1 Identity and relationships with others

Describing people's personalities

Décris ta personnalité	Describe your personality
En général, je suis sympa et drôle.	Generally, I am nice and funny.
Je suis très timide et assez sensible.	I am very shy and quite sensitive.
Je suis travailleur / travailleuse.	I am hard-working.
Je suis une personne sportive.	I am a sporty person.
Mes amis pensent que je suis gentil(le).	My friends think that I am kind.
Mes professeurs disent que je suis trop bavard(e).	My teachers say that I am too chatty.
Parfois, je suis embêtant(e) et négatif / négative.	Sometimes, I am annoying and negative.
Je suis un peu paresseux / paresseuse.	I am a bit lazy.
Je ne suis jamais méchant(e).	I am never mean.
J'essaie toujours d'être sérieux / sérieuse.	I always try to be conscientious.
Je voudrais être calme.	I would like to be calm.

Comment sont tes amis?	What are your friends like?
Mon meilleur ami est vraiment amusant.	My best friend is really funny.
Tous mes amis sont agréables.	All my friends are pleasant.
Ils sont vifs / Elles sont vives.	They are lively.
Un(e) de mes ami(e)s est trop fier/fière.	One of my friends is too proud.

> **GRAMMAR TIP** ★
>
> Most adjectives need to change to agree with the noun they describe. Usually, adjectives follow the noun – but there are some exceptions. See pages 123–124.

> **REVISION TIP** ✅
>
> To save time in the exam, choose a few phrases and adjectives that you can use to describe yourself and one of your friends.

Décris ta personnalité et la personnalité d'un(e) ami(e)
Describe your personality and a friend's personality

Je pense que je suis **extrêmement** travailleuse et **très** responsable. Évidemment, je ne suis pas **complètement** parfaite mais je ne suis jamais méchante. Mon meilleur ami est **plutôt** amusant. Il est sportif et **vraiment** sympa. Généralement, il n'est pas **du tout** sérieux et parfois les profs disent qu'il est **trop** bavard.

I think that I am extremely hard-working and responsible. Obviously, I am not completely perfect, but I am never mean. My best friend is rather funny. He is sporty and really nice. Generally, he is not at all conscientious, and sometimes teachers say that he is too chatty.

> **REVISION TIP** ✅
>
> Use **intensifiers** or **qualifiers** (words like 'extremely', 'very', 'completely' and 'rather') in front of adjectives to add variety.

Describing your family

Ma famille / My family

Ma famille	My family
J'ai un (demi-)frère et une (demi-)sœur.	I have one (half-)brother and one (half-)sister.
Je n'ai pas de frères et sœurs.	I don't have any brothers and sisters.
Je suis fille / fils unique.	I'm an only child.
Il y a sept personnes dans ma famille.	There are seven people in my family.
J'habite avec ma mère et mon père.	I live with my mother and father.
J'ai deux mères / pères.	I have two mums / dads.
Ma belle-mère a deux fils.	My stepmother has two sons.
Mon beau-père a une fille.	My stepfather has a daughter.
Je ne vois pas mes tantes et mes oncles très souvent.	I don't see my aunts and uncles very often.
Nous avons beaucoup de cousin(e)s.	We have lots of cousins.

Les cheveux, les yeux et la taille / Hair, eyes and size

Les cheveux, les yeux et la taille	Hair, eyes and size
Ma mère a les cheveux longs et noirs et les yeux verts.	My mother has long, black hair and green eyes.
Mon père a les cheveux courts et gris et les yeux bleus.	My father has short, grey hair and blue eyes.
Ma petite sœur est forte, avec les cheveux bruns.	My little sister is strong, with brown hair.
Mon frère est plus grand que moi.	My brother is taller than me.
Ma grand-mère est petite et très vieille.	My grandmother is small and very old.
Mon grand-père porte toujours un vieux chapeau.	My grandfather always wears an old hat.

SOUNDS TIP
Take care when saying the words *famille* and *fille*. The *-ille* sound in these words is pronounced differently to *ville* or *mille*.

GRAMMAR TIP
There are three different words for 'my' in French, according to whether the noun that follows is masculine, feminine or plural: *mon*, *ma*, *mes*. See page 126.

You can also use the structure 'the … of …' to indicate possession. For example: *La copine de mon père.* My dad's girlfriend.

SOUNDS TIP
The letter *è* appears in many family words. It is pronounced in the same way as *ê* and *ai*. Try saying: m*è*re / extr*ê*me / non-bin*ai*re.

Décris un membre de ta famille *Describe a member of your family*

J'ai une cousine qui est plus jeune que moi mais qui est ma meilleure copine. Elle est très grande et **elle ressemble** à sa maman. Elle a les cheveux courts et bruns et les yeux verts. **J'aime** bien son style car **elle porte** toujours des vêtements géniaux. **On passe** tout notre temps libre ensemble!

I have a cousin who is younger than me but who is my best friend. She is very tall and she looks like her mum. She has short, brown hair and green eyes. I like her style because she always wears great clothes. We spend all our free time together!

GRAMMAR TIP
The *je* and *il / elle / on* forms of **regular -er verbs in the present tense** have the same -e endings. Revise regular verb forms on page 144.

Décris la photo

Sur la photo, il y a une famille.

Les deux adultes sont les parents.

Je crois que c'est une mère et sa copine.

Je vois un père et une mère.

Ils ont trois enfants.

Je pense que les deux ados sont frère et sœur.

La dame de gauche est peut-être leur grand-mère.

Je crois que le vieil homme de droite est le grand-père.

À mon avis, ils sont mari et femme.

Describe the photo

In the photo, there is a family.

The two adults are the parents.

I think it's a mother and her girlfriend.

I can see a father and a mother.

They have three children.

I think that the two teenagers are brother and sister.

The lady on the left might be their grandmother.

I believe the old man on the right is the grandfather.

In my opinion, they are a husband and wife.

REVISION TIP

In the speaking exam, you might have to talk about photos featuring people who could be related to each other. You can use the family vocabulary you know to help describe pictures like this.

Deux photos de famille

Two family photos

Photo 1

Photo 2

REVISION TIP

Cover up the sentences above and the text below these photos. Try describing the photos yourself in French and then compare your description to the text below.

Parle-moi des photos   *Tell me about the photos*

Sur la première photo, il y a quatre personnes. C'est une famille avec deux parents et deux enfants. Je pense que c'est une femme et son mari avec leur fils et leur fille. Je crois que le petit garçon a environ trois ans et que sa sœur a cinq ou six ans.

Sur la deuxième photo, il y a un jeune couple gay avec une dame qui est peut-être leur mère ou belle-mère. Il y a aussi un père qui a les cheveux gris.

In the first photo, there are four people. It's a family with two parents and two children. I think that it's a woman and her husband with their son and their daughter. I believe that the little boy is about three years old and that his sister is five or six.

In the second photo, there is a young gay couple with a lady who might be their mum or stepmum. There is also a dad who has grey hair.

Vocabulary learning

Learn this vocabulary and then use the 'look, cover, write, check' technique to make sure you really know it. Cover the English first and then the French.

Identity

French	✓	English	✓
s'appeler		to be called	
africain(e)		African	
anglais(e)		English	
arabe		Arabic, Arab	
bi(sexuel / sexuelle)		bi(sexual)	
bouddhiste		Buddhist	
britannique		British	
chinois(e)		Chinese	
chrétien(ne)		Christian	
le copain		friend, boyfriend	
la copine		friend, girlfriend	
différent(e)		different	
divers		varied, diverse	
la diversité		diversity	
la foi		faith	
français(e)		French	
francophone		French-speaking	
gay		gay	
handicapé(e)		disabled	
hétéro		straight / heterosexual	
juif / juive		Jewish	
la langue		language / tongue	
lesbienne		lesbian	
marocain(e)		Moroccan	
musulman(e)		Muslim	
non-binaire		non-binary	
l'origine (f.)		origin, source	
plusieurs		several, many	
queer		queer	
le respect		respect	
transgenre		trans	

Describing personality

French	✓	English	✓
agréable		nice, pleasant	
amusant(e)		fun, funny	
bavard(e)		chatty, talkative	
calme		calm, quiet	
complètement		completely	
dire		to say	
drôle		funny	
embêtant(e)		annoying	
généralement		generally	
essayer (de)		to try (to)	
évidemment		obviously	
fier / fière		proud	
gentil(le)		kind	
méchant(e)		mean, nasty, naughty	
négatif / négative		negative	
paresseux / paresseuse		lazy	
parfait(e)		perfect	
la personnalité		personality	
plutôt		rather	
responsable		responsible	
sensible		sensitive	
sérieux / sérieuse		conscientious, responsible	
sportif / sportive		sporty	
sympathique / sympa		nice, kind, friendly	
timide		shy	
travailleur / travailleuse		hard-working	
vif / vive		lively	

Family members and people

French	✓	English	✓
l'ado(lescent) (m.)		teenager	
l'adulte (m. / f.)		adult	
le beau-père		stepfather, father-in-law	
la belle-mère		stepmother, mother-in-law	
le couple		couple	
le / la cousin(e)		cousin	
la dame		lady	
l'enfant (m. / f.)		child	
la famille		family	
la femme		woman, wife	
la fille		daughter, girl	
le fils		son	
le (demi-)frère		(half-)brother	
le garçon		boy	
la grand-mère		grandmother	
le grand-père		grandfather	
habiter		to live	
l'homme (m.)		man	
la maman		mum	
le mari		husband	
le membre		member	
la mère		mother	
l'oncle (m.)		uncle	
le parent		parent	
le père		father	
la personne		person	
la (demi-)sœur		(half-)sister	
la tante		aunt	
unique		unique, only	
bleu(e)		blue	

Physical descriptions

French	✓	English	✓
brun(e)		brown	
le chapeau		hat	
les cheveux (m.pl.)		hair	
court(e)		short	
fort(e)		strong	
grand(e)		big, tall	
gris(e)		grey	
jeune		young	
long(ue)		long	
noir(e)		black	
petit(e)		small, short	
porter		to wear, carry	
ressembler à		to look like	
la taille		size	
vert(e)		green	
le vêtement		item of clothing	
vieux / vieil / vieille		old	
les yeux (m.pl.)		eyes	

Describing a photo

French	✓	English	✓
à droite		on the right	
à gauche		on the left	
à mon avis,…		in my opinion,…	
deuxième		second	
il y a…		there is / are…	
je crois que…		I believe that…	
je pense que…		I think that…	
je vois…		I (can) see…	
peut-être		maybe, perhaps	
la photo		photo	

Answer the questions below. Cover the answers column with a piece of paper and write down as many answers as you can. Check and repeat.

Questions | Answers

	Questions		Answers
1	Say your name, age and one thing about yourself (e.g. nationality) in French.		*Je m'appelle…, j'ai … ans et je suis…*
2	Translate the following words into French: Buddhist, Christian, Jewish, Muslim.		*Bouddhiste, chrétien(ne), juif/juive, musulman(e)*
3	Say in French which languages you speak.		*Je parle anglais / français / chinois / arabe*, etc.
4	What does *francophone* mean?		French-speaking
5	Say three adjectives in French that best describe your personality.		*Timide; calme; gentil(le)* or any three from the list on page 23
6	Ask a question about friends in French.		*Parle-moi de tes amis / Comment sont tes amis?*
7	What do the following words mean in English: *très, assez, un peu, extrêmement, vraiment, plutôt?*		Very; quite; a bit / a little; extremely; really; rather
8	List as many French words for family members as you can.		*La mère; le père; l'oncle; la tante* or any from the list on page 24
9	Describe your best friend's hair and eyes in French.		Possible answer: *Il / Elle a les cheveux longs / courts et les yeux verts / bleus / bruns*
10	What is the ending for the *je* and *il / elle / on* forms of regular -*er* verbs in the present tense? Give some examples.		-*e*. Possible examples: *j'aime / elle porte / il ressemble / on passe*
11	How do you say in French 'in the first photo, there is / are…'?		*Sur la première photo, il y a…*
12	Say three phrases in French you could give to introduce an opinion.		*Je pense que; je crois que; à mon avis*

(Put paper here)

Previous questions

Use the questions below to check your knowledge from previous chapters.

Questions | Answers

	Questions		Answers
1	When is *le mois prochain*?		Next month
2	Give three positive and three negative adjectives in French.		Possible answers: *facile; génial; sympa / cher; difficile; ennuyeux*
3	Translate into French: it was, it is, it will be.		*C'était; c'est; ce sera*

(Put paper here)

⚙ Knowledge

1.1 Identity and relationships with others

Relationships

Les rapports avec les autres	Relationships with others
J'ai de bonnes relations avec mon copain / ma copine.	I have a good relationship with my boyfriend / girlfriend.
Je m'entends bien avec ma belle-mère.	I get on well with my stepmother.
Je ne m'entends pas (toujours) bien avec mon père.	I don't (always) get on well with my dad.
Je me dispute souvent avec ma sœur.	I often argue with my sister.
Je ne me dispute jamais avec mes amis.	I never argue with my friends.
On se comprend.	We understand each other.
Nous nous parlons de tout.	We talk to each other about everything.
Mes parents se séparent.	My parents are separating.

Comment s'entendre mieux / How to get on better

Il faut…	You have to…
remercier les gens.	thank people.
soutenir tes amis.	support your friends.
apprécier ta famille.	appreciate your family.
avouer tes erreurs.	admit / confess to your mistakes.
s'excuser / dire 'désolé(e)'.	apologise / say sorry.
améliorer la communication.	improve communication.
trouver un accord.	find an agreement.
démontrer ton amour.	show your love.
respecter d'autres opinions.	respect other opinions.

> **GRAMMAR TIP** ⭐
>
> **Reflexive verbs** like *s'entendre* (to get on) and *se séparer* (to separate / break up) are useful to talk about relationships. You can use a **reflexive pronoun** with other verbs as well for an action that is done to 'each other': *nous nous écoutons* (we listen to each other). See page 160.

Tu t'entends bien avec ta famille? *Do you get on well with your family?*

Je m'entends bien avec mon beau-père **qui** est vraiment génial et nous montre toujours son amour. Par contre, je ne m'entends pas très bien avec ma mère, **qui** ne s'excuse jamais. Je me dispute parfois avec ma sœur, **qui** ne respecte pas mes opinions. Heureusement, nous avons ma grand-mère, **qui** nous aide souvent à trouver un accord.

I get on well with my stepdad, who is really great and always shows his love for us. On the other hand, I don't get on very well with my mum, who never apologises. I sometimes argue with my sister, who doesn't respect my opinions. Luckily, we have my grandmother, who often helps us to find an agreement.

> **GRAMMAR TIP** ⭐
>
> Use *qui* (who / which) to extend your sentences and add complexity to your speaking and writing.

> **REVISION TIP** 📝
>
> Learn one sentence in French about who you get on well with and why, and one about who you don't get on with and why not.

Les relations futures — Future relationships

Je vais trouver mon / ma partenaire idéal(e).	*I am going to find my ideal partner.*
Nous allons vivre ensemble, sans nous marier.	*We are going to live together without getting married.*
Je ne sais pas si **je vais me marier**.	*I don't know if I am going to get married.*
Mes amis vont organiser un PACS.	*My friends are going to organise a civil partnership.*
Je voudrais rester célibataire.	*I would like to stay single.*
Je rêve d'un grand mariage.	*I dream of a big wedding.*
J'ai l'intention d'avoir un mariage du même sexe.	*I intend to have a same-sex marriage.*
J'espère rencontrer l'homme / la femme / la personne de mes rêves.	*I hope to meet the man / woman / person of my dreams.*
Je souhaite rester seul(e).	*I wish to remain on my own.*

De bons conseils — Some good advice

Il ne faut pas…	*You mustn't…*
blesser les autres.	*hurt others.*
tromper son partenaire.	*deceive your partner.*
critiquer ses amis.	*criticise your friends.*
mentir à sa famille.	*lie to your family.*
crier après les gens.	*shout / scream at people.*
décevoir ses meilleurs amis.	*disappoint your best friends.*

> **GRAMMAR TIP** ⭐
>
> To talk about the future, you can use *aller* in **the present tense + infinitive:** *Un jour, je vais me marier*. I'm going to get married one day.

> **REVISION TIP** ✓
>
> Learn some different phrases to talk about future plans to add variety to your writing and speaking, for example: I would like to, I dream of, I hope to, I intend to, I wish to.

Veux-tu te marier un jour? *Do you want to get married one day?*

Je ne sais pas si je veux me marier un jour parce que je suis un peu jeune pour décider! Je vois des couples qui se trompent et se blessent donc à mon avis le mariage n'est pas toujours agréable ou facile. Je préfère rester seul et éviter les **histoires de cœur***.

I don't know if I want to get married one day because I am a bit young to decide! I see couples who deceive and hurt each other so in my opinion marriage isn't always pleasant or easy. I prefer to remain on my own and avoid affairs of the heart.

---

*une histoire de cœur = *a love story / an affair of the heart*

Learn this vocabulary and then use the 'look, cover, write, check' technique to make sure you really know it. Cover the English first and then the French.

Useful verbs to talk about relationships

French	✓	English	✓
aider		to help	
améliorer		to improve	
apprécier		to appreciate	
avouer		to admit to, confess to	
blesser		to hurt, injure	
(se) comprendre		to understand (each other)	
crier		to shout, scream	
critiquer		to criticise	
décevoir		to disappoint	
(se) décider		to decide	
démontrer		to show	
se disputer		to argue	
s'entendre (avec)		to get on (with)	
espérer		to hope	
éviter		to avoid	
se marier		to get married	
mentir		to lie	
organiser		to organise	
(se) parler		to talk (to each other)	
protéger		to protect	
remercier		to thank	
rencontrer		to meet	
respecter		to respect	
rester		to stay, remain	
rêver à / de		to dream about / of	
se séparer		to separate, break up	
souhaiter		to wish	
soutenir		to support	
tromper		to deceive, cheat	
vivre		to live	

Relationships

French	✓	English	✓
l'accord (m.)		agreement	
l'amour (m.)		love	
les autres (m.pl. / f.pl.)		others	
célibataire		single, unmarried	
le cœur		heart	
la communication		communication	
le conseil		advice	
désolé(e)		sorry	
l'erreur (f.)		mistake, error	
les gens (m.pl.)		people	
heureusement		luckily	
idéal(e)		ideal	
l'intention (f.)		intention	
le mariage (du même sexe)		(same-sex) marriage	
mieux		better	
le PACS		civil partnership	
par contre		on the other hand	
le/la partenaire		partner	
le rapport		relationship	
la relation		relationship	
le rêve		dream	
je sais		I know	
sans		without	
seul(e)		alone, on one's own, by oneself	
si		if, whether	

SOUNDS TIP

Practise saying the sound *-œu* in the words *cœur* and *sœur*. It's the same open sound as in the words *heure* and *leur*.

REMEMBER !

Watch out for **faux amis** (false friends). These are words that look similar to English words but which have a different meaning, for example: *blesser*, *crier* and *décevoir*.

Answer the questions below. Cover the answers column with a piece of paper and write down as many answers as you can. Check and repeat.

Questions | Answers

#	Questions	Answers
1	Say a sentence in French about one person you get on well with and why.	*Je m'entends bien avec … parce que…*
2	Say a sentence in French about one person you don't get on well with and why.	*Je ne m'entends pas bien avec … parce que…*
3	List as many reflexive verbs (or verbs used reflexively) as possible for the topic of relationships.	*S'entendre; se disputer; se séparer; se marier; (s')écouter; (se) parler; (se) comprendre*
4	Translate this sentence into English: *Il faut avouer tes erreurs.*	You have to admit / confess to your mistakes
5	List three different verbs in the *je* form which can be used with an infinitive to talk about future plans.	Any three from: *je voudrais; je veux; j'espère; je vais; je souhaite*
6	What is a *PACS*?	A civil partnership
7	Answer this question in French: *Veux-tu te marier un jour?*	Possible answer: *Oui, et je rêve d'un grand mariage.* See page 27 for more ideas
8	Translate this sentence into French: You mustn't hurt others.	*Il ne faut pas blesser les autres*
9	Which French words for a family member and a body part rhyme with *heure* and *leur*?	*Sœur; cœur*
10	Which of these verbs is a positive action? *mentir, tromper, soutenir*	*Soutenir* (to support) as *mentir* (to lie) and *tromper* (to deceive) are both negative
11	What do these 'false friends' mean in English? *blesser, crier, décevoir*	To hurt / injure; to shout / scream; to disappoint
12	How do you say 'sorry' in French?	*Désolé(e)*

Put paper here

Previous questions

Use these questions to check your knowledge of previous topics.

Questions | Answers

#	Questions	Answers
1	Give three ways to introduce your opinion in French (e.g. in my opinion, I think that, for me).	*À mon avis; je pense que; pour moi*
2	Ask a question about friends in French.	*Parle-moi de tes amis / Comment sont tes amis?*
3	What do the following words mean in English: *très, assez, un peu, extrêmement, vraiment, plutôt?*	Very; quite; a bit / a little; extremely; really; rather

Put paper here

1.2 Healthy living and lifestyle

Eating and drinking

La nourriture à la maison

Je mange **des** légumes chaque jour.

Je bois **de l'**eau mais je ne bois plus **de** lait.

Au petit-déjeuner, je prends **des** fruits et **du** thé.

Le matin, je ne mange pas beaucoup.

Au déjeuner, je mange **du** pain et **du** fromage.

Je mange souvent **du** gâteau.

Pour le dîner, on mange **de la** viande.

Chez nous, il n'y a personne qui aime faire la cuisine.

Food at home

I eat vegetables every day.

I drink water but I no longer drink milk.

For my breakfast, I have some fruit and some tea.

In the morning, I don't eat a lot.

I eat bread and cheese for lunch.

I often eat some cake.

For dinner, we eat meat.

There isn't anyone who likes doing the cooking at home.

Les repas au café ou au restaurant

Mon plat préféré, c'est du poulet avec des frites.

Je ne prends jamais d'entrée.

Nous ne commandons que des plats végans.

Je suis végétarien(ne) donc je ne mange ni viande, ni poisson.

Comme boisson, je préfère le café.

Ma belle-mère boit du vin quand elle mange au restaurant.

Sur la carte, il y a des glaces.

Meals at the café or restaurant

My favourite meal is chicken with chips.

I never have a starter.

We only order vegan dishes.

I'm a vegetarian, so I eat neither meat nor fish.

As a drink, I prefer coffee.

My stepmother drinks wine when she eats at a restaurant.

On the menu, there are ice-creams.

GRAMMAR TIP ★

Remember that negative expressions go around the verb.

*Je **ne** mange **pas** beaucoup.*
I don't eat a lot.

Watch out for tricky negatives like *ne … que* (only) and *ne … plus* (no longer). See page 157.

GRAMMAR TIP ★

Use *du / de la / de l' / des* in French when talking about what you eat and drink.

After negative expressions, use *de / d'.* See page 121.

REVISION TIP ☑

You might need to use the *il / elle* form of *manger* (to eat) and *boire* (to drink) for a photo card task.

Il / Elle mange / boit…

Qu'est-ce que tu as mangé et bu récemment?
What have you eaten and drunk recently?

Hier, j'ai pris du pain au petit-déjeuner et j'ai bu du café au lait. À midi, j'ai mangé du poulet avec des frites et j'ai bu de l'eau. Le soir, mon grand-père a commandé mon repas préféré à emporter. J'adore la cuisine chinoise – c'était trop bon!

Yesterday, I had some bread for breakfast and I drank some white coffee. At noon, I ate chicken and chips and I drank some water. In the evening, my grandfather ordered my favourite meal to take away. I love Chinese food – it was so good!

REMEMBER ❗

The verb in *je préfère* (I prefer) is pronounced differently to the adjective *préféré(e)* (favourite).

Well-being

Activités pour le bien-être	Activities for well-being
J'ai écouté de la musique.	I listened to music.
Nous avons dansé ensemble.	We danced together.
Il a joué d'un instrument.	He played an instrument.
Elle a écrit un poème.	She wrote a poem.
J'ai lu un livre.	I read a book.
Tu as essayé un nouveau passe-temps.	You tried a new hobby.
Elles ont dessiné.	They drew / did some drawing.
Vous avez partagé des inquiétudes / soucis.	You shared some worries.

Aller dehors	Going outside
Nous avons fait de l'exercice.	We did some exercise.
Ils ont fait du vélo.	They **went** for a bike ride.
Elle a nagé dans la mer.	She swam in the sea.
J'ai couru à la campagne.	I ran in the countryside.
Il a fait une promenade.	He **went** for a walk.
Ils ont passé du temps dans la nature.	They spent time in nature.
Tu as profité du beau temps.	You made the most of the nice weather.

GRAMMAR TIP

Use *avoir* + **a past participle** with these verbs to talk about what you have done in the past. Remember that some past participles are irregular, e.g. *fait* (did / done).

REMEMBER

The verb *faire* does not always translate in English as 'make' or 'do'.

Récemment, qu'est-ce que tu as fait pour ton bien-être?
What have you done recently for your well-being?

Récemment, j'ai essayé **deux** activités pour bouger plus car j'étais un **peu** triste. J'ai nagé dans la mer et j'ai fait une longue promenade à la campagne parce que j'adore passer du temps dans la nature. Ça va beaucoup **mieux** maintenant et je me sens plus **heureux**!

Recently, I tried two activities in order to move more because I was a bit sad. I swam in the sea and I went for a long walk in the countryside because I love spending time in nature. I'm much better now and I feel happier!

SOUNDS TIP

The 'closed' *eu* sound in these words is the same as the sound in the number *deux*:

peu   mieux   heureux

Practise reading the text above out loud.

⚙ Knowledge

1.2 Healthy living and lifestyle

Health problems

Les maladies	Illnesses
Je suis malade.	I am ill.
Je ne me sens pas bien.	I don't feel well.
Je souffre beaucoup.	I'm suffering a lot.
J'ai (trop) chaud et j'ai (vraiment) soif.	I'm (too) hot and I'm (really) thirsty.
J'ai (très) froid et je n'ai pas faim.	I'm (very) cold and I'm not hungry.
Je suis fatigué(e).	I am tired.
J'ai mal au bras et à la main.	My arm and my hand hurt.
J'ai mal au dos.	My back hurts / I have back-ache.
J'ai mal à l'œil / J'ai mal aux yeux.	My eye hurts / My eyes hurt.
J'ai mal à l'oreille.	My ear hurts / I have earache.
J'ai mal aux pieds.	My feet hurt.
J'ai mal à la jambe.	My leg hurts.
J'ai mal à la tête.	My head hurts / I have a headache.

Les accidents	Accidents
Je suis tombé(e).	I fell.
Je me suis coupé à la main avec un couteau.	I cut my hand with a knife.
Il y avait du sang partout et j'avais peur.	There was blood everywhere and I was afraid.
Je me suis cassé le bras.	I broke my arm.
Je me suis blessé(e).	I hurt myself.

Pas de chance! *No luck!*

La semaine dernière, je suis tomb**é** dehors et je me suis cass**é** la jambe. Hier, je suis all**é** dans la cuisine et je me suis coup**é** à la main avec un couteau. Puis, ce matin, mon frère m'a fait mal au bras par accident. En plus, aujourd'hui, j'ai mal à la tête. Je n'ai pas de chance!

Last week, I fell outside and I broke my leg. Yesterday, I went into the kitchen and I cut my hand with a knife. Then, this morning, my brother hurt my arm by accident. Also, I have a headache today. I don't have any luck!

GRAMMAR TIP ⭐

Use *avoir* with these expressions in French, even when they translate differently in English:

avoir mal (to hurt)

avoir chaud / froid (to be hot / cold)

avoir faim / soif (to be hungry / thirsty)

avoir peur (to be afraid)

avoir besoin de (to need)

GRAMMAR TIP ⭐

Some verbs form the perfect tense with *être* rather than *avoir*. This includes verbs like *aller* (to go) and *tomber* (to fall), as well as reflexive verbs like *se couper* (to cut oneself). See page 151.

SOUNDS TIP 🎤

Make sure you pronounce the -**é** sound at the end of past participles. They have the same sound as -**er** and -**ez**, so all the following verb forms sound exactly the same:

all**é**   all**er**   all**ez**

Try reading the text on the left out loud.

Les mauvaises habitudes

Bad habits

Boire beaucoup d'alcool n'est pas bon pour la santé.	*Drinking a lot of alcohol is not good for your health.*
Manger trop de fast-food n'est pas sain.	*Eating too much fast food is not healthy.*
Il est difficile d'arrêter si on prend de la drogue.	*It is difficult to stop if you take drugs.*
Beaucoup de jeunes vapotent et c'est dangereux.	*A lot of young people vape and it's dangerous.*
Fumer est très mauvais pour le corps.	*Smoking is very bad for your body.*
Le tabac peut avoir des effets graves.	*Tobacco can have serious effects.*

J'ai besoin d'aide

I need help

Il faut aller à l'hôpital.	*You have to go to hospital.*
On va prendre un rendez-vous chez le médecin demain.	*We are going to make an appointment with the doctor tomorrow.*
Nous allons acheter des médicaments.	*We're going to buy some medicine.*
Il faut se reposer.	*You have to rest.*
Je vais me coucher.	*I'm going to go to bed.*
Il faut boire plus d'eau.	*You have to drink more water.*
Il faut être moins actif.	*You have to be less active.*

GRAMMAR TIP ⭐

After expressions of quantity, use *de / d'* followed by the noun:

Beaucoup de / d' (a lot of)

Trop de / d' (too much)

Plus de / d' (more)

Moins de / d' (less)

REMEMBER ❗

An infinitive verb in French can be translated as '-ing' in English.

Une crise de santé publique *A public health crisis*

On sait que fumer ou prendre de la drogue est mauvais pour la santé. Cependant, le nombre d'adolescents qui vapotent a augmenté et les risques sont moins compris. Selon une enquête, environ 20% des jeunes de quinze ans vapotent. Le problème, c'est que les effets sont graves et que c'est très difficile d'arrêter.

We know that smoking or taking drugs is bad for your health. However, the number of teenagers who vape has increased and the risks are less understood. According to a survey, about 20% of young people aged 15 vape. The problem is that the effects are serious and it's very difficult to stop.

REVISION TIP ✍️

Cover up the English paragraph above and try translating the French text into English yourself. Then compare your translation with the one above.

1.2 Healthy living and lifestyle

Vocabulary learning

Learn this vocabulary and then use the 'look, cover, write, check' technique to make sure you really know it. Cover the English first and then the French.

Eating and drinking

French	✓	English	✓
la boisson		drink	
la carte		menu	
cependant		however	
la cuisine		cooking, kitchen	
le déjeuner		lunch	
le dîner		dinner	
donc		so, therefore	
l'eau (f.)		water	
l'entrée (f.)		starter	
les frites (f.pl.)		chips	
le fromage		cheese	
le fruit		fruit	
le gâteau		cake	
la glace		ice cream, ice	
le légume		vegetable	
la maison		house, home	
la nourriture		food	
le pain		bread	
le petit-déjeuner		breakfast	
le plat		dish	
le poisson		fish	
le poulet		chicken	
récemment		recently	
le repas		meal	
le thé		tea	
végan(e)		vegan	
végétarien(ne)		vegetarian	
la viande		meat	
le vin		wine	

Useful verbs for eating and drinking

French	✓	English	✓
boire		to drink	
commander		to order	
emporter		to take away	
manger		to eat	
prendre		to take	

Well-being activities

French	✓	English	✓
actif / active		active	
l'activité (f.)		activity	
bouger		to move	
la campagne		countryside	
courir		to run	
danser		to dance	
dehors		outside	
dessiner		to draw	
écrire		to write	
l'exercice (m.)		exercise	
heureux / heureuse		happy	
l'inquiétude (f.)		worry, anxiety	
l'instrument (m.)		instrument	
maintenant		now	
la mer		sea	
nager		to swim	
la nature		nature	
partager		to share	
le poème		poem	
profiter de		to make the most of	
la promenade		walk	
le souci		worry, concern	
le temps		time, weather	
triste		sad	

> **REVISION TIP** 📝
> Use the vocabulary above to say what you eat for breakfast, lunch and dinner, in French.

Vocabulary learning

Parts of the body

French	✓	English	✓
le bras		arm	
le corps		body	
le dos		back	
la jambe		leg	
la main		hand	
l'œil (m.)		eye	
l'oreille (f.)		ear	
le pied		foot	
le sang		blood	
la tête		head	
les yeux (m.pl.)		eyes	

Illnesses, accidents and getting help

French	✓	English	✓
l'accident (m.)		accident	
se blesser		to hurt, injure oneself	
casser		to break	
la chance		luck	
chez		at the place of, with	
se coucher		to go to bed	
couper		to cut	
le couteau		knife	
fatigué(e)		tired	
l'hôpital (m.)		hospital	
malade		ill	
la maladie		illness	
le médecin		doctor	
le médicament		medicine	
le rendez-vous		appointment	
se reposer		to rest	
se sentir		to feel	
souffrir		to suffer	
tomber		to fall	

Expressions with *avoir*

French	✓	English	✓
avoir besoin de		to need	
avoir chaud		to be hot	
avoir faim		to be hungry	
avoir froid		to be cold	
avoir mal		to hurt	
avoir peur		to be afraid	
avoir soif		to be thirsty	

Unhealthy habits

French	✓	English	✓
l'alcool (m.)		alcohol	
l'aide (f.)		help	
arrêter		to stop	
augmenter		to increase	
la cigarette		cigarette	
la crise		crisis	
dangereux / dangereuse		dangerous	
la drogue		drug	
l'effet (m.)		effect	
l'enquête (f.)		survey	
le fast-food		fast food	
fumer		to smoke	
grave		serious	
l'habitude (f.)		habit	
il faut (+ infinitive)		it is necessary	
mauvais(e)		bad	
le nombre		number	
le risque		risk	
sain(e)		healthy	
la santé		health	
savoir		to know	
le tabac		tobacco	
vapoter		to vape	

Retrieval

Answer the questions below. Cover the answers column with a piece of paper and write down as many answers as you can. Check and repeat.

Questions / Answers

#	Questions	Answers
1	Give three foods in French that a vegetarian might eat.	Possible answers: *des légumes*; *des fruits*; *du fromage*
2	Answer this question in French: *Quel est ton plat préféré?*	Possible answer: *Mon plat préféré, c'est du poulet avec des frites*
3	Name five different things people drink in French.	Possible answers: *du café*; *du thé*; *du lait*; *de l'eau*; *du vin*
4	Translate this sentence into French: He is eating and drinking in a café.	*Il mange et boit dans un café*
5	Translate this sentence into English: *Vous avez partagé vos soucis.*	You (have) shared your worries
6	Complete the sentence with the correct past participle: *J'ai passé / couru / fait une promenade.*	*J'ai fait une promenade*
7	Which number between 1 and 5 contains the same sound as in the words *peu* and *dangereux*?	*Deux*
8	In French, give three parts of the body that are above the neck.	*La tête*; *l'œil / les yeux*; *les oreilles*
9	What does *J'ai besoin de* mean in English?	I need
10	Give five examples of unhealthy habits in French.	Any five from: *fumer / vapoter / prendre de la drogue / manger du fast-food / boire beaucoup d'alcool*
11	What is the French for: a lot of, too much, more, less?	*Beaucoup de*; *trop de*; *plus de*; *moins de*
12	Translate this sentence into French: I don't smoke because it's bad for your health.	*Je ne fume pas parce que c'est mauvais pour la santé*

Put paper here

Previous questions

Use these questions to check your knowledge of previous topics.

Questions / Answers

#	Questions	Answers
1	How do you say in French: I have, I am, I do, I go?	*J'ai*; *je suis*; *je fais*; *je vais*
2	Say a sentence in French about one person you get on well with and why.	*Je m'entends bien avec … parce que…*
3	What do these 'false friends' mean in English? *blesser, crier, décevoir*	To hurt / injure; to shout / scream; to disappoint

Put paper here

1.3 Education and work

School subjects and opinions

Les matières et les professeurs	***Subjects and teachers***
J'apprends trois langues: le français, l'allemand et le chinois.	*I'm learning three languages: French, German and Chinese.*
Ma matière préférée, c'est la musique car c'est passionnant.	*My favourite subject is Music because it's exciting.*
J'adore l'informatique parce que c'est intéressant et que le prof est super.	*I love Computer Science because it's interesting and the teacher is great.*
Je n'aime pas l'espagnol parce que c'est nul.	*I don't like Spanish because it's rubbish.*
Nous apprenons la physique parce que c'est utile.	*We are learning Physics because it's useful.*
Je n'aime pas beaucoup la technologie car c'est trop difficile pour moi.	*I don't like Design and Technology much because it's too difficult for me.*

Comparer les matières et les profs	***Comparing subjects and teachers***
J'aime l'anglais car c'est plus facile que les maths.	*I like English because it's easier than Maths.*
Je déteste l'histoire car c'est moins pratique que mes autres matières.	*I hate History because it's less practical than my other subjects.*
À mon avis, les sciences sont pires que les maths.	*In my opinion, Science is worse than Maths.*
Le choix de matières est meilleur que l'année dernière.	*The choice of subjects is better than last year.*
La prof de sport est la prof la plus sympa de l'école.	*The PE teacher is the nicest teacher in the school.*
Les deux matières les plus amusantes sont le théâtre et la géographie.	*The two most fun subjects are Drama and Geography.*

Quelle est ta matière préférée? *Which is your favourite subject?*

Ma matière préférée, c'est la danse car c'est **simple** et **amusant**. Pour moi, c'est plus **passionnant** que le théâtre et le prof est vraiment **super** aussi. Il est le prof le moins **strict** du collège. Je pense que mes autres matières sont plus **dures** et un peu **ennuyeuses**.

My favourite subject is Dance because it's simple and fun. In my opinion, it's more exciting than Drama and the teacher is really great as well. He is the least strict teacher in the school. I think that my other subjects are harder and a bit boring.

GRAMMAR TIP ⭐

Use the comparative **plus / moins + adjective + que** (more / less … than) and **meilleur / pire que** (better / worse than) to compare two things.

Use the superlative to say what is the 'the most…', 'the least…', 'the best…', etc.

Remember that the adjective will need to agree with the first noun See page 125.

REMEMBER ❗

The phrase *pour moi* (for me) can be used to introduce an opinion. In English, this could be translated as 'I think that' or 'in my opinion'.

REVISION TIP 📝

Use a range of different adjectives to describe things and to give your opinions.

⚙ Knowledge VOCABULARY

1.3 Education and work

The school day and school life

La journée scolaire

The school day

Le premier cours commence à neuf heures moins dix.

The first lesson starts at 8:50am.

Les cours finissent à quinze heures trente.

Lessons finish at 3:30pm.

Nous avons quatre leçons le matin et deux l'après-midi.

We have four lessons in the morning and two in the afternoon.

La récré dure un quart d'heure.

Break lasts a quarter of an hour.

Nous avons quarante-cinq minutes pour manger à midi.

We have 45 minutes to eat at noon.

Après le collège, il y a des clubs de sport et de musique.

After school, there are sport and music clubs.

J'attends le bus à seize heures.

I wait for the bus at 4:00pm.

La vie au collège

School life

La rentrée est début septembre.

The start of the school year is at the beginning of September.

J'ai choisi mes matières en quatrième.

I chose my subjects in year 9.

Nous avons nos examens en seconde.

We have our exams in year 11.

Il y a environ deux cents élèves en troisième.

There are about 200 pupils in year 10.

Il y a une grande bibliothèque.

There is a big library.

Je parle avec mes amis dans la cour ou sur le terrain de sport.

I talk to my friends in the playground or on the sports ground.

★ GRAMMAR TIP

Make sure you revise the present tense endings for regular **-re** verbs like *attendre* (to wait) and **-ir** verbs like **finir** (to finish). See page 144.

🎤 SOUNDS TIP

When you see the letter ç, remember that this is a soft 's' sound rather than a hard 'k' sound.

Try saying: *Les garçons reçoivent des leçons de français.* (The boys receive French lessons.)

❗ REMEMBER

The way that school years are named in the French system is different:

- *quatrième* (year 9)
- *troisième* (year 10)
- *seconde* (year 11)
- *première* (year 12).

Comment est ta journée scolaire? *What is your school day like?*

Dans mon collège, les leçons commencent à neuf heures moins le quart et finissent à quinze heures trente. Pendant la récré et à midi, je parle avec mes amis dans la cour. Nous avons de la chance parce qu'il y a beaucoup de clubs après les cours. Normalement, je prends le bus à dix-sept heures pour rentrer chez moi.

In my school, lessons start at 8:45am and finish at 3:30pm. During break time and at noon, I talk to my friends in the playground. We are lucky because there are lots of clubs after the lessons. Normally, I take the bus at 5:00pm to go home.

📋 REVISION TIP

You could adapt the text on the left to describe your own school day by changing the times and form of transport.

School rules and challenges

Le règlement au collège	The rules at school
On doit respecter les règles.	*We must respect the rules.*
Nous devons porter un uniforme avec un pantalon noir.	*We have to wear a uniform with black trousers.*
On ne doit pas manger dans les salles de classe.	*We mustn't eat in the classrooms.*
On doit écouter les professeurs et le directeur.	*We must listen to the teachers and the headteacher.*
On peut utiliser un portable seulement pendant la récré.	*You can only use a mobile phone at break.*
On ne peut pas manquer un cours.	*You can't miss a lesson.*
Il faut apporter tes cahiers.	*You must bring your exercise books.*
Il ne faut pas oublier tes stylos.	*You mustn't forget your pens.*
Il est interdit d'arriver en retard.	*It is forbidden to be late.*
Il est essentiel de travailler en silence pendant les examens.	*It is essential to work in silence during exams.*

Les défis du collège	The challenges of school
Il y a trop de devoirs chaque soir.	*There is too much homework every evening.*
Certains élèves harcèlent les plus jeunes enfants.	*Some pupils bully the younger children.*
Cette année, il y a beaucoup de contrôles.	*This year there are lots of tests.*
La durée de certains cours est un peu longue.	*The length of some lessons is a bit long.*
Je voudrais obtenir de bonnes notes mais il faut travailler dur!	*I would like to get good marks but you have to work hard!*

GRAMMAR TIP
Modal verbs like *devoir* (to have to) and *pouvoir* (to be able to) are often followed by a second verb in the infinitive form. See page 148.

GRAMMAR TIP
You can use the impersonal verb *il faut / il ne faut pas* + infinitive to say what you must and must not do.

The structure *il est + adjective + de + infinitive* is also useful to talk about rules. See page 161.

REVISION TIP
Practise talking about your school, teachers, school rules and school subjects out loud in front of the mirror to build up your confidence with speaking French.

Parle-moi de ton collège. *Talk to me about your school.*

Mon collège est très grand, avec trois mille élèves et beaucoup de bâtiments modernes. Moi, je suis en troisième. Il faut porter un uniforme avec un pantalon noir et chaque soir, on doit faire beaucoup de devoirs. Parfois, il y a aussi trop de contrôles. Je m'entends bien avec mes professeurs mais la directrice est un peu stricte.

My school is very big, with 3000 pupils and lots of modern buildings. Me, I'm in year 10. We must wear a uniform with black trousers and we have to do a lot of homework every evening. Sometimes there are too many tests as well. I get on well with my teachers but the headteacher is a bit strict.

SOUNDS TIP
You know the *oi* sound from the word *trois*. Now practise saying the other words with this sound in the text on the left. Then read the whole text out loud.

1.3 Education and work

Vocabulary learning

Learn this vocabulary and then use the 'look, cover, write, check' technique to make sure you really know it. Cover the English first and then the French.

School subjects and teachers

French	✓	English	✓
l'allemand (m.)		German	
l'anglais (m.)		English	
le chinois		Chinese	
le choix		choice	
le directeur / la directrice		headteacher	
l'espagnol (m.)		Spanish	
le français		French	
la géographie		Geography	
l'histoire (f.)		History	
l'informatique (f.)		Computer Science, Computing	
la langue		language	
les maths (f.pl.)		Maths	
la matière		subject	
la musique		Music	
la physique		Physics	
le / la professeur / prof		teacher	
les sciences (f.pl.)		Science(s)	
le sport		PE / sport	
la technologie		Design and Technology	
le théâtre		Drama	

Opinions for the school topic

French	✓	English	✓
amusant(e)		funny, fun, enjoyable, amusing	
comparer		to compare	
difficile		difficult	
dur(e)		hard	
ennuyeux / ennuyeuse		boring	
facile		easy	
intéressant(e)		interesting	
meilleur(e)		better, best	
moins		less	
nul(le)		rubbish	
passionnant(e)		exciting, thrilling	
pire		worse, worst	
plus		more	
pratique		practical	
préféré(e)		favourite	
simple		simple	
strict(e)		strict	
super		great	
sympa		nice	
utile		useful	

> **REVISION TIP** 📝
>
> Use the vocabulary above to practise giving opinions in French of your school subjects and your teachers.

Vocabulary learning

School life and rules

French	✓	English	✓
apporter		*to bring*	
apprendre		*to learn*	
après		*after*	
arriver		*to arrive*	
attendre		*to wait (for)*	
l'autobus / le bus (m.)		*bus*	
le bâtiment		*building*	
la bibliothèque		*library*	
le cahier		*exercise book*	
certains		*some (people)*	
choisir		*to choose*	
la classe		*class*	
le club		*club*	
le collège		*school*	
commencer		*to start*	
le contrôle		*test*	
la cour		*playground, courtyard*	
le cours		*lesson*	
le début		*beginning*	
le défi		*challenge*	
devoir		*to have to, must*	
les devoirs (m.pl.)		*homework*	
la durée		*length, duration*	
durer		*to last*	
l'élève (m. / f.)		*pupil, student*	
en retard		*late*	
essentiel(le)		*essential*	
l'examen (m.)		*exam*	
finir		*to finish*	
harceler		*to bully*	
il faut + infinitive		*it is necessary*	
interdit(e)		*prohibited, banned, forbidden*	

French	✓	English	✓
la leçon		*lesson*	
manquer		*to miss*	
moderne		*modern*	
la note		*mark, grade*	
obtenir		*to get*	
oublier		*to forget*	
le pantalon		*trousers*	
le portable		*mobile phone*	
pouvoir		*to be able to, can*	
la première		*year 12*	
la quatrième		*year 9*	
recevoir		*to receive*	
la récré(ation)		*break (time)*	
la règle		*rule*	
le règlement		*rule, regulation*	
la rentrée		*the start of the school year*	
rentrer		*to go back (home)*	
respecter		*to respect*	
la salle		*room*	
scolaire		*school (adjective)*	
la seconde		*year 11*	
seulement		*only*	
le silence		*silence*	
le stylo		*pen*	
le terrain		*ground, pitch*	
la troisième		*year 10*	
l'uniforme (m.)		*uniform*	
utiliser		*to use*	
la vie		*life*	

Retrieval

Answer the questions below. Cover the answers column with a piece of paper and write down as many answers as you can. Check and repeat.

Questions

Answers

1 Answer these questions in French: *Quelle est ta matière préférée? Pourquoi?*

Possible answer: *Ma matière préférée, c'est (l'anglais) parce que c'est (plus intéressant que le français)*

2 List as many words as possible to describe school subjects in French.

Possible answers: *difficile; ennuyeux; passionnant* See page 40 for more ideas

3 Answer this question in French: *Que penses-tu de tes profs?*

Possible answer: *Mes profs sont sympas mais très stricts*

4 Translate this phrase into French: English is easier than Maths.

L'anglais est plus facile que les maths

5 Say three things about your school day.

Possible answer: *Les cours commencent à neuf heures et finissent à seize heures. La récré dure vingt minutes*

6 Give the *je* form of these verbs in the present tense: to learn, to wait, to go back (home).

J'apprends; j'attends; je rentre

7 What is *la rentrée*?

The start of the school year

8 Translate these school years into French: year 9, 10, 11, 12.

La quatrième; la troisième; la seconde; la première

9 Give three examples of school rules in French.

Possible answers: *Nous devons porter un uniforme; Il faut apporter les cahiers; On doit écouter les profs*

10 Choose the correct form of *pouvoir* to complete this sentence: *On ne pouvons / peut / peux pas utiliser un portable.*

Peut

11 Translate this sentence into English: *Je voudrais obtenir de bonnes notes.*

I would like to get good grades

12 Say three sentences in French to describe your school.

Possible answer: *Mon collège est très grand. Il y a deux mille élèves. Nous avons beaucoup de bâtiments modernes*

Put paper here

Previous questions

Use these questions to check your knowledge of previous topics.

Questions

Answers

1 List as many reflexive verbs (or verbs used reflexively) as possible for the topic of relationships.

S'entendre; se disputer; se séparer; se marier; (s')écouter; (se) parler; (se) comprendre

2 Answer this question in French: *Quel est ton plat préféré?*

Possible answer: *Mon plat préféré, c'est du poulet avec des frites*

3 Translate this sentence into French: He is eating and drinking in a café.

Il mange et boit dans un café

Put paper here

1.3 Education and work

Future study and travel

Les études futures — *Future studies*

Je veux aller au lycée pour préparer mon bac. — *I want to go to sixth form to do my A Levels.*

Mes amis et moi, nous voulons changer de collège. — *My friends and I want to change school.*

Je sais que je veux quitter le collège pour faire un apprentissage. — *I know I want to leave school to do an apprenticeship.*

Mon meilleur ami veut faire une formation pratique. — *My best friend wants to do practical training.*

Mes copines veulent étudier à l'université. — *My (female) friends want to study at university.*

Tu veux aller à des cours du soir? — *Do you want to go to evening classes?*

Mes projets — *My plans*

Cet été, **j'apprendrai** à conduire. — *This summer, I will learn to drive.*

Après avoir passé le bac, je vais prendre une année sabbatique. — *After having done my A Levels, I am going to take a gap year.*

Après avoir fini mes examens, **je ferai** un stage. — *After having finished my exams, I will do some work experience.*

Après avoir quitté le collège, **je chercherai** un boulot d'été. — *After having left school, I will look for a summer job.*

L'année prochaine, **je voyagerai** en Europe. — *Next year, I will travel to Europe.*

J'irai en vacances avec mes amis et **je** ne **ferai** rien! — *I will go on holiday with my friends and I will do nothing!*

Je ne connais pas encore ma prochaine étape. — *I don't know my next step yet.*

Qu'est-ce que tu veux faire après tes examens?
What do you want to do after your exams?

Si je réussis à mes examens à la fin de la seconde, je veux rester au lycée pour préparer le bac. **Après avoir quitté** le lycée, je vais prendre une année sabbatique pour travailler et pour voyager. Je voudrais aussi apprendre à conduire. **Après avoir fini** mes voyages, j'irai à l'université pour étudier les langues.

If I pass my exams at the end of year 11, I want to go to sixth form to do my A Levels. After having left sixth form, I will take a gap year to work and to travel. I would like to learn to drive as well. After having finished my travels, I will go to university to study languages.

GRAMMAR TIP
Use the modal verb *vouloir* + **infinitive** in the present tense to say what you and other people **want** to do. See page 148.

GRAMMAR TIP
The simple future tense is used to say what you **will** do. See page 154.

SOUNDS TIP
When a word ending in *-s*, *-t*, *-n* or *-x* is followed by a word which starts with a vowel, the sound of the two words runs together with a 'liaison'.
Practise reading aloud these phrases:
- *Après avoir fini…*
- *On doit étudier tout un chapitre.*
- *Dix ans.*

REVISION TIP
To extend your answers, use *après avoir* + **past participle** (after having done).

1.3 Education and work

Jobs and careers

Les emplois créatifs	Creative jobs
Si possible, je travaillerais comme artiste ou auteur.	*If possible, I would work as an artist or author.*
J'aimerais commencer ma propre entreprise d'art.	*I would like to start my own art business.*
J'aimerais surtout devenir influenceur.	*I would especially love to become an influencer.*
Comme acteur, je travaillerais sur scène.	*As an actor, I would work on stage.*
Mon emploi de rêve serait écrivain.	*My dream job would be a writer.*
Je penserais devenir journaliste.	*I would think about becoming a journalist.*

D'autres carrières	Other careers
J'aimerais être facteur.	*I would like to be a postman.*
Je voudrais devenir avocate car les lois m'intéressent.	*I would like to become a lawyer because law interests me.*
J'aimerais être scientifique ou médecin.	*I would like to be a scientist or a doctor.*
Je n'aimerais pas être policier ou soldat.	*I would not like to be a police officer or a soldier.*
Mon travail idéal serait chercheuse.	*My ideal job would be a researcher.*
Dans mon rôle de présidente, je changerais le monde.	*In my role as president, I would change the world.*
Je travaillerais comme serveur ou chef de cuisine.	*I would work as a waiter or chef.*
J'irais à l'étranger pour être secrétaire francophone.	*I would go abroad to be a French-speaking secretary.*

> **REMEMBER** ❗
> In French, you don't need to use the indefinite article (*un* / *une*) before jobs – unlike in English.

> **REMEMBER** ❗
> Remember that some job words have a masculine and a feminine form. For example:
> - *écrivain* / *écrivain(e)* (writer)
> - *influenceur* / *influenceuse* (influencer)

> **GRAMMAR TIP** ★
> To say what you **would** do, use the conditional. With regular **-er** verbs, add the ending **-ais** to the infinitive to make the *je* form.
>
> Some verbs are irregular, for example *je voudrais* (I would like), *j'irais* (I would go). See page 155.

Quel métier aimerais-tu faire? *Which job would you like to do?*

Un jour, j'aimerais être footballeuse professionnelle parce que j'adore le sport et que **ce serait** vraiment bien payé aussi. Si ce n'est pas possible, je pense que je chercherais un emploi dans la construction ou le commerce car **ce serait** intéressant.

One day, I would like to be a professional footballer because I love sport and it would be really well paid as well. If it's not possible, I think that I would look for a job in construction or trade as that would be interesting.

> **REVISION TIP** ☑
> Learn the phrase *ce serait*… (it would be…) so that you can describe what things **would be** like.

Choosing a career

Les lieux de travail	*Workplaces*
J'aimerais travailler dans une ferme.	*I would like to work on a farm.*
Mes parents travaillent dans un bureau.	*My parents work in an office.*
J'aime l'idée de travailler dans un hôpital.	*I like the idea of working in a hospital.*
Beaucoup de gens travaillent de chez eux.	*Lots of people work from home.*
Je ne voudrais pas un travail dans une usine.	*I wouldn't like a job in a factory.*

> **SOUNDS TIP** 🎤
> Take care with the *-aill* / *-ail* sound in *travailler* and *travail*. You don't hear the letter 'l' in these words.

Les avantages et les inconvénients	*Advantages and disadvantages*
Un avantage, ce serait le salaire.	*One advantage would be the salary.*
Un homme ou une femme d'affaires peut gagner beaucoup.	*A businessperson can earn a lot.*
Un inconvénient, c'est qu'il faut se lever très tôt.	*One disadvantage is that you have to get up very early.*
Les heures seraient longues.	*The hours would be long.*
Certains rôles sont trop dangereux.	*Some roles are too dangerous.*
Il y a beaucoup de concurrence.	*There is a lot of competition.*
Un métier professionnel demande beaucoup de responsabilités.	*A professional job involves a great deal of responsibilities.*
Ce serait bien d'avoir des collègues sympas.	*It would be good to have nice colleagues.*
Travailler en équipe est mieux que travailler seul.	*Working in a team is better than working alone.*

> **REVISION TIP** 📝
> Think of one job you are interested in and the pros and cons of the role so you are ready to talk about this in French.

Où voudrais-tu travailler? *Where would you like to work?*

Je voudrais travailler dans un bureau comme femme d'affaires. Je sais que beaucoup de gens travaillent de chez eux mais ce serait bien d'avoir des collègues dans la même pièce! À mon avis, travailler en équipe est mieux que travailler seul. Je n'aimerais pas travailler dehors, surtout en hiver.

I would like to work in an office as a businesswoman. I know that lots of people work from home but it would be good to have some colleagues in the same room! In my opinion, working in a team is better than working alone. I wouldn't like to work outside, especially in the winter.

1.3 Education and work

Vocabulary learning

Learn this vocabulary and then use the 'look, cover, write, check' technique to make sure you really know it. Cover the English first and then the French.

Future study and future plans

French	✓	English	✓
l'année (f.) sabbatique		gap year	
l'apprentissage (m.)		apprenticeship	
après avoir (+ past participle)		after having (done)	
le baccalauréat / bac		high school final exam (like A Levels)	
le boulot		work, job	
changer		to change	
conduire		to drive	
connaître		to know, be familiar with	
encore		yet, again	
l'étape (f.)		step, stage	
l'étude (f.)		study	
étudier		to study	
l'Europe (f.)		Europe	
la fin		end	
la formation		training	
futur(e)		future	
le lycée		college, sixth form	
le projet		plan	
quitter		to leave	
réussir		to succeed, pass	
le stage		work experience	
travailler		to work	
l'université (f.)		university	
les vacances (f.pl.)		holidays	
vouloir		to want (to)	
le voyage		trip, journey	
voyager		to travel	

Jobs

French	✓	English	✓
l'acteur / l'actrice		actor	
l'artiste (m. / f.)		artist	
l'auteur(e)		author	
l'avocat(e)		lawyer	
le chef / la cheffe		boss, cook	
le chercheur / la chercheuse		researcher	
l'écrivain(e)		writer	
le facteur / la factrice		postman / postwoman	
la femme d'affaires		businesswoman	
l'homme d'affaires		businessman	
l'influenceur / l'influenceuse		influencer	
le / la journaliste		journalist	
le médecin		doctor	
le policier / la policière		police officer	
le / la président(e)		president	
le / la scientifique		scientist	
le / la secrétaire		secretary	
le serveur / la serveuse		waiter, server	
le / la soldat(e)		soldier	

> **REVISION TIP** 📝
>
> To get more confident with speaking, try telling a friend, family member or pet which of the jobs above you would like to do or not, and why (in French).

Vocabulary learning

Work and workplaces

French	✓	English	✓
les affaires (f.pl.)		*business, matters*	
l'art (m.)		*art*	
l'avantage (m.)		*advantage*	
le bureau		*office*	
la carrière		*career*	
chercher		*to look for*	
le / la collègue		*colleague*	
le commerce		*trade*	
la concurrence		*competition*	
la construction		*construction, building*	
devenir		*to become*	
l'emploi (m.)		*job*	
l'équipe (f.)		*team*	
l'entreprise (f.)		*company*	
l'étranger (m.)		*abroad*	
la ferme		*farm*	
gagner		*to earn*	
l'idée (f.)		*idea*	
l'inconvénient (m.)		*disadvantage*	
intéresser		*to interest*	
se lever		*to get up*	
le lieu		*place*	
la loi		*law*	
le métier		*job, occupation*	
le monde		*world*	
la pièce		*room*	
possible		*possible*	
professionnel(le)		*professional*	
propre		*own, clean*	
la responsabilité		*responsibility*	
le rôle		*role*	
le salaire		*salary, wage*	

French	✓	English	✓
la scène		*stage*	
seul(e)		*alone*	
tôt		*early*	
le travail		*work, job*	
l'usine (f.)		*factory*	

REVISION TIP

For any words that you find harder to learn, try repeating them out loud ten times to help them to stick in your memory.

Answer the questions below. Cover the answers column with a piece of paper and write down as many answers as you can. Check and repeat.

Questions | Answers

	Questions		Answers
1	How do you say in French: 'I want to' and 'I would like to'?	Put paper here	*Je veux*; *je voudrais / j'aimerais*
2	Translate the following verbs into English: *je chercherai, je voyagerai, j'irai*.		I will look for; I will travel; I will go
3	What is *une année sabbatique*?		A gap year
4	Complete this phrase with the correct word: *Après avoir finis / fini / finir mes examens,...*	Put paper here	*Fini*
5	Answer this question in French: *Qu'est-ce que tu veux faire après tes examens?*		Possible answer: *Je veux aller au lycée pour préparer le bac*
6	List as many jobs in French as you can.	Put paper here	Possible answers: *professeur*; *avocat*; *chercheur*. See page 46 for more examples
7	Give three different places you could work in French.		Possible answers: *dans un bureau*; *dans une ferme*; *dans une usine*
8	What ending do you add to the infinitive of regular *-er* verbs to make the *je* form of the conditional?	Put paper here	*-ais*
9	How do you say 'it would be great' in French?		*Ce serait génial*
10	In French, give one advantage and one disadvantage of being a doctor.		Possible answer: *L'avantage, c'est le salaire mais l'inconvénient, ce sont les responsabilités*
11	Give four different words meaning 'job' in French.	Put paper here	*Le boulot*; *l'emploi*; *le métier*; *le travail*
12	Answer this question in French: *Quel métier aimerais-tu faire?*		Possible answer: *J'aimerais être médecin car j'adore les sciences*

Previous questions

Use these questions to check your knowledge of previous topics.

Questions | Answers

	Questions		Answers
1	Give five examples of unhealthy habits in French.	Put paper here	Possible answers: *fumer*; *vapoter*; *prendre de la drogue*; *manger du fast-food*; *boire beaucoup d'alcool*
2	Say three things about your school day.		Possible answer: *Les cours commencent à neuf heures et finissent à seize heures. La récré dure vingt minutes*
3	Give three examples of school rules in French.		Possible answers: *Nous devons porter un uniforme*; *Il faut apporter les cahiers*; *On doit écouter les profs*

Practice

EXAM

Section A: Listening comprehension

Relationships

You hear some French exchange students talking about relationships.

What is the opinion of the students on the following aspects?

Write   **P** for a **positive** opinion.

N for a **negative** opinion.

P+N for a **positive** and **negative** opinion.

> **EXAM TIP**
> Listen carefully for positive and negative adjectives and adverbs to help you decide on your answer.

1.	Parents		**[1 mark]**
2.	Friends		**[1 mark]**
3.	Partner		**[1 mark]**
4.	Teachers		**[1 mark]**

A French YouTuber

You hear this online documentary about Maxime, a French YouTuber.

Choose the correct answer and write the letter in each box.

> **EXAM TIP**
> You may hear all these options mentioned but only one will be true of Maxime.

Answer both parts of question 5.

5.1   Maxime is a…   **[1 mark]**

A	writer.
B	lawyer.
C	student.

5.2   He shared his school resources to…   **[1 mark]**

A	help his friends.
B	support year 12 students.
C	make some money.

Answer both parts of question 6.

6.1   Maxime's website…   **[1 mark]**

A	was immediately successful.
B	includes memory games.
C	made him well-known internationally.

6.2   Maxime's book…   **[1 mark]**

A	will be written soon.
B	includes well-being advice.
C	is for year 11 students.

7.   Recently, Maxime announced that he…   **[1 mark]**

A	has left university.
B	is going to travel for a year.
C	will work on a government education project.

Theme 1 Listening practice

A lifestyle podcast

You listen to two people on a podcast about their lifestyle.

They are talking about their reasons for wanting to make changes to their life.

A	Saving money
B	Getting fitter
C	Being more sociable
D	Supporting family members
E	Eating more healthily
F	Getting more sleep

What **two** reasons does each person give?

Write the correct letters in the boxes.

8. ☐   ☐   **[2 marks]**

9. ☐   ☐   **[2 marks]**

EXAM TIP

In this type of question, all the options A–F might be referred to in some way, but only **two** options will be true for each person.

Section B: Dictation

You will now hear 5 short sentences.

Listen carefully and using your knowledge of French sounds, write down in **French** exactly what you hear for each sentence.   **[10 marks]**

Sentence 1

....

....

Sentence 2

....

....

Sentence 3

....

....

Sentence 4

....

....

Sentence 5

....

....

EXAM TIP

There will always be a couple of words in the dictation task that do not appear on AQA's set vocabulary list. You may not know what they mean but you can still write them down, using your knowledge of French sounds.

✏ Practice EXAM

Theme 1 Speaking practice

Part 1: Role-play

Prepare the following role-play task. Then listen to the teacher's prompts and respond.

You are talking to your Swiss friend.

Your teacher will play the part of your friend and will speak first.

You should address your friend as *tu*.

When you see – **?** – you have to ask a question.

> **In order to score full marks, you must include at least one verb in your response to each task.**
>
> 1. Describe one member of your family. (Give **two** details.)
>
> 2. Say how you get on with your family. (Give **one** detail.)
>
> 3. Say if you like children and why / why not. (Give **one** opinion and **one** reason.)
>
> 4. Describe an activity you did with your family recently. (Give **two** details.)
>
> **? 5.** Ask your friend a question about marriage.

Part 2: Reading aloud task

Read aloud the following text in **French**.

> Hier, j'ai trouvé un boulot dans un supermarché en ville.
>
> Je commence cet été et c'est pour deux mois.
>
> Mon père pense que les heures sont assez longues.
>
> Heureusement, le salaire n'est pas mal.
>
> Les employés bénéficent d'une réduction de prix quand ils font des achats.
>
> À l'avenir, je travaillerai comme secrétaire dans un bureau.

Then listen and respond to the four questions on the topic of **Education and work**.

In order to score the highest marks, you must try to **answer all four questions as fully as you can**.

EXAM TIP

In order to score full marks, you must include at least one verb in your response to each task.

EXAM TIP

Ask the simplest question you can for task 5 here, using language that you are confident with. For example, you could ask, 'What do you think of marriage?' in French.

EXAM TIP

Notice any liaisons between words that end in 's' or 't' and words that start with a vowel or a silent 'h' in this text. Make sure you pronounce them correctly.

SOUNDS TIP

Remember that many French words end in a silent final **-e**. For example, *ville*, *pense* and *comme* in this text.

EXAM TIP

To get the best marks you should try and extend each response to give three bits of information, including suitable verbs.

Practice

Theme 1 Speaking practice

Part 3: Photo card task

Prepare a description of these two photos. You may make as many notes as you wish and use these notes during the test.

Then record yourself talking about the content of these photos for approximately one and a half minutes. **You must say at least one thing about each photo**.

After you have spoken about the content of the photos, you will be asked questions related to **any** of the topics within the theme of **People and lifestyle**. Listen to and respond to the example questions.

> **EXAM TIP**
>
> You could use your first sentence to say where each photo is set before giving more details. That ensures you have said at least one thing about each photo without worrying about running out of time.

> **EXAM TIP**
>
> Listen carefully to the unprepared questions that your teacher asks during the conversation. You can often adapt the language in the question to help start your answer.
>
> - Question: *Que **penses**-tu de…*
> - Answer: *Je **pense** que…*

Photo 1

Photo 2

Theme 1 Reading practice

Section A: Reading comprehension

Phone apps

You see some apps described on a website.

A	Cœurs et fleurs: club de célibataires à la recherche de l'amour.
B	Conduire sans peur: conseils pour ados inquiets.
C	En cas d'urgence: soutien santé dans les moments de crise.
D	Recettes originales pour la rentrée.
E	Battre le chômage: ouverture d'emplois et de stages.

Which description matches each type of app?

Write the correct letter in each box.

1. A jobs app ☐ **[1 mark]**

2. A dating app ☐ **[1 mark]**

3. A cookery app ☐ **[1 mark]**

Distance learning

You see an article by Léo, a teenage boy who studies from home in Canada.

He describes his experience of distance learning.

> Après le lycée, j'ai décidé de faire des études de commerce international avec un établissement d'enseignement à distance. Pour moi, il y a deux avantages à apprendre chez moi. D'abord, je peux étudier à mon propre rythme. Ensuite, il y a toujours des profs en ligne pour nous encourager.
>
> Par contre, il y a quelques inconvénients. Là où j'habite, Internet ne marche pas toujours bien et c'est extrêmement embêtant. En plus, parfois, je me sens triste et seul.
>
> Comme je souffre d'une maladie et que j'ai souvent froid, je mets **des gants** quand je travaille sur mon ordinateur.

EXAM TIP

To work out the meaning of **des gants**, read the whole sentence carefully to look for clues.

Answer the following questions **in English**.

4. According to Léo, what are **two** advantages of distance learning? **[2 marks]**

1 ....

2 ....

5. What **two** disadvantages does he mention? **[2 marks]**

1 ....

2 ....

6. Read the last sentence again. What would you do with **des gants**?
Write the correct letter in the box.

A	Read them.
B	Eat them.
C	Wear them.

☐

[1 mark]

Theme 1 Reading practice

Part time jobs

You read this online forum.

People are giving advice on finding part-time jobs.

André

Chaque samedi, j'achète le journal local pour voir s'il y a des entreprises qui cherchent des candidats. En ville, je vais dans les petits magasins et je parle aux propriétaires pour savoir s'ils ont un travail pour moi.

Béatrice

Il faut écrire une lettre de demande d'emploi que vous pouvez facilement adapter aux différents métiers. Ensuite, se préparer pour un futur entretien avec un membre de votre famille est toujours une bonne idée.

Cédric

À mon avis, la meilleure façon de trouver un boulot, c'est de regarder des sites de travail en ligne. Vous pouvez aussi proposer de garder les enfants de vos voisins.

Who gives the following advice?

Write   **A** for **André**.

            B for **Béatrice**.

            C for **Cédric**.

Write the correct letter in each box.

7.   Volunteer to babysit.   ☐ **[1 mark]**

8.   Practise your interview skills.   ☐ **[1 mark]**

9.   Find opportunities on the internet.   ☐ **[1 mark]**

10.   Have a draft application ready.   ☐ **[1 mark]**

11.   Speak to shopkeepers.   ☐ **[1 mark]**

Section B: Translation into English

12.   Translate these sentences into **English**.

Mon père est malade et il a souvent froid.   **[2 marks]**

....

....

Demain matin, je vais faire une promenade avec ma tante.   **[2 marks]**

....

....

S'il y avait un plus grand choix de matières, j'étudierais l'allemand ou le chinois.   **[2 marks]**

....

....

> **EXAM TIP** 🎯
>
> Re-read your answers to make sure they make sense and sound like natural English.

J'ai un ami qui ne boit que du thé avec du lait.   **[2 marks]**

....

....

Après avoir fini ses examens, ma demi-sœur voyagera à l'étranger.   **[2 marks]**

....

....

Practice **EXAM**

Theme 1 Writing practice

Section A: Translation into French

1. Translate the following sentences into **French**. **[10 marks]**

I always get on well with my friends.

....

....

He is the strictest teacher but we like his lessons.

....

....

I have hurt myself so I'm going to go to the hospital now.

....

....

This summer, I will learn a new language with an app.

....

....

My parents think that it's really bad to vape.

....

....

> **EXAM TIP**
> Remember that there are two possible ways to translate 'friends' in French. Either option is acceptable here.

Section B

Answer **either** Question 2.1 **or** Question 2.2

Either

Question 2.1

You are emailing your Belgian friend about your school.

Write approximately **90** words in **French**.

You must write something about each bullet point.

Describe:

- what you like about your school
- a recent activity at school
- what you want to do when you leave school. **[15 marks]**

Or

Question 2.2

You are writing an article about friendship for a French website.

Write approximately **90** words in **French**.

You must write something about each bullet point.

Describe:

- what makes a good friend
- a recent outing with friends
- what you will do to make new friends in future. **[15 marks]**

> **EXAM TIP**
> Tick off each bullet point prompt as you answer it.

> **EXAM TIP**
> Use the French you have learned – it doesn't have to be true.

Theme 1 Writing practice

Section C

Answer **either** Question 3.1 **or** Question 3.2

Either

Question 3.1

You are writing a post about health for a French blog.

Your post is about unhealthy lifestyles.

Write approximately **150** words in French.

You must write something about both bullet points.

Describe:

- the dangers of unhealthy habits
- how you improved your lifestyle recently.

Or

Question 3.2

You are writing an article for a French careers website.

Your article is about teenagers choosing a career.

Write approximately **150** words in French.

You must write something about both bullet points.

Describe:

- the importance of choosing the right job
- how you will decide what job to do in the future.

> **EXAM TIP**
> Take a few minutes to plan your answer, making a note of any key vocabulary and phrases you want to use.

[25 marks]

> **EXAM TIP**
> Try to develop some longer, more complex sentences with more than one clause.

[25 marks]

> **EXAM TIP**
> Read through your answers at the end to check for common mistakes. Make sure your verbs and tenses are correct!

2.1 Free-time activities

Music

Écouter de la musique	Listening to music
J'aime écouter de la musique à la radio.	I like listening to music on the radio.
Ma mère télécharge ses chansons préférées.	My mum downloads her favourite songs.
Il y a des services de streaming qui sont gratuits.	There are streaming services which are free.
Une fois par an, nous **allons** à un concert.	We go to a concert once a year.
Ma sœur achète des billets.	My sister is buying tickets.
Elle **va** à une soirée de musique traditionnelle.	She is going to a traditional music evening.
Cet été, je **vais** à un festival.	I'm going to a festival this summer.
Mon chanteur préféré **fait** une tournée en Angleterre.	My favourite singer is touring England.
J'apprécie beaucoup de genres de musique différents.	I appreciate lots of different sorts of music.

Faire de la musique	Making music
Tu joues d'un instrument?	Do you play an instrument?
Oui, je joue du piano / de la guitare.	Yes, I play the piano / the guitar.
Non, je ne joue pas d'un instrument.	No, I don't play an instrument.
Je chante avec un groupe d'amis.	I sing with a group of friends.
Ma copine a une belle voix.	My friend has a beautiful voice.
J'écris des paroles de chanson.	I write song lyrics.
Je fais de la musique car c'est ma passion.	I make music because it's my passion.
Nous faisons des rythmes et des sons.	We make rhythms and sounds.

> **GRAMMAR TIP** ★
> Make sure you know all forms of the irregular verbs *aller* and *faire* in the present tense. See page 146.

> **GRAMMAR TIP** ★
> The verb *jouer* is used with *de* when talking about playing an instrument. Remember that *de* changes to *du / de la / de l' / des* in front of masculine / feminine / plural nouns.

> **REVISION TIP** ☑
> There are no specific instruments on AQA's set vocabulary list but you can learn the French for any instruments that you play if you want to mention this in your own speaking or writing exam.

Tu aimes la musique? *Do you like music?*

J'adore la musique forte parce que c'est super pour ma motivation quand **je** fais de l'exercice. **Je** n'ai **jamais joué** d'un instrument mais tous les **jeudis, je** vais à un club de **jeunes** et nous faisons du karaoké ensemble. Un **jour, je** voudrais être chanteuse.

I love loud music because it's great for my motivation when I do exercise. I have never played an instrument but I go to a youth club every Thursday and we do karaoke together. One day, I would like to be a singer.

> **SOUNDS TIP** 🎤
> The French *j* sound in words like *je*, *jamais* and *joué* is softer than an English 'j'.

2.1 Free-time activities

Sport

Faire du sport	*Doing sport*
Chaque matin, je cours trois kilomètres.	*I run 3km every morning.*
Tous les samedis, je fais de la danse.	*I go dancing every Saturday.*
Nous faisons régulièrement du vélo.	*We regularly go cycling.*
Le mardi soir, mes frères font de la natation.	*My brothers go swimming on Tuesday evenings.*
Je suis membre d'une équipe de netball / rugby.	*I am a member of a netball / rugby team.*
Je joue au foot avec mes copains / copines.	*I play football with my friends.*
Chaque week-end, il y a des matchs.	*There are games / matches every weekend.*
Je vais m'inscrire à un club de vélo.	*I'm going to join a cycling club.*

Faisons une activité sportive!	*Let's do a sporting activity!*
Allons au parc pour courir.	*Let's go to the park to run.*
Jouons un match sur la plage.	*Let's play a match on the beach.*
Nageons dans la piscine ce soir.	*Let's swim in the pool tonight.*
Prenons un cours au centre sportif.	*Let's take a class at the sports centre.*
Regardons le match au stade.	*Let's watch the match at the stadium.*
Pratiquons un sport sur le terrain de jeux.	*Let's play a sport on the playing field.*
Soyons plus actifs cette année.	*Let's be more active this year.*

> **GRAMMAR TIP** ⭐
>
> Use **jouer + à** (to play) for ball sports and **faire + de** (to do) for other sports. Remember that *à* and *de* need to change to agree with the noun that follows.
>
> *Je joue au hockey.*
> I play hockey.
>
> *Je fais du ski.*
> I do skiing. / I ski.

> **REMEMBER** ❗
>
> The only ball game on the AQA vocabulary list is *le foot*. However, lots of other sports are cognates (similar to the English words) and might come up in a reading activity.

> **GRAMMAR TIP** ⭐
>
> The *nous* form of the imperative is used to say 'let's do' something. For most verbs, simply drop the *nous* from the present tense verb. The verb *être* is an exception – *soyons* (let's be). See page 141.

L'importance du sport *The importance of sport*

Voici trois **raisons** pour faire du sport: c'est **amusant**, c'est sain et cela encourage les jeunes à sortir de la **maison**. Faire du sport apprend aux enfants qu'on ne peut pas toujours gagner. Il est important d'accepter qu'on peut quelquefois manquer un but ou perdre un match, et c'est une bonne leçon pour la vie. **Faisons** plus de sport!

Here are three reasons to do sport: it's fun, it's healthy and it encourages young people to get out of the house. Doing sport teaches children that you can't always win. It is important to accept that one can sometimes miss a goal or lose a match and it's a good lesson for life. Let's do more sport!

> **SOUNDS TIP** 🎤
>
> The *s* sound in the middle of *faisons, amusant, raison* and *maison* is more like an English 'z' sound.

Vocabulary learning

Learn this vocabulary and then use the 'look, cover, write, check' technique to make sure you really know it. Cover the English first and then the French.

Music

French	✓	English	✓
le billet		*ticket*	
la chanson		*song*	
chanter		*to sing*	
le chanteur / la chanteuse		*singer*	
le concert		*concert*	
écouter		*to listen (to)*	
le festival		*festival*	
fort(e)		*loud, strong*	
le genre		*type, kind, sort*	
gratuit(e)		*free*	
le groupe		*group*	
l'instrument (m.)		*instrument*	
jouer		*to play*	
la musique		*music*	
les paroles (f.pl.)		*lyrics*	
la passion		*passion*	
la radio		*radio*	
le rythme		*rhythm, rate*	
le service		*service*	
le son		*sound*	
le streaming		*streaming*	
télécharger		*to download*	
la tournée		*tour, round*	
traditionnel(le)		*traditional*	
la voix		*voice*	

Sport

French	✓	English	✓
actif / active		*active*	
le but		*goal*	
le centre sportif		*sports centre*	
le club		*club*	
courir		*to run*	
danser		*to dance*	
l'équipe (f.)		*team*	
faire		*to do, make*	
le foot(ball)		*football*	
la forme		*form, shape*	
gagner		*to win*	
le jeu		*game*	
le kilomètre		*kilometre*	
manquer		*to miss*	
le match		*match*	
le membre		*member*	
nager		*to swim*	
la natation		*swimming*	
le parc		*park*	
perdre		*to lose*	
la piscine		*swimming pool*	
la plage		*beach*	
pratiquer		*to do, play*	
régulièrement		*regularly*	
s'inscrire à		*to join*	
le sport		*sport*	
le stade		*stadium*	
le terrain		*ground, terrain*	
le vélo		*bike, bicycle*	

REVISION TIP

When learning vocabulary, notice how some words are identical in both French and English (e.g. *le match*), while others are very similar (e.g. *le groupe*).

⇄ Retrieval VOCABULARY

Answer the questions below. Cover the answers column with a piece of paper and write down as many answers as you can. Check and repeat.

Questions

Answers

1 List in French five musical things you could listen to.

Possible answers: *un instrument / un concert / une chanson / une voix / un groupe / un rythme / un chanteur / une chanteuse / la musique / un son*

2 Translate these verbs into French: to listen to, to download, to join.

Écouter; télécharger; s'inscrire à

3 What does *faire une tournée* mean?

To tour / go on tour

4 What little words follow the verb *jouer* when talking about playing an instrument?

De (du; de la; de l'; des)

5 What little words follow the verb *jouer* when talking about playing a sport involving balls?

À (au; à la; à l'; aux)

6 Translate this sentence into French: I make music because it's my passion.

Je fais de la musique car c'est ma passion

7 List five places where you could do sport in French.

Possible answers: *au centre sportif / au stade / à la piscine / sur la plage / au parc / au terrain de jeux*

8 What does the verb *courir* mean?

To run

9 Translate this sentence into French: I am a member of a football team.

Je suis membre d'une équipe de foot

10 What do these suggestions mean in French? *nageons, faisons, soyons*

Let's swim; let's do / make; let's be

11 Answer this question in French: *Est-ce que tu aimes faire du sport? Pourquoi / pourquoi pas?*

Possible answers: *J'aime faire du sport car c'est amusant. / Je déteste jouer au foot parce que je n'aime pas perdre*

12 Give two examples of words where the 's' sound in the middle sounds a bit like an English 'z' (for example: *mai<u>s</u>on*).

Possible answers: *fai<u>s</u>ons, amu<u>s</u>ant, rai<u>s</u>on*

Put paper here

Previous questions

Use these questions to check your knowledge of previous topics.

Questions

Answers

1 How do you say 'the best thing' and 'the worst thing' in French?

Le mieux / le pire

2 Answer this question in French: *Qu'est-ce que tu veux faire après tes examens?*

Possible answer: *Je veux aller au lycée pour préparer le bac*

3 Translate the following verbs into English: *je chercherai, je voyagerai, j'irai.*

I will look for; I will travel; I will go

Put paper here

2.1 Free-time activities

Viewing habits

Qu'est-ce que tu regardes pendant ton temps libre?

What do you watch in your free time?

Mon émission préférée s'appelle…

My favourite programme is called…

Je **la** regarde avec mes sœurs.

*I watch **it** with my sisters.*

Je n'aime pas la télé-réalité.

I don't like reality TV.

J'aime regarder un influenceur qui raconte des blagues.

I like watching an influencer who tells jokes.

Je **le** regarde tous les jours.

*I watch **him** every day.*

Je préfère les films d'action.

I prefer action films.

Je **les** regarde parce que j'aime les effets spéciaux.

*I watch **them** because I like the special effects.*

Les pubs sont embêtantes donc je ne **les** regarde pas.

*The adverts are annoying so I don't watch **them**.*

La nouvelle série? Mes parents **l'**enregistrent.

*The new series? My parents are recording **it**.*

Nous regardons la météo.

We watch the weather forecast.

> **GRAMMAR TIP** ⭐
>
> Use the direct object pronouns **le** (it / him), **la** (it / her) and **les** (them) before the verb to avoid repeating a masculine, feminine or plural noun.
>
> Other direct object pronouns are *me* (me), *te* (you), *nous* (us) and *vous* (you). See page 132.

Devant l'écran

In front of the screen

Quand j'**étais** petit(e), je **regardais** la télé chaque matin.

When I was little, I used to watch TV every morning.

C'**était** amusant car les personnages **étaient** un peu fous.

It was funny because the characters were a bit crazy.

Mon grand frère **regardait** des vidéos sur son ordinateur.

My big brother used to watch videos on his computer.

On **faisait** les devoirs devant l'écran.

We used to do homework in front of the screen.

Nous **allions** au cinéma une fois par semaine.

We used to go to the cinema once a week.

> **GRAMMAR TIP** ⭐
>
> You can use the imperfect tense to say what you and other people used to do. See page 152.

Ma série préférée *My favourite series*

J'aime regarder des films en langues étrangères en streaming avec ma mère. Quand j'étais plus jeune, on diffusait ma série préférée à la télé tous les vendredi soirs. Mes amis et moi, nous la regardions chaque semaine pour nous relaxer. C'était parfait pour la fin de la semaine parce que chaque épisode nous faisait rire.

I like watching foreign language films on a streaming service with my mum. When I was younger, my favourite series used to be broadcast on TV every Friday evening. My friends and I used to watch it every week in order to relax. It was perfect for the end of the week because every episode used to make us laugh.

> **REVISION TIP** 📝
>
> Think about what you like to watch, and how, why, when and who with. Prepare some sentences in French that you could use in speaking or writing tasks on this topic.

2.1 Free-time activities

Shopping and going out

Le shopping	Shopping
Je cherche un cadeau.	I'm looking for a present.
Je vais acheter un sac **pour lui** et un chapeau **pour elle**.	I'm going to buy a bag for him and a hat for her.
Je vais faire des achats en ligne **avec vous**.	I'm going to make some online purchases with you.
Ils sont allés aux magasins **sans moi**.	They went to the shops without me.
Ils vont livrer les vêtements **chez nous**.	They are going to deliver the clothes to our house.
Ça coûte trop cher **pour eux** – c'est cent livres!	It's too expensive for them – it's £100!
Je veux acheter quelque chose avec mon argent de poche.	I want to buy something with my pocket money.
Tu vas payer pour un manteau de marque?	Are you going to pay for a designer coat?

Sortons!	Let's go out!
Est-ce que tu veux…	Do you want to…
sortir avec moi?	go out with me?
aller en ville?	go into town?
voir une pièce au théâtre?	see a play at the theatre?
voir un spectacle?	see a show?
manger dans un restaurant?	eat in a restaurant?
aller à un événement culturel?	go to a cultural event?
faire du shopping au centre commercial?	go to the shopping centre?

> **GRAMMAR TIP** ★
>
> Emphatic pronouns are often used after prepositions such as *avec* (with), *pour* (for) and *sans* (without). The emphatic pronouns are *moi* (me), *toi* (you), *lui* (him), *elle* (her), *nous* (us), *vous* (you), *eux* (them) and *elles* (them).

> **SOUNDS TIP** 🎤
>
> The **ch** sound in French is more like a 'shh' sound in English. Try saying these words:
>
> **ch**er**ch**er, **ch**ose, **ch**er, **ch**apeau, a**ch**eter, po**ch**e.

> **REVISION TIP** ☑
>
> Practise asking questions on different topics to prepare for the role-play task.

Où fais-tu du shopping? *Where do you shop?*

Je vais **souvent** au marché qui a lieu en ville **toutes les semaines**. Il y a **toujours** des vêtements à la mode pour moins de vingt euros. **Normalement**, on ne peut pas les essayer donc **parfois** je préfère aller au centre commercial avec mes copains. **De temps en temps**, j'achète et je vends des choses en ligne aussi.

I often go to the market, which takes place in town every week. There are always some fashionable clothes for less than 20 euros. Normally, you can't try them on, so sometimes I prefer to go to the shopping centre with my friends. I buy and sell things online as well from time to time.

> **GRAMMAR TIP** ★
>
> Use adverbs of frequency to say how often things happen. For other types of adverbs and where to place them in a sentence, see page 128.

Vocabulary learning

Learn this vocabulary and then use the 'look, cover, write, check' technique to make sure you really know it. Cover the English first and then the French.

Viewing habits

French	✓	English	✓
l'action (f.)		action	
la blague		joke	
le cinéma		cinema	
devant		in front of	
diffuser		to broadcast	
l'écran (m.)		screen	
l'effet (m.)		effect	
l'émission (f.)		TV programme	
enregistrer		to record	
étranger / étrangère		foreign	
fou / folle		crazy	
la météo		weather forecast	
l'ordinateur (m.)		computer	
le personnage		character	
la publicité / pub		advert / ad	
raconter		to tell	
la réalité		reality	
se relaxer		to relax	
rire		to laugh	
la série		series	
spécial(e)		special	
la télé		TV	
la vidéo		video	

Going out

French	✓	English	✓
culturel(le)		cultural	
l'événement (m.)		event	
la pièce		play	
le spectacle		show	
le théâtre		theatre	

Shopping

French	✓	English	✓
l'achat (m.)		purchase	
acheter		to buy	
l'argent (m.)		money	
le cadeau		present	
le centre		centre	
le chapeau		hat	
cher / chère		expensive	
chercher		to look for	
chez		at the place of, at	
la chose		thing	
commercial(e)		commercial, shopping	
coûter		to cost	
de temps en temps		from time to time	
l'euro (m.)		euro	
la livre		pound	
livrer		to deliver	
le magasin		shop	
le manteau		coat	
le marché		market	
la marque		brand	
la mode		fashion	
avoir lieu		to take place	
payer		to pay (for)	
la poche		pocket	
quelque		some	
le sac		bag	
le shopping		shopping	
vendre		to sell	
le vêtement		garment, item or article of clothing	

Retrieval

Answer the questions below. Cover the answers column with a piece of paper and write down as many answers as you can. Check and repeat.

Questions | Answers

	Questions		Answers
1	Answer this question in French: *Quelle est ton émission préférée?*	Put paper here	*Mon émission préférée s'appelle…*
2	List five things you could watch on TV in French.		Possible answers: *un film d'action; la télé-réalité; les pubs; une série; la météo*
3	What do the direct object pronouns *le, la* and *les* mean?	Put paper here	It / him; it / her; them
4	Translate this sentence into English: *Quand j'étais petit(e), je regardais la télé chaque matin.*		When I was little, I used to watch TV every morning
5	What is the name of the tense used to say what you and other people used to do?		The imperfect tense
6	Which verb is the odd one out and why? *diffuser, enregistrer, rire*	Put paper here	*Rire* (to laugh) as *diffuser* (to broadcast) and *enregistrer* (to record) are both things you can do with a programme
7	Translate these phrases into French: for me, with him, without us.		*Pour moi; avec lui; sans nous*
8	Where is *chez eux*?	Put paper here	At their place / house
9	List three words related to clothing in French.		Possible answers: *un manteau / un vêtement / un chapeau / une poche*
10	Translate this question into French: Do you want to go shopping?		Possible answer: *Est-ce que tu veux faire du shopping?*
11	List as many adverbs of frequency as you can in French.	Put paper here	Possible answers: *souvent; toutes les semaines; toujours; normalement; parfois; de temps en temps*
12	Answer this question in French: *Où fais-tu du shopping?*		Possible answer: *Je fais du shopping au centre commercial avec mes amis*

Previous questions

Use these questions to check your knowledge of previous topics.

Questions | Answers

	Questions		Answers
1	Give one advantage and one disadvantage of learning Maths.	Put paper here	Possible answer: *L'avantage, c'est que c'est intéressant mais l'inconvénient, c'est que c'est difficile*
2	What ending do you add to the infinitive of regular *-er* verbs to make the *je* form of the conditional?		*-ais*
3	List five places where you could do sport in French.		Possible answers: *au centre sportif / au stade, à la piscine / sur la plage / au parc / au terrain de jeux*

2.2 Customs, festivals and celebrations

Family celebrations

Les anniversaires	***Birthdays***
L'année dernière, ma famille a organisé une fête surprise.	*Last year, my family organised a surprise party.*
Pour mon anniversaire, ils ont invité tous mes copains.	*They invited all my friends for my birthday.*
J'ai reçu beaucoup de cadeaux et c'était très sympa.	*I received lots of presents and it was very nice.*
Tout le monde m'a souhaité 'Joyeux anniversaire'.	*Everyone wished me 'Happy birthday'.*
Ils ont chanté et puis on a mangé du gâteau.	*They sang and then we ate some cake.*

REVISION TIP ☑

Prepare what you would say in French to talk or write about your own birthday.

Célébrer en famille	***Celebrating as a family***
Pour la Saint-Valentin, mon père a offert des fleurs à ma mère.	*For Valentine's Day, my dad gave my mum some flowers.*
J'ai célébré le Nouvel An avec mes cousins.	*I celebrated New Year with my cousins.*
Le 5 novembre, nous avons fait un feu dans le jardin.	*On 5 November, we made a fire in the garden.*
Les jours fériés, mes pères ont toujours préparé un repas spécial.	*On public holidays, my dads have always prepared a special meal.*
J'ai acheté une carte pour féliciter mon frère pour ses résultats d'examen.	*I bought a card to congratulate my brother for his exam results.*

SOUNDS TIP 🎤

Practise pushing your lips forward to make the low, round *ou* sound and say these words: *nous, tous, jour, nouveau, beaucoup* and *toujours*.

Joyeuses Fêtes *Season's greetings*

À Noël, ma famille **m'**a offert un nouveau portable. Ma sœur aime la lecture donc je **lui** ai donné un roman. Mes grands-parents étaient à l'étranger mais nous **leur** avons envoyé une carte. Ils **nous** ont promis qu'ils seraient là l'année prochaine. Je **vous** souhaite une bonne année!

At Christmas, my family gave me a new mobile phone. My sister likes reading so I gave her a novel. My grandparents were abroad but we sent them a card. They promised us that they would be here next year. I wish you a Happy New Year!

GRAMMAR TIP ★

The **indirect object pronouns** *me* (me), *te* (you), *lui* (him / her / it), *nous* (us), *vous* (you) and *leur* (them) are used with verbs that are followed by *à* to convey the idea of doing something **to** someone. See page 132.

REMEMBER ❗

Notice how the word order differs in French and English. Indirect object pronouns in French go **before** the auxiliary verb. See page 132.

⚙ Knowledge VOCABULARY

2.2 Customs, festivals and celebrations

Religious customs, festivals and events

Les fêtes religieuses	*Religious festivals*
À l'Aïd, j'adore donner et recevoir des cadeaux.	*At Eid, I love giving and receiving presents.*
À Pâques, on va à l'église pour prier Dieu.	*At Easter, we go to church to pray to God.*
Aller à la synagogue est une tradition familiale.	*Going to the synagogue is a family tradition.*
Nous allons ensemble à la mosquée.	*We go to the mosque together.*
Des millions de personnes célèbrent la fête des Lumières.	*Millions of people celebrate the Festival of Lights.*
Les jours de fête, ma famille va au temple.	*My family goes to the temple on festival days.*

Les festivals et les événements	*Festivals and events*
On va voir le feu d'artifice.	*We are going to see the firework display.*
Nous allons assister à **cet événement** français.	*We're going to attend this French event.*
Cette année, nous regarderons le Tour de France.	*This year, we will watch the Tour de France.*
Ces gâteaux sont pour la fête des Rois.	*These cakes are for the festival of Kings / Twelfth Night.*
Ce festival a lieu le 6 janvier.	*This festival takes place on 6 January.*
Cet été, je vais participer à la Fête de la Musique.	*I'm going to take part in the Music Festival this summer.*
Pour la fête nationale, il y a toujours des défilés.	*There are always parades for Bastille Day.*
Je m'intéresse à **ce festival** de cuisine, Goût de France.	*I'm interested in this cooking festival, Taste of France.*

La fête nationale à Paris *Bastille Day in Paris*

J'allais à Paris pour la fête nationale quand j'ai rencontré mon ami dans le train. **Nous parlions** encore quand le train est arrivé donc nous sommes allés en ville ensemble. **Tout le monde attendait** le défilé militaire quand nous avons trouvé un bon endroit pour nous arrêter. **Je regardais** les soldats quand le feu d'artifice a commencé. **C'était** formidable!

I was going to Paris for Bastille Day when I met my friend on the train. We were still talking when the train arrived so we went into town together. Everyone was waiting for the military parade when we found a good place to stop. I was watching the soldiers when the firework display started. It was terrific!

GRAMMAR TIP ⭐

To say 'this' or 'these' in French, use the **demonstrative adjectives** *ce* (before a masculine, singular noun), *cette* (before a feminine, singular noun) or *ces* (before a plural noun). *Cet* is used before a masculine noun beginning with a vowel or a silent 'h'.

SOUNDS TIP 🎤

When the letter 'c' is followed by an 'i' or an 'e' in French, it always makes a soft 's' sound rather than a hard 'k' sound. Remember that a 'ç' (with a cedilla accent) also makes an 's' sound. Try saying: *ce, cette, ces, français, leçon, reçois*.

GRAMMAR TIP ⭐

The imperfect tense can be used to describe what you **were** doing or what **was** happening when other events took place. See page 152.

66 2.2 Customs, festivals and celebrations

Vocabulary learning

Learn this vocabulary and then use the 'look, cover, write, check' technique to make sure you really know it. Cover the English first and then the French.

Celebrations and festivals

French	✓	English	✓
l'an (m.) / l'année (f.)		year	
l'anniversaire (m.)		birthday	
le cadeau		present	
la carte		card	
célébrer		to celebrate	
donner		to give	
envoyer		to send	
féliciter		to congratulate	
férié(e)		public holiday	
la fête		party, festival	
le feu		fire	
la fleur		flower	
formidable		terrific, astounding	
inviter		to invite	
joyeux / joyeuse		merry, joyful, happy	
million (m.)		million	
nouveau / nouvelle		new	
offrir		to offer, to give	
organiser		to organise	
promettre		to promise	
recevoir		to receive	
le résultat		result	
le roman		novel	
la Saint-Valentin		Valentine's Day	
souhaiter		to wish	
la surprise		surprise	

> **REVISION TIP**
> Make sure you come back to revise any words you were not sure of the first time you reviewed them. You could mark these with a dot in the columns above.

Religious celebrations

French	✓	English	✓
Aïd (m.)		Eid	
le dieu		god	
l'église (f.)		church	
la lumière		light	
la mosquée		mosque	
Noël (m.)		Christmas	
Pâques (m.)		Easter	
prier		to pray	
religieux / religieuse		religious	
la synagogue		synagogue	
le temple		temple	
la tradition		tradition	

Festivals and events

French	✓	English	✓
arrêter		to stop	
assister à		to attend	
ce / cet / cette / ces		this / these	
le défilé		parade	
l'endroit (m.)		place, spot	
le festival		festival	
la fête nationale		Bastille Day, French national holiday	
le feu d'artifice		firework display	
le goût		taste	
s'intéresser à		to be interested in	
participer à		to take part in	
rencontrer		to meet	
le roi		king	
le train		train	
le Tour de France		Tour de France	
tout le monde		everybody, everyone	

Retrieval

Answer the questions below. Cover the answers column with a piece of paper and write down as many answers as you can. Check and repeat.

Questions	Answers
1 Answer this question in French: *Qu'est-ce que tu as fait pour célébrer ton dernier anniversaire?*	Possible answer: *J'ai organisé une fête, on a mangé du gâteau et j'ai reçu des cadeaux et des cartes*
2 What is *un jour férié*?	A public holiday (or bank holiday)
3 What are the six indirect pronouns in French?	*Me* (me); *te* (you); *lui* (him/her/it); *nous* (us); *vous* (you) and *leur* (them)
4 When would you use an indirect pronoun?	With verbs that are followed by *à*, to convey the idea of doing something <u>to</u> someone
5 Translate this sentence into English: *Nous leur avons envoyé une carte.*	We sent them a card
6 List four places of worship in French.	*La mosquée; l'église; le temple; la synagogue*
7 Choose the correct word to complete this sentence: *Nous allons assister à ce / cet / cette événement.*	*Cet* (in front of a masculine noun that starts with a vowel)
8 What is *la fête nationale*?	Bastille Day (French national holiday)
9 Translate these words into French: a parade, a fire, a king.	*Un défilé; un feu; un roi*
10 Answer this question in French: *Quelle est ta fête préférée et pourquoi?*	Possible answer: *J'adore célébrer Noël avec ma famille parce que c'est sympa*
11 Translate the following verbs into English: *assister à, s'intéresser à, participer à.*	To attend; to be interested in; to take part in
12 What tense would you use to describe what you were doing or what was happening?	The imperfect tense

Put paper here

Previous questions

Use these questions to check your knowledge of previous topics.

Questions	Answers
1 Translate this sentence into French: I don't smoke because it's bad for your health.	*Je ne fume pas parce que c'est mauvais pour la santé*
2 How do you say 'it would be great' in French?	*Ce serait génial*
3 List as many adverbs of frequency as you can in French.	Possible answers: *souvent; toutes les semaines; toujours; normalement; parfois; de temps en temps*

Put paper here

2.3 Celebrity culture

Celebrities

Qui est ta célébrité préférée et pourquoi?
Who is your favourite celebrity and why?

Qui est ta célébrité préférée et pourquoi?	Who is your favourite celebrity and why?
Ma célébrité préférée s'appelle…	My favourite celebrity is called…
C'est mon héros / héroïne.	They are my hero.
Je l'adore parce que c'est un(e) acteur / actrice génial(e).	I love him / her because he / she is a great actor / actress.
Je le / la suis en ligne car il / elle est drôle.	I follow him / her online because he / she is funny.
Je le trouve beau. Je la trouve belle.	I find him handsome. I find her beautiful.
C'est un sportif / une sportive étonnant(e).	He / She is an amazing sportsperson.
Je m'inspire de son style.	I'm inspired by his / her style.
Il / Elle est porte-parole pour la jeunesse.	He / She is a spokesperson for young people.
Il / Elle a eu une grande influence culturelle.	He / She has had a big cultural influence.

Parle-moi de ta célébrité préférée
Tell me about your favourite celebrity

Parle-moi de ta célébrité préférée	Tell me about your favourite celebrity
Il / Elle est en train de faire une tournée internationale.	He / She is in the middle of doing an international tour.
Il / Elle est en train d'écrire un livre.	He / She is in the middle of writing a book.
Il / Elle vient de lancer sa propre marque de vêtements.	He / She has just launched his / her own clothes brand.
Il / Elle vient d'obtenir un rôle dans un nouveau film.	He / She has just got a role in a new film.

Ma célébrité préférée *My favourite celebrity*

Ma célébrité préférée, c'est un chanteur afric**ain** qui a fait beaucoup pour lutter contre la f**aim** dans le monde. Il vient de donner un concert avec des groupes améric**ain**s et m**ain**tenant il est en tr**ain** d'enregistrer un nouvel album. C'est un **in**dividu **in**telligent qui fait un travail **im**portant. Il m'**in**spire!

My favourite celebrity is an African singer who has done a lot to fight against global hunger. He has just given a concert with American bands and now he is in the middle of recording a new album. He's an intelligent individual who does important work. He inspires me!

REVISION TIP

Choose one celebrity you could describe in a writing or speaking task. Prepare to give your opinion and a reason why you like them in French.

GRAMMAR TIP

The phrase *être en train de + infinitive* means 'to be in the middle of (do)ing'.

The phrase *venir de + infinitive* means 'to have just (done)'.

SOUNDS TIP

The letter combinations *ain / in / aim / im* are all pronounced in the same way in French. Try making this nasal sound in the following words: *afric**ain**, **in**telligent, f**aim**, **im**portant.*

2.3 Celebrity culture

Fame

Les avantages et les inconvénients de la célébrité	The advantages and the disadvantages of fame
Un avantage, c'est qu'on peut devenir riche.	One advantage is that you can become rich.
Par contre, il faut apprendre à gérer la presse.	On the other hand, you have to learn to deal with the press.
On peut se marier avec une star.	You can marry a star.
Cependant, on ne peut plus vivre une vie normale.	However, you can't live a normal life any more.
Mais les inconvénients sont les critiques et les scandales.	But the disadvantages are criticism and scandals.
On peut utiliser son succès pour faire une différence.	You can use your success to make a difference.
Malheureusement, il faut toujours penser à son image.	Unfortunately, you always have to think about your image.

Comment devenir célèbre	How to become famous
Gagne / Gagnez un concours.	Win a competition.
Écris / Écrivez une chanson populaire.	Write a popular song.
Développe / Développez une compétence extraordinaire.	Develop an extraordinary skill.
Invente / Inventez un produit.	Invent a product.
Fais / Faites des vidéos pour aider les gens.	Make videos to help people.
Va / Allez dans l'espace.	Go into space.
Sois / Soyez original(e).	Be original.

> **REVISION TIP**
> Learn some key words to describe pros and cons of any topic, as well as to contrast opposing points of view.

> **GRAMMAR TIP**
> The imperative in the *tu* and *vous* forms is used for giving instructions and orders. Use the present tense of the verb, without the *tu* / *vous* in front of it. With **-er** verbs, drop the final **-s** from the *tu* form of the verb. See page 141.

> **REMEMBER**
> The verb *être* (to be) is irregular in the imperative: *sois / soyez…* (be…).

La vie d'un influenceur   *The life of an influencer*

Je suis célèbre **depuis** six mois mais je travaille dur **depuis** longtemps pour réaliser cet objectif. **Depuis** deux ans, je poste des selfies avec mon chien sur les réseaux sociaux. Cependant, c'est seulement récemment que les gens ont commencé à me reconnaître dans la rue. Maintenant, je gagne suffisamment d'argent pour nourrir ma famille.

I have been famous for six months but I've been working hard for a long time to achieve this goal. I've been posting selfies with my dog for two years on social media. However, it's only recently that people have started to recognise me in the street. Now, I earn sufficient money to feed my family.

> **GRAMMAR TIP**
> Use *depuis* with the present tense in French to say how long you **have been doing** something.

Vocabulary learning

Learn this vocabulary and then use the 'look, cover, write, check' technique to make sure you really know it. Cover the English first and then the French.

French	✓	English	✓
américain(e)		American	
l'avantage (m.)		advantage	
la célébrité		celibrity / fame	
le chien		dog	
la compétence		skill	
le concours		competition	
la critique		criticism	
depuis		for, since	
développer		to develop	
devenir		to become	
la différence		difference	
l'espace (m.)		space	
étonnant(e)		surprising, amazing, incredible	
être en train de (+ infinitive)		to be in the middle of + verb	
extraordinaire		extraordinary	
la faim		hunger	
gérer		to manage / deal with	
le héros (m.) / l'héroïne (f.)		hero	
l'image (f.)		image	
important(e)		important	
l'inconvénient (m.)		disadvantage	
l'individu (m.)		individual	
l'influence (f.)		influence	
inspirer		to inspire	
s'inspirer de		to be inspired by	
intelligent(e)		intelligent	
international(e)		international	

French	✓	English	✓
inventer		to invent	
la jeunesse		youth	
lancer		to launch	
longtemps		a long time	
lutter		to fight	
malheureusement		unfortunately	
la marque		brand	
mondial(e)		worldwide, global	
normal(e)		normal	
l'objectif (m.)		goal, objective	
original(e)		original	
populaire		popular	
le / la porte-parole		spokesperson	
poster		to post	
la presse		press	
le produit		product	
réaliser		to achieve	
reconnaître		to recognise	
le réseau		network	
riche		rich	
la rue		street	
le scandale		scandal	
le selfie		selfie	
social(e)		social	
la star		star, celebrity	
le style		style	
le succès		success	
suivre		to follow	
suffisamment		sufficient(ly)	
venir de (+ infinitive)		to have just (done)	

Answer the questions below. Cover the answers column with a piece of paper and write down as many answers as you can. Check and repeat.

Questions | Answers

	Questions		Answers
1	Answer this question in French: *Qui est ta célébrité préférée et pourquoi?*	Put paper here	Possible answer: *Ma célébrité préférée s'appelle … et je l'adore car il / elle est drôle*
2	Translate this sentence into French: I find her beautiful.		*Je la trouve belle*
3	What is *un(e) porte-parole*?		A spokesperson
4	What is the French phrase meaning 'to be in the middle of (do)ing'?	Put paper here	*Être en train de* + infinitive
5	Translate this sentence into English: *Je viens d'écrire un livre.*		I have just written a book
6	What do all these words have in common? *train, intelligent, faim, important*	Put paper here	They all include the same sound in French (made by the letter combinations *ain / in / aim / im*)
7	What are the French words for 'advantage' and 'disadvantage'?		*L'avantage*; *l'inconvénient*
8	List three French words or phrases you could use to contrast pros and cons.	Put paper here	*Par contre*; *cependant*; *malheureusement*
9	Translate the following sentence into French: I have been posting selfies for two years.		*Je poste des selfies depuis deux ans*
10	Translate this sentence into French: You can't live a normal life any more.		Possible answer: *On ne peut plus vivre une vie normale*
11	What does *sois original(e)* mean?	Put paper here	Be original
12	What is the name of the grammatical form used to give instructions and orders?		The imperative

Previous questions

Use these questions to check your knowledge of previous topics.

Questions | Answers

	Questions		Answers
1	List three different verbs in the *je* form that can be used with an infinitive to talk about future plans.	Put paper here	Any three from: *je voudrais / je veux / j'espère / je vais / je souhaite*
2	What do these suggestions mean in French? *nageons, faisons, soyons*		Let's swim; let's do / make; let's be
3	Answer this question in French: *Qu'est-ce que tu as fait pour célébrer ton dernier anniversaire?*		Possible answer: *J'ai organisé une fête, on a mangé du gâteau et j'ai reçu des cadeaux et des cartes*

Practice EXAM

Theme 2 Listening practice

Section A: Listening comprehension

A local event

You hear this event mentioned on the radio.

Write

A if only statement **A** is correct.

B if only statement **B** is correct.

A+B if both statements **A** and **B** are correct.

Write the correct letter(s) in each box.

Answer both parts of question 1.

5.1 The festival is to celebrate… [1 mark]

A	the start of summer.
B	the role of Mother Nature.

EXAM TIP

Don't leave any answer boxes empty, even if you are not totally sure of the correct response.

5.2 There will be… [1 mark]

A	fireworks in the evening.
B	children taking part in parades.

2. You could… [1 mark]

A	dress up.
B	win a prize.

Online influencer

You hear this review of an online influencer.

Complete the sentences in **English**.

Answer both parts of question 3.

3.1 Every day she tells us… [1 mark]

....

3.2 The best thing is that… [1 mark]

....

Answer both parts of question 4.

4.1 She always shares… [1 mark]

....

4.2 Sometimes in her videos she adds… [1 mark]

....

Theme 2 Listening practice

An entertainment podcast

You are listening to an entertainment podcast.

Choose the **two** correct statements. Write the correct letters in the boxes.

5.

A	The play opened at the end of the month.
B	The play will run until the Easter holidays.
C	The main actor recently starred in a film.
D	The play will also be performed in London.

[2 marks]

> **EXAM TIP**
>
> Listen carefully for verbs in different tenses to help identify when these events take place.

6.

A	The event will take place outside.
B	It takes place every summer.
C	Teenagers will watch their favourite films.
D	There is a chance to meet some film stars.

[2 marks]

Section B: Dictation

You will now hear 5 short sentences.

Listen carefully and using your knowledge of French sounds, write down in **French** exactly what you hear for each sentence.   [10 marks]

Sentence 1

....

....

Sentence 2

....

....

Sentence 3

....

....

Sentence 4

....

....

Sentence 5

....

....

✏ Practice EXAM

Theme 2 Speaking practice

Part 1: Role-play

Prepare the following role-play task. Then listen to the teacher's prompts and respond.

You are talking to your Moroccan friend.

Your teacher will play the part of your friend and will speak first.

You should address your friend as *tu*.

When you see this – **?** – you will have to ask a question.

> **In order to score full marks, you must include at least one verb in your response to each task.**
>
> **2.** Say what type of sport you prefer and why. (Give **one** type and **one** reason.)
>
> **3.** Describe your favourite TV programme. (Give **two** details.)
>
> **4.** Say something you did in town recently. (Give **two** details.)
>
> **5.** Give **one** advantage of pocket money.
>
> **? 6.** Ask your friend a question about music.

EXAM TIP 🎯

For the type of sport you prefer, you could name a specific sport or be more general (e.g. team sports, water sports, winter sports).

Part 2: Reading aloud task

Read aloud the following text in **French**.

> Avant de choisir un film, je lis les critiques.
>
> Je préfère le regarder sur le grand écran.
>
> Ma sœur vient de télécharger une série sur son ordinateur.
>
> Malheureusement, elle a utilisé toute la mémoire.
>
> Nous partageons les mêmes goûts.
>
> Demain, quand je la garderai, on jouera à un jeu ensemble.

EXAM TIP 🎯

If you make a mistake, you can correct your pronunciation or start again. It is the final, corrected, version that will be assessed.

Then listen and respond to the four questions on the topic of **Free-time activities**.

In order to score the highest marks, you must try to **answer all four questions as fully as you can**.

SOUNDS TIP 🎤

Make sure you pronounce *un* and *une* differently: ***un** film*, ***une** série*. Try contrasting these sounds as they appear in words like *b**run*** / *b**rune*** (brown) and *chac**un*** / *chac**une*** (each person).

Theme 2 Speaking practice

Part 3: Photo card task

Prepare a description of these two photos. You may make as many notes as you wish and use these notes during the test.

Then record yourself talking about the content of these photos for approximately one and a half minutes. **You must say at least one thing about each photo.**

After you have spoken about the content of the photos, you will be asked questions related to **any** of the topics within the theme of **Popular culture**. Listen to and respond to the example questions.

> **EXAM TIP** 🎯
>
> Try to answer each of the unprepared questions that your teacher asks during the conversation with two or three sentences.

> **EXAM TIP** 🎯
>
> You could use *venir de* **+ infinitive** to say what seems to have just happened in the photo and *être en train de* **+ infinitive** to say what people in the photo are in the middle of doing.

Photo 1

Photo 2

EXAM

Theme 2 Reading practice

Section A: Reading comprehension

A wedding in Morocco

You read this article about weddings in Morocco, a country in North Africa.

Quand on organisait notre mariage au Maroc, on nous a dit de choisir entre les saisons du printemps et de l'automne car l'été est trop chaud. Avant d'acheter nos billets, on a dû faire une demande officielle pour obtenir l'accord du gouvernement marocain.

Pour réduire les coûts, célébrer le mariage sur la plage ou dans un jardin public en ville sont deux possibilités également populaires. Ça vaut la peine de visiter le quartier le lendemain aussi – sans se lever trop tôt le matin!

EXAM TIP

Start by reading the options for question 1 **before** you look for the answer near the start of the text. Then read question 2 and find the answer – and so on.

Complete these sentences. Write the correct letter in each box.

1. It's best to avoid getting married in Morocco in the... **[1 mark]**

A	spring.
B	summer.
C	autumn.

2. An official request to get married in the country should be submitted... **[1 mark]**

A	on arrival in Morocco.
B	for government approval.
C	after buying tickets.

3. Compared to celebrating in a park, celebrating on the beach is... **[1 mark]**

A	equally popular.
B	less popular.
C	more popular.

4. It's worth visiting the area... **[1 mark]**

A	early in the morning.
B	the day before.
C	the next day.

A teenage model

You read an article about a young model, Zimo.

What does the article say about these events?

Write **P** for something that happened **in the past**

N for something that is happening **now**

F for something that will happen **in the future**.

Write the correct letter in each box.

5. Sharing selfies **[1 mark]**

6. Appearing on posters **[1 mark]**

7. Living in London **[1 mark]**

8. Studying fashion **[1 mark]**

9. Becoming a spokesperson **[1 mark]**

Zimo ne partage plus de selfies mais, depuis un mois, on le voit partout sur les affiches. Cet adolescent britannique a eu la chance de sa vie quand **une réalisatrice*** l'a remarqué dans le métro à Londres. Maintenant, il mène une vie de célébrité à Paris, tout en continuant ses études de mode en ligne. Malgré son succès, il n'a qu'un objectif pour l'avenir: devenir le porte-parole des jeunes qui, comme lui, vivent avec un handicap.

*une réalisatrice = a film director

Theme 2 Reading practice

Free-time activities

You see a French website where people talk about their free-time activities.

Emma	Nager m'apporte beaucoup de paix. L'inconvénient, c'est l'eau froide!
Mathieu	J'apprécie mon club de vélo. J'ai déjà amélioré ma vitesse.
Fathia	Mon équipe de foot m'a déçue à cause de son manque d'énergie. Dommage!
Lucas	J'ai toujours adoré jouer d'un instrument et je ne regrette pas mon choix de passe-temps.
Toni	Chanter en public me fait peur mais c'est ma passion.

What do these people think about their activities?

Write **P** for a **positive** opinion

N for a **negative** opinion

P + N for a **positive** and **negative** opinion.

Write the correct letter(s) in each box.

10. Emma ⬚ **[1 mark]**

11. Mathieu ⬚ **[1 mark]**

12. Fathia ⬚ **[1 mark]**

13. Lucas ⬚ **[1 mark]**

14. Toni ⬚ **[1 mark]**

Section B: Translation into English

15. Translate these sentences into **English**.

Nous faisons de la natation toutes les semaines. **[2 marks]**

....

....

Quand il était plus jeune, il jouait d'un instrument. **[2 marks]**

....

....

Ce soir, après le spectacle, il y aura un feu d'artifice. **[2 marks]**

....

....

Depuis six mois, je partage mes pensées sur des réseaux sociaux. **[2 marks]**

....

....

À la fête, elles nous ont donné un cadeau et une carte. **[2 marks]**

....

....

Theme 2 Writing practice

Section A: Translation into French

1.   Translate the following sentences into **French**.   **[10 marks]**

I like to follow celebrities online.

....

....

She is going to join a football team this year.

....

....

We went shopping in town but unfortunately, we didn't buy anything.

....

....

Do you want to spend a day in London with me?

....

....

I was watching my favourite programme on TV when everyone arrived.

....

....

Section B

Answer **either** Question 2.1 **or** Question 2.2

Either

Question 2.1

You are emailing your Canadian friend about your birthday.

Write approximately **90** words in **French**.

You must write something about each bullet point.

Describe:

- what you like about your birthday
- how you celebrated last year
- what presents you hope to receive in future.   **[15 marks]**

Or

Question 2.2

You are writing an article about films and TV for a French website.

Write approximately **90** words in **French**.

You must write something about each bullet point.

Describe:

- your favourite actor
- a recent trip to the cinema
- what you will watch at home this weekend, on TV or online.   **[15 marks]**

> **EXAM TIP** 🎯
> Check you have used verbs in three different time frames (present, past and future).

> **EXAM TIP** 🎯
> If you can't think of a specific actor, you can give any name or avoid giving a name altogether.

Practice

Theme 2 Writing practice

Section C

Answer **either** Question 3.1 **or** Question 3.2

Either

Question 3.1

You are writing a post about fame.

Your post is about the challenges of being and becoming famous.

Write approximately **150** words in **French**.

You must write something about both bullet points.

Describe:

- the negative aspects of being a celebrity
- how you will become successful in the future.

[25 marks]

> **EXAM TIP**
>
> Break up the task by aiming to write three paragraphs of about 50 words each. You don't have to write the same amount about each bullet point.

Or

Question 3.2

You are writing an article about shopping.

Your article is for a social media post.

Write approximately **150** words in **French**.

You must write something about both bullet points.

Describe:

- the advantages of shopping online
- how you chose some presents recently.

[25 marks]

> **EXAM TIP**
>
> Show off the grammar and vocabulary you know by using a range of different structures, tenses and words.

3.1 Travel and tourism, including places of interest

Weather and countries

Quel temps fait-il aujourd'hui?	***What's the weather like today?***
Dans le nord de la Belgique, il y a du soleil.	*In the north of Belgium, it's sunny.*
Dans le sud de la France, il pleut.	*In the south of France, it's raining.*
Dans les Pyrénées, il y a du brouillard.	*In the Pyrenees, it's foggy.*
La pluie arrive **dans l'est** de l'Afrique.	*Rain is arriving in the east of Africa.*
Dans l'ouest, **au Sénégal**, il fait froid.	*In the west, in Senegal, it's cold.*
En Suisse, la neige arrive dans les Alpes.	*In Switzerland, snow is arriving in the Alps.*
La météo dit qu'il fait chaud **au Maroc**.	*The weather forecast says it's hot in Morocco.*
Au Québec, le ciel est gris.	*In Quebec, the sky is grey.*
À Londres, il fait mauvais.	*In London it's bad weather.*

Le temps pendant les vacances	***The weather during the holiday***
Tu préfères passer tes vacances dans un pays chaud?	*Do you prefer spending your holidays in a hot country?*
Pour moi, le climat est parfait.	*The climate is perfect for me.*
L'année dernière, il faisait beau.	*Last year, the weather was nice.*
Il y avait tous les jours du soleil.	*It was sunny every day.*
Il y aura un peu de vent.	*There will be a bit of wind.*
J'espère qu'il fera chaud demain!	*I hope it will be hot tomorrow!*

> **REMEMBER** ❗
>
> In French, there are different ways to say 'in', depending on the context:
> - for feminine countries, use *en* and for masculine countries, use *au*
> - for towns or cities, use *à*
> - for points of the compass, use *dans*.

> **REVISION TIP** 🗹
>
> Make sure you can describe the weather in the past, present and future.

> **SOUNDS TIP** 🎤
>
> The letter combinations *en / an / em / am* are all pronounced in the same way in French. Practise the sound they make in this sentence:
>
> Mam**an**, qu**and** tu faisais du c**am**ping **en** Fr**an**ce, le t**em**ps était comm**ent**?

Que fais-tu pendant les vacances d'été?
What do you do during the summer holidays?

Normalement, **si** c'est possible, on part en vacances pendant une semaine en été. **S'**il fait beau cette année, nous ferons du camping au bord de la mer. Cependant, **s'**il pleut, nous dormirons chez mes grands-parents. **Si** on avait plus d'argent, j'aimerais traverser la Manche pour aller dans le sud de l'Europe parce que j'adore le soleil!

Normally, if it's possible, we go away on holiday for one week in the summer. If it's nice weather this year, we will go camping by the sea. However, if it rains, we will sleep at my grandparents' house. If we had more money, I would like to cross the English Channel to go to the south of Europe because I love the sun!

> **GRAMMAR TIP** ⭐
>
> You can use 'if' (*si*) clauses to develop more complex sentences.
> - *Si* + present tense is followed by a second clause in the present or in a future tense.
> - *Si* + imperfect tense is followed by a second clause in the conditional.

3.1 Travel and tourism, including places of interest

Planning a trip

Les logements	Accommodation
J'aimerais passer / réserver deux nuits…	I would like to spend / book two nights…
dans un appartement de vacances.	in a holiday apartment.
dans un hôtel cinq étoiles.	in a five-star hotel.
dans un village de vacances.	in a holiday village.
dans une ferme.	on a farm.
dans un endroit tranquille.	in a quiet place.
à la montagne.	in the mountains.
à la campagne.	in the countryside.
dans une forêt.	in a forest.
sur la côte.	on the coast.
au bord de la mer.	at the seaside.
près d'une plage.	near a beach.

> **SOUNDS TIP**
>
> The **-gn-** sound in the middle of the French words *campagne* and *montagne* is a bit like the sound we use in English when we say 'lasa**gn**a'.

Les moyens de transports	Means of transport
Le voyage est plus rapide en avion qu'en train.	The journey is quicker by plane than by train.
Vous devez arriver à l'aéroport deux heures avant votre vol.	You must arrive at the airport two hours before your flight.
On peut acheter des billets à la gare.	You can buy tickets at the station.
Je n'aime pas voyager en bateau.	I don't like travelling by boat.
À Paris, on peut voyager en métro ou en bus.	In Paris, you can travel by underground or by bus.
Je préfère voyager en voiture / à vélo / à pied.	I prefer to travel by car / by bike / on foot.
Les transports publics sont moins chers.	Public transport is less expensive.

> **GRAMMAR TIP**
>
> To say how you travel, use *à* in front of individual forms of transport: *à pied*, *à vélo*. Use *en* in front of forms of transport that can take more than one person: *en métro*, *en bus*, etc.

Des vacances plus 'vertes'   *A 'greener' holiday*

Pour partir en vacances cette année, on a voulu voyager **sans prendre l'avion**. C'est beaucoup mieux pour l'environnement! On a pris un train **pour aller** au port et puis un petit bateau **pour arriver** sur l'île. Pendant notre séjour, nous avons découvert beaucoup d'endroits différents **sans utiliser** une voiture.

To go on holiday this year, we wanted to travel without flying. It's much better for the environment! We took a train to go to the port and then a little boat to arrive on the island. During our stay, we discovered lots of different places without using a car.

> **REMEMBER**
>
> Notice different ways that infinitive structures can be used and translated. For example, *pour* + infinitive means '(in order) to do' and *sans* + infinitive means 'without doing'.

Holiday activities and problems

Des activités pour les vacances	Holiday activities
organiser des visites pour les touristes	to organise visits for tourists
voir tous les sites **historiques**	to see all the historic sites
visiter un château	to visit a castle
aller à un musée d'art	to go to an art museum
visiter un ancien champ de bataille	to visit a former battlefield
monter en **haut** d'une vieille tour	to climb to the top of an old tower
découvrir la culture locale	to discover the local culture
se relaxer sur la plage	to relax on the beach
faire un tour de la ville	to do a tour of the town
c'est / c'était gratuit / très **haut**	it's / it was free / very high
la vue est / était formidable	the view is / was terrific

Les problèmes pendant les vacances	Problems during the holiday
Il y avait une grève des trains.	There was a train strike.
Notre vol était en retard.	Our flight was late.
Ils ont perdu nos bagages.	They lost our luggage.
Quelqu'un a volé ma carte d'identité.	Someone stole my identity card.
Il n'y avait personne à l'accueil.	There was nobody at reception.
Notre chambre n'était pas propre.	Our bedroom was not clean.
Le matin, il **n**'y avait **aucun** serveur.	There wasn't a waiter in the morning.
Nous n'avons pas eu une seule plainte!	We haven't had a single complaint!

SOUNDS TIP 🎤

In French, 'h' at the start of a word is usually silent. Try saying these words: *historique* (historic), *hôtel* (hotel), *haut* (high).

REMEMBER ❗

Some words have more than one meaning. For example: *vol* (flight, theft) and *voler* (to fly, to steal); *propre* (clean, proper, own) and *ancien* (former, ancient).

GRAMMAR TIP ⭐

The negative expression *ne … aucun(e)* means 'no, not one, not any'. It agrees with the gender of the noun that follows: **aucun** *serveur*, **aucune** *plainte*.

Avant de partir *Before leaving*

Avant de partir en vacances, vous devez préparer vos bagages. Faites une liste de choses à prendre **avant de** les mettre dans votre sac. N'oubliez pas que certaines choses sont interdites.

Avant d'aller à l'aéroport, vous devez peser votre valise car dans les avions, il y a des limites strictes. Après, vous pouvez vous relaxer.

Before leaving on your holiday, you must prepare your luggage. Make a list of things to take before putting them in your bag. Don't forget that some things are forbidden.

Before going to the airport, you must weigh your suitcase because there are strict limits on aeroplanes. Afterwards, you can relax.

GRAMMAR TIP ⭐

Use *avant de* + infinitive to mean 'before doing'. See page 137.

⚙ Knowledge VOCABULARY

3.1 Travel and tourism, including places of interest

Vocabulary learning

Learn this vocabulary and then use the 'look, cover, write, check' technique to make sure you really know it. Cover the English first and then the French.

Countries and other geographical locations

French	✓	English	✓
l'Afrique (f.)		Africa	
les Alpes (f.pl.)		the Alps	
la Belgique		Belgium	
l'est (m.)		east	
la France		France	
la Manche		English Channel	
le Maroc		Morocco	
le nord		north	
l'ouest (m.)		west	
le pays		country	
les Pyrénées (f.pl.)		the Pyrenees	
le Québec		Quebec	
le Sénégal		Senegal	
le sud		south	
la Suisse		Switzerland	

Weather

French	✓	English	✓
le brouillard		fog, mist, haze	
chaud(e)		hot, warm	
le ciel		sky	
le climat		climate	
froid(e)		cold	
gris(e)		grey	
il fait (beau / mauvais)		it is / it's (nice / bad weather)	
la neige		snow	
il pleut		it's raining / it rains	
la pluie		rain	
le soleil		sun	
le temps		time, weather	
le vent		wind	

Places to stay

French	✓	English	✓
l'appartement (m.)		apartment, flat	
le bord		edge, side	
la campagne		countryside	
la chambre		bedroom	
la côte		coast	
l'endroit (m.)		place, spot	
l'étoile (f.)		star	
la ferme		farm	
la forêt		forest	
l'hôtel (m.)		hotel	
l'île (f.)		island	
le logement		accommodation	
la mer		sea	
la montagne		mountain	
la plage		beach	
près (de)		near (to)	
réserver		to reserve, book	
le séjour		stay	
tranquille		quiet	
le village		village	

Verbs to talk about travelling

French	✓	English	✓
mettre		to put (on)	
partir		to leave	
perdre		to lose	
peser		to weigh	
préparer		to prepare	
traverser		to cross	
voler		to fly, steal	
voyager		to travel	

Vocabulary learning

Travelling and transport

French	✓	English	✓
l'accueil (m.)		*reception*	
l'aéroport (m.)		*airport*	
avant		*before*	
l'avion (m.)		*aeroplane*	
le bagage		*luggage / baggage*	
le bateau		*boat, ship*	
le billet		*ticket*	
le bus		*bus*	
en retard		*late*	
l'environnement (m.)		*environment*	
la gare		*station*	
la grève		*strike*	
l'identité (f.)		*identity*	
la limite		*limit*	
la liste		*list*	
le métro		*underground / metro*	
le pied		*foot*	
la plainte		*complaint*	
propre		*clean, proper, own*	
public / publique		*public*	
le serveur / la serveuse		*waiter, server*	
le train		*train*	
le transport		*transport*	
la valise		*suitcase*	
le vélo		*bike*	
vite		*quickly, fast*	
la voiture		*car*	
le vol		*flight, theft*	
le voyage		*trip, journey*	

Holiday activities

French	✓	English	✓
ancien(ne)		*former, ancient*	
l'art (m.)		*art*	
la bataille		*battle*	
le camping		*camping*	
le champ		*field*	
le château		*castle*	
la culture		*culture*	
découvrir		*to discover*	
gratuit(e)		*free*	
haut(e)		*high*	
historique		*historic*	
local(e)		*local*	
monter		*to go up, climb*	
le musée		*museum*	
organiser		*to organise*	
se relaxer		*to relax*	
le site		*site*	
la tour		*tower*	
le tour		*tour*	
le / la touriste		*tourist*	
la visite		*visit, tour*	
visiter		*to visit*	
la vue		*view*	

REMEMBER !

Le tour means 'tour' but *la tour* means 'tower' – for example, *la tour Eiffel* (the Eiffel tower).

Answer the questions below. Cover the answers column with a piece of paper and write down as many answers as you can. Check and repeat.

Questions	Answers
1 List as many countries as possible in French.	*La Belgique*; *la France*; *le Maroc*; etc. See page 84 for more ideas
2 Say three things about today's weather.	Possible answer: *Il fait froid, il pleut et il y a du vent* See page 84 for more ideas
3 Choose the correct word for 'in' to complete this sentence: *Je vais passer mes vacances dans / en / à Paris.*	*À* (before a town or city)
4 Answer this question in French: *Que fais-tu pendant les vacances d'été?*	Possible answer: *Normalement, si c'est possible, on fait du camping*
5 In French, name four different places where you could stay for your holiday.	*Un hôtel*; *un appartement*; *un village de vacances*; *une ferme*
6 List as many different ways to travel as possible in French.	*En bus*; *en train*; *en métro*; *en avion*; *en bateau*; *à pied*; *à vélo*
7 Translate the following sentence into English: *Pour découvrir l'île, on a voyagé sans prendre la voiture.*	To discover the island, we travelled without taking the car
8 Answer this question in French: *Qu'est-ce que tu aimes faire pendant tes vacances?*	Possible answer: *J'aime découvrir la culture locale* See page 85 for more ideas
9 What do you know about the pronunciation of the letter 'h' in the French words *historique*, *hôtel* and *haut*?	It is silent / not pronounced
10 Translate the following sentence into French: There was a train strike.	*Il y avait une grève de trains* / *Il y a eu une grève de trains*
11 Give all the possible English meanings of the French words *vol* and *voler*.	Flight; theft *(vol)* and to fly; to steal *(voler)*
12 Which structure would you use in French to translate the idea of 'before doing' something?	*Avant de* + infinitive

Put paper here

Previous questions

Use the questions below to check your knowledge from previous chapters.

Questions	Answers
1 Say the French question words for 'what', 'where', 'when', 'who' and 'why'.	*Que / Quoi / Qu'est-ce que*; *où*; *quand*; *qui*; *pourquoi*
2 Answer this question in French: *Est-ce que tu aimes faire du sport? Pourquoi / pourquoi pas?*	Possible answers: *J'aime faire du sport car c'est amusant / Je déteste jouer au foot parce que je n'aime pas perdre*
3 What is the French phrase meaning 'to be in the middle of (do)ing'?	*Être en train de* + infinitive

Put paper here

3.2 Media and technology

Media

Les médias	Media
lire des articles / des journaux	to read articles / newspapers
écrire un blog	to write a blog
chatter / tchatter avec mes amis	to chat with my friends
communiquer avec ma famille	to communicate with my family
jouer à des jeux vidéo	to play video games
écouter la radio	to listen to the radio
envoyer des SMS	to send texts
recevoir des e-mails	to receive emails
prendre / poster des photos	to take / post photos
regarder des émissions	to watch programmes
enregistrer / partager des vidéos	to record / share videos
télécharger des films	to download films
cliquer sur une publicité / pub	to click on an advert
voir des images dans la presse	to see pictures in the press

La technologie numérique	Digital technology
un streaming / un service de streaming	streamed / via streaming
à la télévision / télé	on television / TV
sur mon portable	on my mobile phone
sur mon ordinateur (portable)	on my (laptop) computer
sur une appli / application	on an app
sur les réseaux sociaux	on social media

SOUNDS TIP 🎤
The -*er* endings on infinitives are pronounced in the same way as -*é* and -*ez*. The following words all sound exactly the same: *écouter, écouté, écoutez*.

REMEMBER ❗
You need to conjugate infinitives to say who is doing the actions. For example, *je lis des articles* (I read articles); *nous prenons des photos* (we take photos).

Comment utilises-tu ton portable? *How do you use your mobile phone?*

Normalement, j'utilise mon portable pour tchatter avec mes amis et pour partager mes photos sur les réseaux sociaux. Je ne dois jamais oublier de le recharger – c'est indispensable!

Hier, j'ai joué à des jeux vidéo en ligne. C'était bien mais demain je vais télécharger un film. Ce sera génial!

Normally, I use my mobile phone in order to chat with my friends and to share my photos on social media. I must never forget to charge it – it's essential!

Yesterday, I played video games online. It was good but tomorrow I'm going to download a film. It will be great!

GRAMMAR TIP ⭐
Practise using the same verbs and vocabulary in different time frames to prepare for speaking and writing tasks. See pages 144–156 to revise tenses.

3.2 Media and technology

Changes in technology and media

Dans le passé	In the past
Il n'y avait pas d'Internet.	There wasn't any internet.
Les gens envoyaient plus de lettres.	People used to send more letters.
Mes parents achetaient un journal quotidien.	My parents used to buy a daily newspaper.
On ne diffusait les émissions qu'à la télé.	Programmes were only broadcast on TV.
Nous parlions souvent au téléphone.	We often used to talk on the telephone.
Mes parents recherchaient des informations à la bibliothèque.	My parents used to look for information in the library.
La plupart des gens allaient aux magasins locaux.	Most people used to go to local shops.

Maintenant	Now
Nous sommes toujours sur nos appareils.	We are always on our devices.
J'envoie des messages avec une appli.	I send messages with an app.
On reçoit des pubs pour des événements.	We get adverts for events.
Nous faisons souvent nos courses en ligne.	We often do our food shopping online.
Je regarde des vidéos sur mon ordinateur.	I watch videos on my computer.
On communique sur les réseaux sociaux.	We communicate on social media.
Nous faisons des recherches sur Internet.	We do research on the internet.
La plupart des jeunes font des achats sur leur portable.	Most young people make purchases on their mobile phones.

> **GRAMMAR TIP** ★
>
> Use the **imperfect tense** to say what used to happen or to describe what things were like in the past:
>
> *Je regardais –* I used to watch
>
> *Nous allions –* We used to go
>
> *C'était amusant –* It was fun
>
> *Ils étaient étonnants –* They were amazing

> **LINK** 🔗
>
> Find out more about the imperfect tense on page 152.

Maintenant ou dans le passé? *Now or in the past?*

Ce siècle, chacun a dû rapidement s'adapter aux changements dans le monde de la technologie numérique. **Dans le passé**, les jeunes n'avaient ni portable ni ordinateur. **À l'époque**, on regardait la télé ou bien on trouvait un passe-temps. **Actuellement**, notre comportement est très différent et on bénéficie d'un réseau de communautés virtuelles.

This century everyone has had to adapt quickly to changes in the world of digital technology. In the past, young people had neither a mobile phone nor a computer. At the time, you watched TV or you found a hobby. At present, our behaviour is very different and we benefit from a network of virtual communities.

> **REVISION TIP** ☑
>
> Learn to recognise time phrases as well as verb tenses to identify what happened in the past and what happens / is happening now.

Vocabulary learning

Learn this vocabulary and then use the 'look, cover, write, check' technique to make sure you really know it. Cover the English first and then the French.

Different forms of media and technology

French	✓	English	✓
l'appareil (m.)		device	
l'application / appli (f.)		app	
l'article (m.)		article, item	
le blog		blog	
les courses (f.pl.)		food shopping	
l'e-mail (m.)		email	
l'émission (f.)		TV / radio programme	
l'image (f.)		image, picture	
indispensable		essential	
les informations (f.pl.)		information	
Internet (m.)		internet	
le jeu		game	
le journal		newspaper	
la lettre		letter	
en ligne		online	
le message		message	
numérique		digital	
l'ordinateur (m.)		computer	
le portable		mobile phone, laptop	
la presse		press	
la publicité / pub		advert, ad	
quotidien(ne)		daily	
la recherche		research, search	
le réseau social		social network	
le SMS		SMS / text	
le streaming		streaming	
la technologie		technology	
le téléphone		telephone	
la vidéo		video	

Useful verbs for this topic

French	✓	English	✓
adapter; s'adapter à		to adapt / adjust; to get used to	
bénéficier de		to benefit from	
cliquer		to click	
commander		to order	
communiquer		to communicate	
diffuser		to broadcast	
écrire		to write	
enregistrer		to record, to save	
envoyer		to send	
lire		to read	
partager		to share	
poster		to post	
recevoir		to receive	
recharger		to charge (an appliance)	
rechercher		to look for, to collect	
tchatter / chatter		to chat	
télécharger		to download	

Other useful words for this topic

French	✓	English	✓
actuellement		at present	
la bibliothèque		library	
chacun(e)		each person	
la communauté		community	
le comportement		behaviour	
l'époque (f.)		era, period, time	
le passé		past	
la plupart (de)		most, the majority (of)	
le siècle		century	

⇄ Retrieval

Answer the questions below. Cover the answers column with a piece of paper and write down as many answers as you can. Check and repeat.

Questions / Answers

Questions	Answers
1 In French, list as many activities that you can do online as you can.	*Écrire un blog*; *jouer à des jeux vidéo*; *poster des photos* or any from the list on page 89
2 Translate this question into English: *Comment utilises-tu ton portable?*	How do you use your mobile phone?
3 Translate this sentence into French: I use my mobile phone in order to chat with my friends.	*J'utilise mon portable pour tchatter / chatter avec mes amis / copains*
4 In French, list six things that you can read.	Any six from: *un blog / un journal / une lettre / un e-mail / un article / un SMS / un message / des informations / la presse*
5 In French, list five ways of watching something at home using a different technology.	Any five from: *en ligne / sur Internet / en streaming / à la télé / sur un portable / sur un ordinateur / sur une appli*
6 How do you say 'tomorrow, I'm going to download a film' in French?	*Demain, je vais télécharger un film*
7 Translate these opinions into English: *c'était bien*; *c'est indispensable*; *ce sera génial*.	It was good; it's essential; it will be great
8 How do you say 'digital technology' in French?	*La technologie numérique*
9 What does *actuellement* mean?	At present, at the moment
10 How do you say 'in the past, there wasn't any internet' in French?	*Dans le passé, il n'y avait pas d'Internet*
11 What are two uses of the imperfect tense?	To say what used to happen or describe things in the past
12 Translate this sentence into English: *La plupart des gens communiquaient par téléphone*.	Most people used to communicate by telephone

Put paper here

Previous questions

Use the questions below to check your knowledge from previous chapters.

Questions / Answers

Questions	Answers
1 What does *J'ai besoin de* mean in English?	I need
2 Answer this question in French: *Quelle est ton émission préférée?*	*Mon émission préférée s'appelle…*
3 Which structure would you use in French to translate the idea of 'before doing' something?	*Avant de* + infinitive

Put paper here

3.2 Media and technology

The advantages of technology

Je suis pour la technologie! — *I am for technology!*

Internet **est utilisé par** 67% de la population mondiale. — *The internet is used by 67% of the global population.*

La technologie **est appréciée par** des personnes de tous les âges. — *Technology is appreciated by people of all ages.*

Des millions de portables **sont vendus** chaque année. — *Millions of mobile phones are sold each year.*

Les informations de Wikipedia **sont lues par** tout le monde. — *Information on Wikipedia is read by everyone.*

Plusieurs applis **sont utilisées par** toutes les filles de ma classe. — *Several apps are used by all the girls in my class.*

Comment est-ce que la technologie nous aide? — *How does technology help us?*

La technologie peut aider les personnes en situation de handicap. — *Technology can help people with disabilities.*

Il y a des outils pour soutenir les étudiants. — *There are tools to support students.*

On peut utiliser une appli pour traduire une langue étrangère. — *You can use an app to translate a foreign language.*

Quand j'écris, l'ordinateur corrige mon travail. — *When I write, the computer corrects my work.*

Les employés peuvent travailler de chez eux. — *Employees can work from home.*

Les scientifiques peuvent partager leurs découvertes. — *Scientists can share their discoveries.*

GRAMMAR TIP

The **passive** is formed from the present tense of the verb *être* (to be) and a past participle. The past participle must agree with the subject of the sentence. You can add *par* (by) to say who is doing the action. See page 158.

REMEMBER

Some indefinite adjectives never change, for example, *chaque* (each) and *plusieurs* (several). However, make sure you use the correct form of *tout* (all) to agree with the noun that follows it: **tout** le temps, **toute** la classe, **tous** les jeunes, **toutes** les filles.

Les avantages de la technologie moderne *Advantages of modern technology*

Je pense que certains ont peur de la nouvelle technologie, comme l'intelligence artificielle (IA), par exemple. Cependant, moi, je crois qu'on peut bénéficier de tous ces changements. Je n'entends pas très b**ien** mais j'ai un appareil numérique qui m'aide **au quotidien***. C'est un grand sout**ien** et je ne manque r**ien** de la conversation autour de moi.

I think that some people are afraid of new technology, like artificial intelligence (AI), for example. However, I believe that we can benefit from all these changes. I can't hear very well but I have a digital device that helps me in my daily life. It's a big support and I don't miss anything from the conversation around me.

SOUNDS TIP

Practise the -*ien* sound in these words: *bien*, *rien*, *soutien*, *quotidien*. Then read the text on the left out loud.

*****au quotidien** = in daily life

Les dangers de la technologie

Je passe trop de temps sur mon portable.

Ce n'est pas bien d'être tout le temps devant un écran.

Je trouve que sur Internet, les gens sont souvent méchants.

Certains élèves harcèlent les autres en ligne.

Il me semble qu'Internet est trop puissant.

À mon avis, on risque d'être victime d'un crime.

Je suis contre les commentaires racistes en ligne.

The dangers of technology

I spend too much time on my mobile phone.

It's not good to be in front of a screen all the time.

I find that people are often mean on the internet.

Some students bully others online.

It seems to me that the internet is too powerful.

In my opinion, you risk being the victim of a crime.

I am against racist comments online.

REVISION TIP

Use a variety of phrases to introduce different opinions. For example, *je trouve que…* (I find that), *à mon avis …* (in my opinion), and *il me semble que…* (it seems to me that…).

Pour ou contre?

Un avantage, c'est que…

Un inconvénient, c'est que…

Je suis d'accord avec…

Je ne suis pas d'accord avec…

Pourtant, il faut admettre que…

Certains disent que c'est…

Cependant, d'autres pensent que c'est…

Par contre, il ne faut pas oublier que…

For or against?

One advantage is that…

One disadvantage is that…

I agree with…

I disagree with…

Yet, you have to admit that…

Some people say that it's…

However, others think that it's…

On the other hand, we mustn't forget that…

REVISION TIP

These kinds of phrases can help you structure an answer that asks for both advantages and disadvantages of any topic.

SOUNDS TIP

Remember that the -**ent** ending on third person plural verbs in the present tense is **not** pronounced. Try saying: *ils dis**ent*** (they say), *ils pens**ent*** (they think).

Quelle est ton opinion sur les réseaux sociaux?
What is your opinion of social media?

Pour moi, un avantage des réseaux sociaux, c'est que je peux facilement rester en contact avec mes copains et ma famille. Je dois admettre que je passe des heures en ligne et que mes parents disent que c'est trop! Par contre, je ne suis pas d'accord avec les gens qui utilisent leurs comptes pour harceler les autres. Quelle honte!

For me, an advantage of social media is that I can stay in touch easily with my friends and family. I must admit that I spend hours online and that my parents say it's too much! On the other hand, I don't agree with people who use their accounts to bully others. Shame on them!

REVISION TIP

Practise giving your opinion of social media, the internet and mobile phones in French. Remember to add reasons or give pros and cons to extend your answers.

Vocabulary learning

Learn this vocabulary and then use the 'look, cover, write, check' technique to make sure you really know it. Cover the English first and then the French.

Pros and cons of technology

French	✓	English	✓
l'accord (m.)		*agreement*	
admettre		*to admit*	
l'âge (m.)		*age*	
l'avantage (m.)		*advantage*	
cependant		*however*	
le changement		*change*	
comme		*like, as*	
le commentaire		*comment, remark*	
le compte		*account*	
contre		*against*	
la conversation		*conversation*	
corriger		*to correct*	
le crime		*crime*	
la découverte		*discovery*	
l'employé(e) (m. / f.)		*employee, worker*	
entendre		*to hear*	
l'étudiant(e) (m. / f.)		*student*	
facilement		*easily*	
le handicap		*disability*	
harceler		*to bully*	
la honte		*shame*	
l'inconvénient (m.)		*disadvantage*	
mondial(e)		*worldwide, global*	
oublier		*to forget*	
l'outil (m.)		*tool*	
par contre		*on the other hand*	
la population		*population*	
pour		*for*	
pourtant		*yet, nevertheless*	
puissant(e)		*powerful*	

French	✓	English	✓
raciste		*racist*	
risquer		*to risk*	
le / la scientifique		*scientist*	
sembler		*to seem*	
la situation		*situation*	
soutenir		*to support*	
le soutien		*support*	
traduire		*to translate*	
le / la victime		*victim*	

REVISION TIP

Saying the French words out loud can help you to memorise them – and to practise your pronunciation at the same time!

Answer the questions below. Cover the answers column with a piece of paper and write down as many answers as you can. Check and repeat.

	Questions		Answers
1	Translate this sentence into English: *Des millions de portables sont vendus chaque année.*	Put paper here	Millions of mobile phones are sold each year
2	How do you form the passive in French (in the present tense)?		Use the verb *être* in the present tense + a past participle (with agreements if needed)
3	What are the four different ways in which the French word for 'all' might be spelled? When is each one used?	Put paper here	*Tout* (followed by a masculine singular noun); *toute* (feminine singular); *tous* (masculine plural); *toutes* (feminine plural)
4	What does the word *plusieurs* mean in English?		Several
5	Give two ways that technology helps us in everyday life.		*Pour traduire des langues*; *pour corriger notre travail sur un ordinateur*, or any from the list on page 91
6	Translate the following sentence into French: We can benefit from all these changes.	Put paper here	*On peut bénéficier de tous ces changements*
7	Say three words that include the *-ien* sound in French.		Possible answers: *b<u>ien</u>* (well); *r<u>ien</u>* (nothing); *sout<u>ien</u>* (support); *quotid<u>ien</u>* (daily)
8	In French, give one reason why the internet can be dangerous.		Possible answer: O*n risque d'être victime d'un crime*
9	List as many different ways to introduce your opinion in French as possible.	Put paper here	*Je trouve que*; *à mon avis*; *il me semble que*; or any from the list on page 92
10	Translate the following words / phrases into French: *pourtant*, *cependant*, *par contre.*		Nevertheless / yet; however; on the other hand
11	Answer the following question in French: *Quelle est ton opinion sur les réseaux sociaux?*	Put paper here	Possible answer: *Un avantage, c'est qu'ils sont amusants. Par contre, je passe trop de temps en ligne*
12	What must you remember about the verb endings when reading the following phrases aloud? *Ils disent*, *ils pensent*.		The *-ent* endings are silent (not pronounced)

Previous questions

Use the questions below to check your knowledge from previous chapters.

1	How do you form the near future tense in the 'I' form?	Put paper here	*Je vais* + infinitive
2	List five things you could watch on TV in French.		Possible answers: *un film d'action*; *une émission de télé-réalité*; *des pubs*; *une série*; *la météo*
3	Translate this sentence into French: I use my mobile phone in order to chat with my friends.		*J'utilise mon portable pour tchatter / chatter avec mes amis / copains*

3.3 The environment and where people live

My local environment

Les problèmes écologiques dans ma ville

Environmental problems in my town

Il y a trop de circulation.	There is too much traffic.
Les voitures polluent de l'air.	The cars pollute the air.
Il n'y a pas beaucoup d'espaces verts.	There are not many green spaces.
Les habitants jettent des papiers dans la rue.	Residents drop litter in the streets.
Il y a des déchets dans le lac.	There is rubbish in the lake.
On a besoin de plus de poubelles.	We need more bins.
Les bâtiments sont sales.	The buildings are dirty.
Les transports en commun sont nuls.	The public transport is rubbish.
C'est une ville industrielle avec des usines.	It's an industrial town with factories.

> **SOUNDS TIP**
>
> In French, the sound **-tion** is pronounced a bit like 'see' followed by the nasal sound 'on'. Practise saying this sound in French words like *circulation* (traffic), *pollution* (pollution) and *action* (action).

Chacun(e) peut faire une différence

Each person can make a difference

Ça vaut la peine de…	It's worth…
faire de petites actions positives.	making small, positive actions.
mettre des déchets dans la poubelle.	putting rubbish in the bin.
porter le verre au centre de recyclage.	taking glass to the recycling centre.
préserver nos espaces verts.	protecting our green spaces.
Il vaut mieux…	It's better to…
aller en ville à vélo ou à pied.	go into town by bike or on foot.
faire ses courses au marché local.	shop at the local market.
éviter les produits en plastique.	avoid plastic products.

> **GRAMMAR TIP**
>
> Use the phrases *il vaut mieux* + infinitive (it's better to…) and *ça vaut la peine de* + infinitive (it's worth…) to impress the examiners.

Un village 'vert' *A 'green' village*

Dans mon village, je suis membre d'un groupe de bénévoles. Ça vaut la peine de faire quelque chose pour améliorer l'environnement là où on habite. Il vaut mieux travailler ensemble, créer une association. Récemment, nous avons mis en place une nouvelle poubelle près du magasin local et nous avons nettoyé la rue principale. Je suis fier du résultat!

In my village, I am a member of a group of volunteers. It's worth doing something to improve the environment where you live. It's better to work together, create a residents' association. Recently, we installed a new bin near the local shop and we cleaned the main street. I am proud of the result!

> **REVISION TIP**
>
> Think about the environmental issues in the area where you live and which ones you could talk about in French, using the language that you have learned.

3.3 The environment and where people live

Everyday ecological actions

De récentes actions pour l'environnement

J'ai décidé de devenir végétarien(ne).

J'ai évité d'acheter des sacs et boîtes en plastique.

J'ai essayé d'utiliser mon vélo plus souvent.

J'ai arrêté d'allumer la lumière pendant la journée.

J'ai commencé à recycler le papier et le verre.

J'ai continué à aller au collège à pied.

J'ai réussi à utiliser moins d'eau.

Des actions pour protéger l'environnement

Je vais aider à nettoyer la plage.

Je vais m'inscrire à une association de bénévoles.

Je vais éviter de prendre des bains.

Je vais encourager mes parents à faire du recyclage.

Je vais participer à une manifestation avec mes amis.

Recent actions for the environment

I decided to become a vegetarian.

I have avoided buying plastic bags and boxes.

I have tried to use my bike more often.

I have stopped switching the light on during the day.

I have started to recycle paper and glass.

I have continued to go to school on foot.

I have succeeded in using less water.

Some actions to protect the environment

I'm going to help to clean the beach.

I'm going to join a volunteer organisation.

I'm going to avoid taking baths.

I'm going to encourage my parents to recycle.

I'm going to take part in a demonstration with my friends.

> **GRAMMAR TIP** ⭐
>
> Some verbs take _à_ or _de_, followed by an infinitive. For example, _arrêter de_ + infinitive (to stop) and _commencer à_ + infinitive (to start).

Qu'est-ce que tu as fait récemment pour protéger la planète?

What have you done recently to protect the planet?

Récemment, j'ai décidé de devenir végan(e) car je pense que manger de la viande n'est pas bon pour la planète. Ensuite, j'ai arrêté de prendre des bains pour éviter d'utiliser trop d'eau. J'ai toujours fait du recyclage mais à l'avenir, je ne vais plus acheter de produits en plastique parce que le plastique pollue la mer.

Recently, I decided to become a vegan because I think that eating meat is not good for the planet. In addition, I have stopped taking baths to avoid using too much water. I have always done some recycling but in future, I am no longer going to buy plastic products because plastic pollutes the sea.

> **REVISION TIP** 📝
>
> Prepare some sentences in French to say what you normally do for the environment, what you have done recently and what you plan to do in future.

Problems and solutions for the planet

Les problèmes pour la planète	Problems for the planet
Le réchauffement de la planète change le climat.	*Global warming is changing the climate.*
Le niveau des mers est en train de monter.	*The sea level is in the process of rising.*
La destruction de nos forêts menace les animaux.	*The destruction of our forests threatens animals.*
Beaucoup d'espèces d'oiseaux risquent de disparaître.	*Lots of bird species risk disappearing.*
La pollution des eaux a des conséquences graves sur les poissons.	*Water pollution has serious consequences for fish.*
La population de la planète joue aussi un rôle.	*The population of the planet also plays a role.*

Des solutions possibles	Possible solutions
On peut peut-être améliorer la situation…	*We can perhaps improve the situation…*
en utilisant moins de gaz.	*by using less gas.*
en choisissant des énergies propres.	*by choosing clean energy.*
en évitant l'énergie nucléaire.	*by avoiding nuclear energy.*
en protégeant les arbres et les animaux.	*by protecting trees and animals.*
en faisant plus pour préserver la nature.	*by doing more to protect nature.*
en étant plus actifs.	*by being more active.*

L'espoir pour l'avenir *Hope for the future*

Il est vrai qu'il y a beaucoup de défis pour la Terre et pour l'humanité. Cependant, j'espère qu'on pourra sauver la planète, en changeant nos habitudes et en faisant plus pour protéger la nature. En développant la technologie pour l'énergie propre, nous pouvons faire une grande différence.

It is true that there are lots of challenges for the Earth and for humanity. However, I hope that we will be able to save the planet, by changing our habits and by doing more to protect nature. By developing the technology for clean energy, we can make a big difference.

SOUNDS TIP

Practise the French sound in bold in these words: *au*ssi, *eau*, n*o*s, r*ô*le. Although the spelling patterns look different, it's the same vowel sound in each of these words.

GRAMMAR TIP

You can recognise the present participle from the 'en … -ant' structure in French. It translates into English as 'by doing' something. For example, *en utilis**ant*** (by using). See page 142.

REVISION TIP

Test your recall by covering this page and writing as many environmental problems and solutions as you can, in French.

⚙ Knowledge   VOCABULARY

3.3 The environment and where people live

Vocabulary learning

Learn this vocabulary and then use the 'look, cover, write, check' technique to make sure you really know it. Cover the English first and then the French.

Useful verbs

French	✓	English	✓
allumer		to turn on	
améliorer		to improve	
arrêter (de + infinitive)		to stop (+ verb)	
changer		to change	
choisir		to choose	
commencer (à + infinitive)		to start (+ verb)	
continuer (à + infinitive)		to continue (+ verb)	
décider (de + infinitive)		to decide (+ verb)	
développer		to develop	
disparaître		to disappear	
encourager (à + infinitive)		to encourage (+ verb)	
éviter (de + infinitive)		to avoid (+ verb)	
s'inscrire à		to join, to enrol in (+ noun)	
menacer		to threaten	
monter		to go up, climb	
nettoyer		to clean	
participer à (+ noun)		to participate in / to take part in	
polluer		to pollute	
préserver		to preserve, to protect	
protéger		to protect	
recycler		to recycle	
réussir (à + infinitive)		to succeed (in) (+ verb)	
sauver		to save	

Environmental problems

French	✓	English	✓
le bain		bath	
la circulation		traffic	
la conséquence		consequence	
le danger		danger	
les déchets (m.pl.)		rubbish	
le défi		challenge	
la destruction		destruction	
l'espace (m.)		space	
être en train de (+ infinitive)		to be in the middle of (+ verb)	
le gaz		gas	
l'habitude (f.)		habit	
industriel(le)		industrial	
jeter		to throw	
le niveau		level	
nucléaire		nuclear	
le papier		paper	
la pollution		pollution	
la poubelle		rubbish bin	
le problème		problem	
le réchauffement		warming	
sale		dirty	
les transports (en commun) (m.pl.)		(public) transport	
l'usine (f.)		factory	

REVISION TIP

Use some of the vocabulary on this page to write five French sentences about the environment.

Vocabulary learning

Environmental solutions

French	✓	English	✓
l'action (f.)		action	
l'association (f.)		association	
l'avenir (m.)		future	
le / la bénévole		volunteer	
la boîte		box	
la communauté		community	
la différence		difference	
l'énergie (f.)		energy	
l'espoir (m.)		hope	
fier / fière		proud	
l'habitant (m.)		resident	
ça vaut la peine de (+ infinitive)		it's worth (+ verb)	
il vaut mieux (+ infinitive)		it's better (+ verb)	
la lumière		light	
la manifestation		demonstration, event	
le marché		market	
la place		place, square	
le plastique		plastic	
positif / positive		positive	
principal(e)		main	
le produit		product	
le recyclage		recycling	
le résultat		result	
la rue		street	
le sac		bag	
la solution		solution	
le verre		glass	
vert(e)		green	

The natural world

French	✓	English	✓
l'air (m.)		air	
l'animal (m.)		animal	
l'arbre (m.)		tree	
le climat		climate	
l'environnement (m.)		environment	
l'espèce (f.)		species	
la forêt		forest	
l'humanité (f.)		humanity	
le lac		lake	
la nature		nature	
la mer		sea	
l'oiseau (m.)		bird	
la planète		planet	
la terre		earth	

REVISION TIP

Remember to learn the gender of every noun, even those beginning with a vowel.

Answer the questions below. Cover the answers column with a piece of paper and write down as many answers as you can. Check and repeat.

Questions	Answers
1 Give an environmental problem that affects your area.	Possible answer: *Il y a trop de circulation*
2 List three things that you could recycle.	*Le papier; le verre; le plastique*
3 Translate the following sentence into English: *Ça vaut la peine de préserver nos espaces verts.*	It's worth protecting our green spaces
4 Translate the following sentence into French: It's best to go into town by bike.	*Il vaut mieux aller en ville à vélo*
5 What is a *bénévole*?	A volunteer
6 Answer the question: *Qu'est-ce que tu as fait récemment pour protéger la planète?*	Possible answer: *Récemment, j'ai décidé de devenir végétarien(ne)*
7 Say two things you will do to help the environment in future.	Possible answers: *Je vais éviter de prendre des bains; Je vais aider à nettoyer la plage*
8 Give three problems facing the planet.	Possible answers: *le réchauffement de la planète; la destruction de nos forêts; la pollution des eaux*
9 In French, list as many words related to the natural world as possible.	Possible answers: *l'oiseau; l'arbre; l'air*; or any from the list on page 99
10 What is the grammatical name for the following verb forms? *en évitant, en choisissant, en faisant*	The present participle
11 Choose the correct verb to complete this sentence: *On peut aider la nature en protégeant / utilisant / étant les animaux.*	*Protégeant*
12 Does the verb *arrêter* (to stop) take *à*, *de* or nothing at all before an infinitive?	*De*

Put paper here

Previous questions

Use these questions to check your knowledge of previous topics.

1 Answer this question in French: *Que penses-tu de tes profs?*	Possible answer: *Mes profs sont sympas mais très stricts*
2 Translate this sentence into English: *Nous leur avons envoyé une carte.*	We sent them a card
3 How do you form the passive in French (in the present tense)?	Use the verb *être* in the present tense + a past participle (with agreements if needed)

Put paper here

3.3 The environment and where people live

Social problems

Les problèmes dans la société	*Problems in society*
La pauvreté est un vrai problème.	*Poverty is a real problem.*
Le taux de chômage est en train d'augmenter.	*The unemployment rate is going up.*
La drogue représente un problème grave partout.	*Drugs represent a serious problem everywhere.*
Il n'y a rien à faire pour les ados ici.	*There's nothing for teenagers to do here.*
Il y a beaucoup de crimes.	*There are a lot of crimes.*
La crise économique crée des difficultés.	*The economic crisis creates difficulties.*
Je vois de nombreuses personnes sans abri dans la rue.	*I see many homeless people in the streets.*
Les gens qui sont un peu différents ne sont pas toujours acceptés.	*People who are a bit different are not always accepted.*

Que penses-tu des problèmes sociaux?	*What do you think of social problems?*
Je déteste l'inégalité dans notre société.	*I hate the inequality in our society.*
Je m'inquiète de tous les problèmes de notre pays	*I worry about all our country's problems.*
Je voudrais voir une société plus égale et moins injuste.	*I would like to see a more equal and less unfair society.*
À mon avis, on doit partager les richesses entre tout le monde.	*In my opinion, we must share wealth between everyone.*
Pour moi, les attaques au couteau sont très inquiétantes.	*For me, knife attacks are very worrying.*

SOUNDS TIP
The French *r* is a rasping sound in the back of your throat. Practise saying it in these words: *r*ue (street), *r*ien (nothing), *r*eprésenter (to represent).

REVISION TIP
To avoid repeating *beaucoup de* (a lot of), you could use the expression *de nombreux / de nombreuses* (many / numerous) with countable nouns. This expression needs to agree with the gender of the noun that follows it.

REMEMBER
Some words can be changed to mean the opposite by adding *in-*. For example:
juste (fair) – *in*juste (unfair)
égalité (equality) – *in*égalité (inequality)

La pauvreté dans ma ville *Poverty in my town*

Dans la ville **où** j'habite, il y a beaucoup de pauvreté parmi les jeunes. **Quand** je vais en ville, je vois toujours des personnes sans abri dans la rue. Il y a une dame **que** je vois souvent et je lui donne parfois quelque chose à manger. Je lui parle aussi. C'est quelqu'un **qui** a vécu beaucoup de difficultés.

In the town where I live, there is a lot of poverty among young people. When I go into town I always see some homeless people in the streets. There is a lady who I see often and I give her something to eat sometimes. I talk to her as well. She's someone who has lived through a lot of difficulties.

GRAMMAR TIP
Use *où*, *que*, *quand* and *qui* to develop more complex sentences. See page 133.

3.3 The environment and where people live

Solutions for social problems

Comment améliorer les problèmes sociaux?

How do we improve social problems?

Il faut trouver des boulots pour les personnes sans emploi.

We must find jobs for unemployed people.

Il faut construire plus de logements pas chers.

We need to build more inexpensive accommodation.

Il faut créer des clubs pour les ados.

We need to create some clubs for teenagers.

On doit soutenir les familles en difficulté.

We must support families in difficulty.

Il faut trouver des solutions à cette crise.

We need to find solutions to this crisis.

Le changement politique

Political change

Le gouvernement doit écouter ses électeurs.

The government must listen to its voters.

Les ministres doivent nous défendre.

Ministers must stand up for us.

Le parlement doit créer de nouvelles lois.

Parliament must create new laws.

Il faut obliger les personnes riches à payer plus d'impôts.

We must force rich people to pay more taxes.

On peut voter pour élire un nouveau candidat.

You can vote to elect a new candidate.

Dans une démocratie, les citoyens peuvent manifester.

Citizens can demonstrate in a democracy.

> **REVISION TIP** ☑
>
> Many political words are similar in French and English. It is easy to recognise the meanings of these words, for example: *le vote* (vote), *démocratique* (democratic) and *président*(e) (president).

> **REVISION TIP** ☑
>
> Try learning 'word families' together, for example: *élire* (to elect), *élection* (election), *électeur* (elector / voter).

Des solutions internationales *International solutions*

Pour **améliorer** notre société, l'État doit **travailler** avec les gouvernements d'autres pays. **Trouver** des solutions, c'est un objectif qu'on ne peut **réaliser** qu'en travaillant ensemble. **Changer** les lois serait un moyen de **réduire** les problèmes de drogues et d'attaques au couteau.

In order to improve our society, the State must work with the governments of other countries. Finding solutions is a goal that we can only achieve by working together. Changing the laws would be one way of reducing the problems with drugs and knife attacks.

> **REMEMBER** ❗
>
> Notice the different ways that infinitives are used in this paragraph and how they are translated into English.

Vocabulary learning

Learn this vocabulary and then use the 'look, cover, write, check' technique to make sure you really know it. Cover the English first and then the French.

Social problems and solutions

French	✓	English	✓
l'abri (m.)		shelter	
accepter		to accept	
l'attaque (f.)		attack	
le chômage		unemployment	
construire		to build	
le couteau		knife	
créer		to create	
la crise		crisis	
la difficulté		difficulty	
la drogue		drug(s)	
économique		economic	
égal(e)		equal	
l'égalité (f.)		equality	
grave		serious	
l'inégalité (f.)		inequality	
s'inquiéter (de)		to be worried (about)	
juste		fair	
de nombreux / nombreuses		many, numerous	
parmi		among	
partout		everywhere	
la pauvreté		poverty	
représenter		represent	
la richesse		wealth	
social(e)		social	
la société		society	
soutenir		to support	
le taux		rate	
vécu		lived	

Political change

French	✓	English	✓
le / la candidat(e)		candidate	
le changement		change	
le / la citoyen(ne)		citizen	
défendre		to defend, stand up for	
la démocratie		democracy	
démocratique		democratic	
réduire		to lower, decrease	
l'électeur (m.)		elector, voter	
l'élection (f.)		election	
élire		to elect	
l'État		state	
le gouvernement		government	
l'impôt (m.)		tax	
la loi		law	
manifester		to protest, demonstrate	
le ministre		minister	
le moyen		means, way	
obliger		to oblige, force	
le parlement		parliament	
politique		political	
le / la président(e)		president	
réaliser		to realise, achieve	
le vote		vote	
voter		to vote	

REVISION TIP

Try writing ten words you find hard to remember on sticky notes and sticking them up where you brush your teeth. Spend two minutes every morning memorising them until you are confident.

Answer the questions below. Cover the answers column with a piece of paper and write down as many answers as you can. Check and repeat.

Questions | Answers

#	Questions	Answers
1	Translate the following sentence into French: There's nothing for teenagers to do here.	*Il n'y a rien à faire pour les adolescents / ados ici*
2	What is *le chômage*?	Unemployment
3	Give an alternative expression that you could use with a countable noun instead of *beaucoup de*.	*De nombreux / de nombreuses* (many)
4	What is *une personne sans abri*?	A homeless person
5	Give the French words for 'equal', 'equality' and 'inequality'.	*Égal(e)*; *l'égalité*; *l'inégalité*
6	Translate the following phrase into English: *parmi les jeunes*.	Among young people
7	Ask a question about social problems.	Possible answer: *Comment peut-on améliorer les problèmes sociaux?*
8	Give the opposites of the following words in French: *juste, la pauvreté, le problème*.	*Injuste* (unfair); *la richesse* (wealth); *la solution*
9	Which word is the odd one out and why? *loi / dame / ado*	*Loi* (law) as the other words are specifically to do with people ('lady' and 'teenager')
10	Suggest one way to improve social problems.	Possible answer: *On doit soutenir les familles en difficulté*
11	Translate the following adjectives into French: serious, worrying, expensive.	*Grave, inquiétant(e), cher / chère*
12	List as many French words related to politics as you can.	*Les électeurs*; *le gouvernement*; *voter*; or any from the list on page 103

Put paper here

Previous questions

Use the questions below to check your knowledge from previous chapters.

Questions | Answers

#	Questions	Answers
1	In French, give one advantage and one disadvantage of being a doctor.	Possible answer: *L'avantage, c'est le salaire mais l'inconvénient, ce sont les responsabilités*
2	Say three things about today's weather.	Possible answer: *Il fait froid, il pleut et il y a du vent* See page 84 for more ideas
3	Say two things you will do to help the environment in the future.	Possible answers: *Je vais éviter de prendre des bains*; *Je vais aider à nettoyer la plage*

Put paper here

3.3 The environment and where people live

Where you live

L'endroit où j'habite

J'habite dans une grande ville / un petit village.

Nous **y** habitons depuis dix ans.

J'habite dans une cité dans la capitale.

Ma famille habite dans la banlieue.

Ma ville se situe dans le sud-ouest de l'Angleterre.

Mon village se trouve dans le nord-est de la France.

Tous mes copains **y** habitent aussi.

The place where I live

I live in a big town / a little village.

We have lived there for ten years.

I live on a council estate in the capital city.

My family lives in the suburbs.

My town is situated in the south-west of England.

My village is situated in the north-east of France.

All my friends live there too.

Que penses-tu de ta ville / ton village?

C'est un lieu calme avec des voisins sympas.

J'aimerais vivre dans un endroit plus central.

J'aime habiter près du centre-ville.

Il y a toujours beaucoup de bruit.

J'aimerais vivre ailleurs.

Il n'y a rien à faire ici.

Il y a beaucoup de magasins.

Il manque un centre commercial.

C'est nul car il n'y a ni poste, ni bibliothèque.

What do you think of your town / village?

It's a quiet place with nice neighbours.

I would like to live in a more central place.

I like living near the town centre.

There is always a lot of noise.

I would like to live somewhere else.

There is nothing to do here.

There are lots of shops.

It is missing a shopping centre.

It's rubbish because there is neither a post office nor a library.

> **GRAMMAR TIP** ⭐
>
> The pronoun **y** means 'there' in French and is useful to avoid repetition. For example:
>
> *J'adore mon village et je voudrais **y** habiter pour toujours.* (I love my village and I would like to live there forever.) See page 134.

> **SOUNDS TIP** 🎤
>
> The French sound for the letters *i* and *y* sounds like 'ee' in English. Practise saying these phrases:
>
> *Il vit ici* (he lives here), *ma ville* (my town), *j'**y** habite* (I live there), *on **y** va* (let's go there).

> **REVISION TIP** ✅
>
> Use a variety of structures in your speaking and writing. For example, you can use the impersonal verb *il manque* or the negative structure *ne … ni … ni …* to highlight any facilities that are lacking in your town or village.

Parle-moi de ta ville / ton village *Tell me about your town / your village*

J'habite dans un petit village qui se situe dans l'ouest de l'Angleterre. Ma famille et moi, nous y habitons depuis deux ans. L'avantage d'habiter ici, c'est qu'on peut faire des promenades à la campagne. Nous **en** faisons tous les week-ends. On peut aussi faire du vélo et j'**en** fais souvent avec mes amis. Cependant, l'inconvénient, c'est qu'il manque un supermarché.

I live in a little village that is situated in the west of England. My family and I have lived there for two years. The advantage of living here is that you can go on walks in the countryside. We go on them every weekend. You can also go cycling and I do this often with my friends. However, the disadvantage is that it is missing a supermarket.

> **GRAMMAR TIP** ⭐
>
> Notice how the pronoun **en** is used to avoid repetition in this paragraph, replacing the activities **des promenades à la campagne** and **du vélo**. See page 134 to find out more about how **en** can be used in different contexts.

Chez moi	At my place
Notre appartement est moderne.	Our flat is modern.
Nous habitons une vieille maison en pierre.	We live in an old house made of stone.
Il y a une entrée, un salon et une salle à manger.	There is an entrance, a lounge and a dining room.
Au premier étage, il y a trois chambres.	On the first floor, there are three bedrooms.
Nous avons aussi une salle de bain et des toilettes.	We also have a bathroom and a toilet.
Le bureau de ma mère se trouve au deuxième étage.	My mum's office is on the second floor.
On mange autour de la table dans la cuisine.	We eat around the table in the kitchen.
Il y a onze pièces, en tout.	There are eleven rooms altogether.

REVISION TIP

Count how many rooms there are in your house and practise describing them in French.

Ma chambre — My bedroom

J'ai ma propre chambre.	I have my own bedroom.
Je partage une chambre avec ma sœur.	I share a bedroom with my sister.
La chambre de mes parents est plus grande.	My parents' bedroom is bigger.
Les murs sont bleus.	The walls are blue.
La porte est en bois.	The door is made of wood.
Il y a un grand lit.	There is a double bed.
J'ai un bureau et une chaise.	I have a desk and a chair.
Je vois notre jardin de la fenêtre.	I can see our garden from the window.

REMEMBER

Remember that in French, you need to use the structure 'the bedroom of my parents' (*la chambre de mes parents*) to express the idea of 'my parents' bedroom'.

Comment serait ta maison idéale? *What would your ideal house be like?*

Si j'avais beaucoup d'argent, **j'aimerais** construire ma propre maison, peut-être en forme de château, avec beaucoup d'espace. **Si j'étais** riche, je pense que **j'aurais** une piscine énorme dans le jardin. **Il y aurait** des sièges où s'asseoir et des petites lumières dans les arbres. **Si j'invitais** mes amis pour une fête, **on nagerait** sous les étoiles.

If I had a lot of money, I would like to build my own house, perhaps in the shape of a castle, with lots of space. If I were rich, I think that I would have an enormous swimming pool in the garden. There would be seats where one could sit and little lights in the trees. If I invited my friends for a party, we would swim under the stars.

REVISION TIP

To talk about what you **would** do, **if** the conditions **were** right, use the structure:

Si + imperfect tense + conditional.

A visit to a town

Qu'est-ce qu'il y a dans cette ville? *What is there in this town?*

On peut y trouver beaucoup de restaurants.	*You can find lots of restaurants there.*
Il ne faut pas manquer le marché.	*You mustn't miss the market.*
Il y a une bonne boulangerie.	*There is a good bakery.*
Ça vaut la peine de visiter le musée et le château.	*It's worth visiting the museum and the castle.*
Est-ce qu'il y a une banque ici?	*Is there a bank here?*
Oui, il y en a deux.	*Yes, there are two (of them).*
Il y a un hôtel et il y en aura bientôt un autre.	*There is one hotel and there will soon be another one (of them).*
Il n'y a plus de cinéma mais avant, il y en avait deux.	*There is no longer a cinema, but before there were two (of them).*

Les directions *Directions*

Où est la place principale?	*Where is the main square?*
Continuez jusqu'au pont.	*Carry on up to the bridge.*
Traversez la rivière et puis ce n'est pas loin.	*Cross the river and then it's not far.*
Prenez la première rue à droite.	*Take the first street on the right.*
Tournez à gauche après cent mètres.	*Turn left after 100 metres.*
La place sera devant vous.	*The square will be in front of you.*
Le magasin le plus proche est au coin.	*The nearest shop is on the corner.*
Le théâtre est près de la gare.	*The theatre is near the station.*
Le parc est derrière la banque.	*The park is behind the bank.*
La poste est entre deux cafés.	*The post office is in between two cafés.*

Décris ta ville *Describe your town*

Dans ma ville, il y a un grand centre commercial où j'aime aller avec mes copines. Malheureusement, il n'y a plus de piscine parce que le centre sportif a fermé récemment. Cependant, pour faire du sport, on peut aller au stade ou au parc. Il n'y a qu'un cinéma qui n'est pas loin du centre-ville, avec un café derrière.

In my town, there is a big shopping centre where I like to go with my friends. Unfortunately, there is no longer a swimming pool because the sports centre closed recently. However, to do sport, you can go to the stadium or the park. There is only one cinema, which is not far from the town centre, with a café behind it.

GRAMMAR TIP ★

The pronouns **y** and **en** can be used together in the phrases *il y en a, il y en avait* and *il y en aura*. For example:

Il y en a beaucoup.
There are a lot (of them).

Il y en avait plusieurs dans le passé.
There used to be several (of them) in the past.

Un supermarché? Il y en aura un à l'avenir.
A supermarket? There will be one (of them) in the future.

GRAMMAR TIP ★

When using the prepositions *près de* (near to) and *loin de* (far from), remember that *de + le* becomes **du** and *de + les* becomes **des**. For example:

*Le marché est près **de la** banque, pas loin **du** parc et **des** cafés.* The market is near the bank, not far from the park and the cafés. See page 136.

REVISION TIP

Practise describing your town or village in French, including what facilities there are, where they are and what you can do there. Try to also include some negatives to say what your town or village does **not** offer.

Qu'est-ce qu'il y a à faire ici?

Dans ma région, il y a beaucoup de choses à faire.	*In my region, there are lots of things to do.*
On peut faire du bowling.	*You can go bowling.*
On peut aller au lac ou à la mer.	*You can go to the lake or the sea.*
Si vous êtes sportif / sportive, vous pouvez monter en haut d'une montagne.	*If you are sporty, you can climb to the top of a mountain.*
Quand il fait beau, on peut faire une promenade.	*When it's nice, you can go for a walk.*
Vous pouvez aller à un café pour prendre un thé.	*You can go to a café to have a tea.*
On peut aller au théâtre ou à un concert.	*You can go to the theatre or to a concert.*

Mes activités en ville — *My activities in town*

Normalement, le week-end, je vais en ville.	*Normally, I go into town at the weekends.*
J'y vais avec mon frère ou mes amis.	*I go (there) with my brother or my friends.*
On aime faire les magasins.	*We like to go shopping.*
Nous allons souvent à un petit café.	*We often go to a little café.*
Le week-end prochain, je vais aller au cinéma avec ma copine.	*Next weekend, I'm going to go to the cinema with my girlfriend.*
Ce sera génial parce qu'il y aura un film d'horreur.	*It will be great because there will be a horror film.*
J'adore aller au centre-ville car ce n'est jamais ennuyeux.	*I love going into the town centre because it's never boring.*

Parle-moi d'une récente visite *Tell me about a recent visit*

Récemment, je suis allée à une ville de ma région. J'y suis allée avec mon beau-père pour passer la journée. Nous nous sommes perdus dans les petites rues étroites du vieux quartier et nous avons dû demander notre chemin pour trouver la voiture. Nous avons beaucoup ri et c'était très amusant.

Recently, I went to a town in my region. I went there with my stepdad for a day trip. We got lost in the little narrow streets in the old district and we had to ask our way in order to find the car. We laughed a lot and it was really fun.

GRAMMAR TIP ⭐

Remember, when *à* is followed by *le*, it becomes **au**. When it is followed by *les*, it becomes **aux**. For example:

*J'aime aller **au** lac, **à la** mer et **aux** rivières de la région*. I like going to the lake, to the sea and to the rivers of our region.

SOUNDS TIP 🎤

The French **th** sound is like 't' in English. Practise saying the words **th**é and **th**éâtre.

REVISION TIP ☑

You can develop longer answers about activities by mentioning when you do them, where, how often and who with. You could also add an opinion and a reason.

REVISION TIP ☑

If you want to speak or write about activities in the exam that are not on AQA's vocabulary list, you can do so.

For example: *faire du **bowling*** (to go bowling), *voir un film d'**horreur*** (to see a horror film).

However, you don't have to learn any words beyond the set list.

Vocabulary learning

Learn this vocabulary and then use the 'look, cover, write, check' technique to make sure you really know it. Cover the English first and then the French.

Where you live

French	✓	English	✓
ailleurs		somewhere else, elsewhere	
l'Angleterre (f.)		England	
la banlieue		suburbs, outskirts	
le bruit		noise	
calme		calm, quiet	
la capitale		capital, capital city	
central(e)		central	
le centre		centre	
la cité		council estate	
l'endroit (m.)		place, spot	
étroit(e)		narrow	
habiter		to live (somewhere)	
ici		here	
le lieu		place	
il manque…		…is missing / it lacks	
ne … ni … ni …		neither … nor …	
ne … plus		no longer, not any more	
ne … que		only	
le quartier		district, quarter	
la région		region, area	
se situer		to be situated	
se trouver		to be situated	
le village		village	
la ville		town	
vivre		to live	
le / la voisin(e)		neighbour	
y		there	

House and bedroom

French	✓	English	✓
l'appartement (m.)		apartment, flat	
s'asseoir		to sit down	
autour		around	
le bois		wood	
le bureau		office, desk	
la chaise		chair	
la chambre		bedroom	
énorme		enormous	
l'entrée (f.)		entrance	
l'étage (m.)		floor	
la fenêtre		window	
le jardin		garden	
le lit		bed	
la lumière		light	
la maison		house, home	
moderne		modern	
le mur		wall	
partager		to share	
la pièce		room	
la pierre		stone	
la porte		door	
propre		clean, proper, own	
la salle		room	
la salle à manger		dining room	
la salle de bain		bathroom	
le salon		lounge / living room	
le siège		seat, bench	
le sol		ground, floor	
la table		table	
les toilettes		toilet	

Knowledge

3.3 The environment and where people live

Vocabulary learning

Places in town

French	✓	English	✓
la banque		*bank*	
la bibliothèque		*library*	
bientôt		*soon*	
la boulangerie		*bakery*	
le café		*café, coffee*	
le centre commercial		*shopping centre*	
le centre sportif		*sports centre*	
le château		*castle*	
le cinéma		*cinema*	
fermer		*to close, shut*	
la gare		*station*	
l'hôtel (m.)		*hotel*	
le lac		*lake*	
le magasin		*shop*	
le marché		*market*	
le musée		*museum*	
le parc		*park*	
la piscine		*swimming pool*	
la place		*place, square*	
le pont		*bridge*	
la poste		*post office*	
le restaurant		*restaurant*	
la rivière		*river*	
le stade		*stadium*	
le supermarché		*supermarket*	
le théâtre		*theatre*	

Directions

French	✓	English	✓
le chemin		*way, path*	
le coin		*corner*	
continuer		*to continue, carry on*	
demander		*to ask (for)*	
devant		*in front (of)*	
derrière		*behind*	
la direction		*direction*	
la droite		*right*	
entre		*between*	
la gauche		*left*	
jusque		*until, to, up to*	
loin (de)		*far (from)*	
le mètre		*metre*	
où		*where*	
se perdre		*to get lost*	
près (de)		*near (to)*	
prendre		*to take*	
proche		*nearby, close*	
rire		*to laugh*	
la rue		*street*	
traverser		*to cross*	
trouver		*to find*	

REVISION TIP

Practise talking in French for one minute to describe what there is (or isn't) in your nearest town. Use as many words as possible from the vocabulary list on the left.

Answer the questions below. Cover the answers column with a piece of paper and write down as many answers as you can. Check and repeat.

Questions | Answers

	Questions		Answers
1	Answer the question: *Où habites-tu et depuis quand?*	Put paper here	Possible answer: *J'habite dans une ville du nord de l'Angleterre depuis trois ans*
2	What is the French pronoun that means 'there'?		*Y* (pronounced 'ee')
3	Translate the following sentence into French: I would like to live somewhere else.		*Je voudrais / J'aimerais habiter / vivre ailleurs*
4	Choose the correct word to complete the sentence: *Il manquent / manque / manquer des magasins.*	Put paper here	*Manque* (*Il manque des magasins*: It is missing some shops)
5	Give one advantage and one disadvantage of where you live.		Possible answer: *L'avantage d'habiter ici, c'est qu'on peut faire des promenades; l'inconvénient, c'est que c'est trop calme*
6	In French, list as many rooms in a house as possible.	Put paper here	*La chambre*; *le salon*; *la cuisine*; or any from the list on page 109
7	Describe your bedroom in French.		Possible answer: *Ma chambre est grande avec des murs bleus*
8	Say an 'if' sentence in French using both the imperfect tense and conditional.		Possible answer: *Si j'étais riche, j'aurais une piscine dans le jardin*
9	List as many places in town as you can in French.	Put paper here	*Le stade*; *la banque*; *la gare*; or any from the list on page 110
10	Translate the following sentence into English: *Il y a un hôtel et il y en aura bientôt un autre.*		There is one hotel and there will soon be another one (of them)
11	What do you need to remember when using the prepositions *près de* and *loin de*?	Put paper here	*De* + *le* becomes *du* and *de* + *les* becomes *des*
12	Answer the question: *Parle-moi d'une récente visite en ville.*		Possible answer: *Récemment, je suis allé(e) en ville avec mon père et on a fait du bowling. C'était très amusant*

Previous questions

Use the questions below to check your knowledge from previous chapters.

Questions | Answers

	Questions		Answers
1	Say three sentences in French to describe your school.	Put paper here	Possible answer: *Mon collège est très grand. Il y a deux mille élèves. Nous avons beaucoup de bâtiments modernes*
2	Translate this sentence into English: *Je viens d'écrire un livre.*		I have just written a book
3	Translate the following sentence into French: There's nothing for teenagers to do here.		*Il n'y a rien à faire pour les adolescents / ados ici*

Theme 3 Listening practice

Section A: Listening comprehension

Digital technology

You hear a Canadian grandfather talking about digital technology.

What is his opinion on the following aspects?

Write   **P** for a positive opinion.

           N for a negative opinion.

           P+N for a positive and negative opinion.

Write the correct letter(s) in each box.

5.	Entertainment		**[1 mark]**
6.	Digital communication		**[1 mark]**
7.	Online news		**[1 mark]**
8.	Shopping		**[1 mark]**

> **EXAM TIP**
> Positive adjectives can be used in negative sentences (e.g. if something is '**not** good') so listen to the whole extract carefully.

Gap year travels

You hear this interview with Max, who went travelling after doing his A Levels.

Answer the questions in **English**.

9. For Max, what were the **two** best moments of his travels?   **[2 marks]**

     1   ....

     2   ....

> **EXAM TIP**
> This task has an interview format. Focus on the answers to each interview question in the audio.

Answer both parts of question 6.

6.1 What problem does he mention?   **[1 mark]**

....

6.2 What advice does Max give about accommodation?   **[1 mark]**

....

7. What worried his parents the most?   **[1 mark]**

A	His safety	
B	Lack of communication	
C	The political situation	

A volunteer from Paris

You listen to this podcast about Mohammed, a volunteer with a charity in Paris.

Choose the correct answer and write the letter in each box.

Answer both parts of question 8.

8.1 Mohammed started volunteering because… **[1 mark]**

A	he wanted some work experience.
B	his grandmother encouraged him to.
C	he saw someone sleeping on the street.

8.2 Mohammed helps by… **[1 mark]**

A	giving out hot drinks.
B	volunteering at a support centre.
C	making food in the evenings.

EXAM TIP

You may well hear items of vocabulary that appear in all the three options so listen carefully to the whole extract to work out which **one** statement is true.

Answer both parts of question 9.

9.1 Mohammed thinks one solution would be to… **[1 mark]**

A	create more jobs.
B	build a council estate.
C	help city charities.

9.2 Mohammed likes volunteering because… **[1 mark]**

A	it has given him hope.
B	it has made him more confident.
C	it has helped him make new friends.

Section B: Dictation

You will now hear 5 short sentences. Listen carefully and using your knowledge of French sounds, write down in **French** exactly what you hear for each sentence. **[10 marks]**

SOUNDS TIP

The letter combinations *on* and *om* make the same sound. Listen out for this sound in these sentences.

Sentence 1

....

....

Sentence 2

....

....

Sentence 3

....

....

Sentence 4

....

....

Sentence 5

....

....

✏️ Practice

Theme 3 Speaking practice

Part 1: Role-play

Prepare the following role-play task. Then listen to the teacher's prompts and respond.

You are talking to your French friend.

Your teacher will play the part of your friend and will speak first.

You should address your friend as *tu*.

Whan you see – **?** – you will have to ask a question.

In order to score full marks, you must include at least one verb in your response to each task.

1. Describe your phone. (Give **two** details.)

2. Say if you like playing video games and why / why not. (Give **one** opinion and **one** reason.)

? 3. Ask your friend a question about social media.

4. Say how much time you spent online yesterday. (Give **one** detail.)

5. Say how people use technology for work. (Give **two** details.)

> **EXAM TIP** 🎯
> Remember to respond using a full sentence.

Part 2: Reading aloud task

Read aloud the following text in **French**.

Notre appartement est dans un village.

J'y habite depuis deux ans mais il n'y a pas beaucoup de choses à faire.

On m'a dit qu'ils allaient ouvrir une salle de jeux dans le café.

Si j'avais le choix, je choisirais plutôt d'avoir un cinéma.

Quand je serai riche, je trouverai une maison ailleurs.

> **SOUNDS TIP** 🎤
> Take care with the French sounds made by the letters *a*, *e*, *i*, *o*, and *u*. Try saying these words from the text to warm up: *ha*bi*te*, *le*, *ici*, *no*tre, *plutôt*.

> **EXAM TIP** 🎯
> Read each sentence slowly and clearly, using your knowledge of French sounds.

Then listen and respond to the four questions on the topic of **The environment and where people live**.

In order to score the highest marks, you must try to **answer all four questions as fully as you can**.

Part 3: Photo card task

- Prepare a description of these two photos. You may make as many notes as you wish and use these notes during the test.

- Then record yourself talking about the content of these photos for approximately **one and a half minutes. You must say at least one thing about each photo**.

- After you have spoken about the content of the photos, you will be asked questions related to **any** of the topics within the theme of **Communication and the world around us**. Listen to and respond to the example questions.

EXAM TIP

When making notes for this task during the preparation time, organise them clearly into two sections, labelled 'photo 1' and 'photo 2'.

EXAM TIP

Make sure you are familiar with which topics fall within each theme so that you can anticipate what you might be asked during the conversation.

Photo 1

Photo 2

Theme 3 Reading practice

Section A: Reading comprehension

Reading habits

What does Mahmoud say about each type of reading material?

Write   **P** for something he read **in the past**

           N for something he reads **now**

           F for something he is going to read **in the future**.

EXAM TIP

Look for clues in the tenses and time phrases used in the text.

> Je suis un garçon qui aime la lecture. Je vais aller à la bibliothèque plus souvent pour lire des romans importants, car à l'université je vais étudier l'anglais. En ce moment, je passe trop de temps à répondre à mes e-mails.
>
> Depuis quelques mois, je lis le journal quotidien en ligne et je trouve ça intéressant. L'année dernière, j'ai lu beaucoup de blogs et j'aimais bien ça aussi.
>
> Quand j'étais plus jeune, j'adorais acheter des magazines mais, malheureusement, je n'avais pas les moyens de continuer.

1. Novels   ☐ **[1 mark]**   4. Blogs   ☐ **[1 mark]**

2. Emails   ☐ **[1 mark]**   5. Magazines   ☐ **[1 mark]**

3. Newspapers   ☐ **[1 mark]**

Digital life

You read this article by Sara, who shares her ideas about technology.

> Au début de l'année, j'ai décidé de faire certains changements en ce qui concerne mon utilisation de la technologie. Avant, j'allumais mon portable au milieu de la nuit pour lire des commentaires sur mes réseaux sociaux donc j'étais tout le temps fatiguée. Maintenant, je ne fais plus ça et je dors beaucoup mieux.
>
> J'ai annulé tous mes **abonnements*** aux services de streaming et j'ai arrêté de regarder tous les épisodes de ma série préférée en une seule soirée! J'ai réussi à trouver des moyens pour contrôler mon comportement.
>
> Il y a de nombreux avantages mais une conséquence positive, c'est que j'arrive enfin à bien me concentrer sur mon travail scolaire.
>
> ---
> ***abonnements** = subscriptions

Answer the following questions in **English**.

6. What did Sara use to do in the night? Give **two** details.   **[2 marks]**

    1 ....

    2 ....

7. What has Sara stopped doing in the evening?   **[1 mark]**

....

8. How have these changes benefitted Sara?   **[1 mark]**

....

EXAM TIP

Read the three questions **before** you read the text so that you know what key information to look out for.

An adventure holiday

You read an article about a tropical holiday on a travel website.

Avez-vous déjà rêvé de partir en vacances sur une île tropicale? C'était le souhait de deux amis, Sami et Marie, depuis leur enfance.

Dès l'âge de 13 ans, Marie a commencé à mettre son argent de poche de côté pour s'offrir un voyage à la Réunion. Pour gagner de l'argent, Sami a aidé ses grands-parents. Comme elle a toujours voulu pratiquer le surf, Marie désirait aller dans l'ouest de l'île où les conditions seraient meilleures. Son copain préférait l'idée de la côte est, loin des villes.

Quand le jour du départ est enfin arrivé, ils sont partis en priant, tous les deux, pour avoir du beau temps pendant leurs vacances. La jeune femme a pu profiter pleinement des vagues puissantes. Sami n'osait pas l'accompagner dans l'eau, même pour un essai, donc il s'est relaxé sur la plage.

EXAM TIP

In reading texts, there may be a couple of cognates (French words that look like English words and which have the same meaning). It's easy to guess what *tropicale* and *surf* mean!

Who do the following statements refer to?

Write **M** for **Marie**

S for **Sami**

M+S for **Marie** and **Sami**.

9.   Who saved up money for the trip?   [1 mark]

10. Who wanted to stay on the east coast?   [1 mark]

11. Who was praying for good weather?   [1 mark]

12. Who went into the sea?   [1 mark]

Section B: Translation into English

13. Translate these sentences into **English**.

Le taux du chômage continue à augmenter.   **[2 marks]**

....

Cette application est utilisée par tout le monde.   **[2 marks]**

....

L'hôtel était sale et il n'y avait aucune clé pour la chambre.   **[2 marks]**

....

Il faut visiter ce bel endroit que j'ai trouvé hier en ligne.   **[2 marks]**

....

Si nous avions plus de temps, nous travaillerions comme bénévoles.   **[2 marks]**

....

EXAM TIP

Think about how to translate short phrases within each sentence rather than focusing only on each individual word.

Theme 3 Writing practice

Section A: Translation into French

1. Translate the following sentences into **French**.   **[10 marks]**

In the south, it's cold and it's foggy.

....

I used to read my emails before going to bed.

....

In my little town, there is neither a bank nor a post office.

....

This summer, we will organise a stay in the mountains.

....

I think they can improve the situation by protecting animals and birds.

....

> **EXAM TIP** 🎯
>
> Before starting to translate, try to identify which grammar point is being tested in each sentence. For example, the structure of 'before doing' something in French in sentence 2 (*avant de* + infinitive).

Section B

Answer **either** Question 2.1 **or** Question 2.2

Either

Question 2.1

You are writing a blog about your online activities.

Write approximately **90** words in **French**.
You must write something about each bullet point.

Describe:

- how you use technology to communicate with people   **[15 marks]**
- how you have used the internet for school work recently
- what you will do online this weekend.

Or

Question 2.2

You are writing an email to a French friend about your home.

Write approximately **90** words in **French**.
You must write something about each bullet point.

Describe:

- your house   **[15 marks]**
- what you did with your family at home last week
- where you will live in the future.

> **EXAM TIP** 🎯
>
> Make your choice about which question to pick fairly quickly, based on your knowledge of the topics outlined in each bullet point.

> **EXAM TIP** 🎯
>
> Check you have used verbs in three different time frames (present, past and future).

Section C

Answer **either** Question 3.1 **or** Question 3.2

Either

Question 3.1

You are writing an article about the environment.

Your article is about problems and solutions.

Write approximately **150** words in **French**.
You must write something about both bullet points.

Describe:

- some current environmental problems
- what people are going to do to improve the situation in the future.

[25 marks]

Or

Question 3.2

You are writing a blog about your local area.

Your post is designed for tourists visiting the region.

Write approximately **150** words in **French**.
You must write something about both bullet points.

Describe:

- the positive aspects of the region
- something fun that you have done in the area recently.

[25 marks]

EXAM TIP

Plan which problems and solutions you want to mention **before** you start to write. Spend a minute jotting down key words in French on the environment topic that you want to include.

EXAM TIP

Try to extend your sentences, using several clauses or connectives.

⚙ Knowledge `GRAMMAR`

Nouns and articles

Nouns: gender and plurals

Gender of nouns

- A noun is a word that refers to people, places, things or concepts. In French, all nouns have a gender: they are either masculine or feminine.

  For example, the word *père* (father) is a masculine noun while *mère* (mother) is a feminine noun.

- Even nouns referring to objects or concepts have a gender. Here are some examples:

Masculine nouns	Feminine nouns
conflit (conflict) *détail* (detail) *esprit* (mind, spirit)	*concurrence* (competition) *diversité* (diversity) *époque* (era, period, time)

REVISION TIP ✓

When you learn a new noun, always learn its gender (m. / f.) at the same time.

Nouns that change gender

- Some nouns, such as job titles, change their ending to refer to people of different genders.

Masculine form	Ending change	Feminine form
écrivain (male writer) *directeur* (male headteacher or manager) *chanteur* (male singer) *citoyen* (male citizen)	Add -*e* Change -*teur* to -*trice* Change -*eur* to -*euse* Change -*en* to -*enne*	*écrivaine* (female writer) *directrice* (female headteacher or manager) *chanteuse* (female singer) *citoyenne* (female citizen)

REMEMBER !

If the prefixes *in-* or *im-* are added to some nouns, it can change their meaning to the opposite: *sécurité* (security) – *insécurité* (insecurity).

- Other nouns do not change their spelling but can be used to refer to people of any gender, for example: *professeur* (teacher), *élève* (pupil).

Plural nouns

- To form the plural of nouns, you usually just add an -*s*: *deux professeur**s*** (two teachers).
- If a noun ends in -*eau*, -*au* or -*eu*, add an -*x* to form the plural instead:
  - *un bateau* = one boat – *deux bateau**x*** = two boats
  - *un jeu* = one game – *deux jeu**x*** = two games
- If a noun already ends in -*s* or -*x* in the singular form, it does not change in the plural form:
  - *un cours* = one lesson – *deux cours* = two lessons
  - *un choix* = one choice – *deux choix* = two choices
- A few nouns have irregular plural forms: *un œil* (one eye) – *deux yeux* (two eyes).

EXAM TIP ◎

You can work out the meaning of some nouns ending in -*eur* or -*euse* from your knowledge of verbs:

jouer (to play) – *joueur / joueuse* (player)

Definite and indefinite articles

- The definite article in English is the word 'the'. The indefinite article in English is 'a' or 'an'.

- In French, articles need to 'agree' with the noun, by matching its gender and number.

- The definite articles in French are *le* (m.), *la* (f.) and *les* (plural): *le frère* (the brother), *la sœur* (the sister), *les parents* (the parents).

  Le and *la* become *l'* in front of a masculine or feminine noun that starts with a vowel or silent 'h': *l'ennemi* (enemy), *l'humanité* (humanity).

- The indefinite articles in French are *un* (m.) or *une* (f.): *un collège* (a school), *une famille* (a family).

Uses of the definite article

- The definite articles (*le*, *la* and *les*) tend to be used more often in French than they are in English. For example, they are needed when giving opinions or talking about things in general:

  *J'adore **la** natation.* I love swimming.
  ***Le** sport est important.* Sport is important.

- Languages and school subjects also take the definite article in French:

  ***L'**espagnol est une belle langue.* Spanish is a beautiful language.
  *J'étudie **la** géographie.* I study Geography.

Partitive articles

- The partitive article in English is the word 'some'. In French, the partitive articles agree with the noun that follows: *du* (m.), *de la* (f.) or *des* (plural): ***du** poisson, **de la** viande et **des** légumes* (some fish, some meat and some vegetables).

  Du and *de la* become *de l'* in front of a masculine or feminine noun that starts with a vowel or silent 'h': ***de l'**eau* (some water).

- After negative expressions and expressions of quantity, the partitive articles become **de** (or *d'* before a vowel): *Je n'ai pas **de** frères ou **de** sœurs mais j'ai beaucoup **de** cousins.* (I don't have any brothers or sisters but I have a lot of cousins.)

Other uses of partitive articles

- Partitive articles are also used after *jouer* (to play) with musical instruments and after *faire* (to make / do) with sports and other activities.

  *Je joue **du** piano et je fais **de la** danse.* I play the piano and I do dance.

> **REMEMBER** !
>
> Notice how *le* in front of a French day of the week changes the meaning in English:
>
> *Mercredi, j'ai un club.* On Wednesday, I have a club.
>
> ***Le** mercredi, j'ai un club.* On Wednesday**s** (every Wednesday), I have a club.

> **REMEMBER** !
>
> Notice the difference between ***un** pain* (a loaf of bread) and ***du** pain* (some bread).

Retrieval

Answer the questions below. Cover the answers column with a piece of paper and write down as many answers as you can. Check and repeat.

Questions | Answers

#	Questions		Answers
1	In French, list four masculine nouns and four feminine nouns.	Put paper here	Possible answers: *père*; *conflit*; *détail*; *esprit* (masculine nouns) and *mère*; *concurrence*; *diversité* and *époque* (feminine nouns)
2	How do the prefixes *in-* or *im-* change the meaning of some nouns in French? Give an example.	Put paper here	Adding these prefixes changes the meaning of the nouns to its opposite, for example: *sécurité* (security) – *insécurité* (insecurity)
3	What is the feminine spelling of the noun *directeur* (headteacher, manager)?	Put paper here	*Directrice*
4	What is the masculine spelling of the noun *citoyenne* (female citizen)?	Put paper here	*Citoyen*
5	Can you work out the meaning of this job role, from your knowledge of French verbs? *Vendeur / vendeuse*	Put paper here	Salesperson (from the verb *vendre*, to sell)
6	How do you form the plural of a noun that already ends in *-s* or *-x*?	Put paper here	Nouns that already end in *-s* or *-x* do not change in the plural form
7	How do you translate the words 'the' and 'a / an' into French?	Put paper here	*Le / la / l' / les* (the) and *un* or *une* (a / an)
8	Translate the following sentence into French: I love sport.	Put paper here	*J'adore / J'aime le sport*
9	Translate the following sentence into English: *Le samedi, je fais de la natation.*	Put paper here	I do / go swimming on Saturdays / every Saturday
10	What are the French words for 'some' (the partitive articles)?	Put paper here	*Du / de la / de l' / des*
11	Translate the following sentence into French: I have never done (any) sport.	Put paper here	*Je n'ai jamais fait de sport*
12	Choose the correct word to complete this sentence: J'ai beaucoup des / de / du copains.	Put paper here	*De*

Previous questions

Use these questions to check your knowledge of previous topics.

Questions | Answers

#	Questions		Answers
1	Say the months of the year in French.	Put paper here	*Janvier; février; mars; avril; mai; juin; juillet; août; septembre; octobre; novembre; décembre*
2	Which tense are these verbs in? *J'ai joué / je suis allé(e) / j'ai fait*	Put paper here	The perfect tense (a past tense) – I played / I went / I did
3	Describe your best friend's hair and eyes in French.	Put paper here	Possible answer: *Il / Elle a les cheveux longs / courts et les yeux verts / bleus / bruns*

Adjectives

Adjective agreement

Agreement of regular adjectives

- Adjectives are describing words, like *intéressant* (interesting) and *amusant* (funny).

- In French, most adjectives change their spelling in some way to 'agree' with the noun they describe in gender and number.

- Many adjectives follow this pattern of endings:

Masculine singular	Feminine singular	Masculine plural	Feminine plural
- *un garçon bavard*	*-e* *une fille bavarde*	*-s* *des garçons bavards*	*-es* *des filles bavardes*

- Adjectives that already end in a silent *-e* in the masculine singular do not take another *-e* in the feminine singular or plural forms: *une tâche facile* (an easy task).

- Adjectives that already end in *-s* in the masculine singular do not take another *-s* in the masculine plural form: *ils sont québécois* (they are from Quebec).

- A few adjectives never change their ending, for example: *marron* (brown).

Other adjectival agreement patterns

- Look at the patterns of endings in the examples below.

Masculine singular	Feminine singular	Masculine plural	Feminine plural
dangereux	*dangereuse*	*dangereux*	*dangereuses*
naturel	*naturelle*	*naturels*	*naturelles*
végétarien	*végétarienne*	*végétariens*	*végétariennes*
sportif	*sportive*	*sportifs*	*sportives*
premier	*première*	*premiers*	*premières*
normal	*normale*	*normaux*	*normales*

> **REMEMBER** !
>
> Before a masculine, singular noun starting with a vowel or silent 'h', some adjectives are spelled differently to make them easier to pronounce: *vieil* (old), *bel* (beautiful) and *nouvel* (new).

Irregular adjective agreements

- Some adjectives are completely irregular and need to be learned, for example:

English meaning	Masculine singular	Feminine singular	Masculine plural	Feminine plural
old	*vieux*	*vieille*	*vieux*	*vieille*
beautiful	*beau*	*belle*	*beaux*	*belles*
new	*nouveau*	*nouvelle*	*nouveaux*	*nouvelles*
good	*bon*	*bonne*	*bons*	*bonnes*
all	*tout*	*toute*	*tous*	*toutes*

Adjectives

Position of adjectives

Adjectives after a noun or verb

– Unlike in English, most French adjectives **follow** the noun they are describing:

*Nous avons une maison **bleue**.* We have a blue house.

– Adjectives can also follow a verb such as *être* (to be), *sembler* (to seem) or *devenir* (to become). However, the adjective must still agree with the noun it describes.

*Elles sont **prêtes**.* They are ready.

Adjectives before a noun

– Some adjectives usually go **before** the noun, for example:

- *beau* = beautiful
- *bon* = good
- *faux* = false
- *grand* = big
- *haut* = high
- *jeune* = young
- *joli* = pretty
- *mauvais* = bad
- *nouveau* = new
- *petit* = small
- *premier* = first
- *vieux* = old

– A few adjectives can go before **or** after the noun, but change their meaning according to their position. For example, *propre* can mean 'own' or 'clean':

- *ma **propre** chambre* = my own bedroom
- *une chambre **propre*** = a clean bedroom

Some other adjectives in this category include *ancien* (former / ancient) and *seul* (only / alone).

> **REVISION TIP**
> The question word *quel* (which / what) is an adjective and must agree with the noun that follows (*quel / quelle / quels / quelles*).

Quelles sont tes activités préférées? *What are your favourite activities?*

Je **n'**ai **aucune** activité préférée mais en ce moment, je cherche de **nouveaux** passe-temps. Je suis **incapable** de décider! Une activité pas trop **chère** serait **préférable**.

I don't have any favourite activity but I'm looking for new hobbies at the moment. I am incapable of deciding! An activity that isn't too expensive would be preferable.

> **REMEMBER**
> In the negative expression *ne … aucun(e)*, meaning 'no / not one / not any', an **-e** is added here to agree with the feminine noun that follows.

> **EXAM TIP**
> In the Reading paper, you may see adjectives ending in **-able** / **-eable** that are created from a verb stem. In the text above, *préférable* comes from the verb *préférer* (to prefer).

Comparatives

- To compare two things in French, use the following comparative phrases:

  - *plus ... que*
    = more ... than
  - *moins ... que*
    = less ... than
  - *aussi ... que*
    = as ... as

- The adjective you use with these comparatives must agree with the noun it describes:

  La physique est plus intéressante que l'allemand.
  Physics is more interesting than German.
  Les maths sont plus difficiles que le théâtre.
  Maths is more difficult than Drama.
  La géographie est aussi amusante que la musique.
  Geography is as fun as Music.

Irregular comparatives

- To say that something is 'better' or 'worse', use these irregular comparative phrases, making sure you add the correct agreements:

  - *meilleur(e)(s) que* = better than
  - *pire(s) que* = worse than

  La géographie est meilleure que l'histoire. Geography is better than History.
  Les sciences sont pires que la technologie. Science is worse than Technology.

Superlatives

- To say that something is 'the most + adjective' or 'the least + adjective', use the superlative structures:

  - *le plus (intéressant)* = the most (interesting)
  - *le moins (difficile)* = the least (difficult)

- Make sure that the adjective and the word for 'the' agree with the noun:

  *C'est la matière **la** plus intéressante.* It's the most interesting subject.
  *Les cours d'aujourd'hui sont **les** moins difficiles.*
  Today's lessons are the least difficult.

Irregular superlatives

- To say that something is 'the best' or 'the worst', use these irregular superlatives:

  - *le / la / les meilleur(e)(s)* = the best
  - *le / la / les pire(s)* = the worst

  Nos profs sont les meilleurs. Our teachers are the best.
  Les sciences sont les pires leçons. The sciences are the worst lessons.

REMEMBER ❗

To translate words like 'easier' into French, you have to say *plus facile* ('more easy'). 'Cheaper' would translate as *moins cher* ('less expensive').

LINK 🔗

To revise adjective agreement, go to page 123.

REMEMBER ❗

You can't use the adjectives *bon* (good) or *mauvais* (bad) with the structure *plus ... que*. Use *meilleur que* (better than) or *pire que* (worse than) instead.

REVISION TIP ✅

Practise describing some of your own school subjects using comparative and superlative structures and a range of different adjectives.

Adjectives

Possessive, demonstrative and indefinite adjectives

– Possessive adjectives are used to say who things belong to. There are different words for 'my', 'your', etc. in French because they must agree with the noun that follows them:

English	Masculine singular	Feminine singular	Plural
my	mon	ma	mes
your (informal, singular)	ton	ta	tes
his / her / its	son	sa	ses
our	notre	notre	nos
your (formal / plural)	votre	votre	vos
their	leur	leur	leurs

– Use *mon*, *ton* and *son* before a singular noun that starts with a vowel or a silent 'h', even if it is feminine, to make it easier to pronounce: *mon amie* (my girlfriend), *ton histoire* (your story).

Demonstrative adjectives

– Demonstrative adjectives mean 'this' or 'that' (in the singular forms) and 'these' or 'those' (in the plural forms). They must agree with the noun that follows them:

Masculine singular	Masculine singular before a vowel	Feminine singular	Plural
ce	cet	cette	ces

– Use *cet* before a singular, masculine noun that starts with a vowel or silent 'h' to make it easier to pronounce / say: *cet endroit* (this place), *cet hôtel* (this hotel).

Indefinite adjectives

– Indefinite adjectives are words like *chaque* (every) and *plusieurs* (several). These two examples never change their endings: *chaque semaine* (every week), *plusieurs personnes* (several people).

– However, the indefinite adjectives *quelque* (some) and *autre* (other) do take an -*s* if followed by a plural noun: *quelques livres* (some books), *mes autres amis* (my other friends).

Notre programme d'exercice *Our exercise schedule*

Nous faisons **ces** exercices à la maison **plusieurs** fois **chaque** semaine pour augmenter **notre** énergie. **Ceci** est plus facile que d'aller au centre sportif.

We do these exercises at home several times each week to increase our energy. This is easier than going to the sports centre.

REMEMBER ❗

Remember that *son / sa / ses* could **all** mean either 'his / her / its', depending on the context: *Il aime sa grand-mère, son grand-père et ses cousins.* (He loves **his** grandmother, **his** grandfather and **his** cousins.)

REVISION TIP ☑

Try saying the possessive adjectives out loud as a rap or rhyme: *mon, ma, mes*; *ton, ta, tes...* etc.

REMEMBER ❗

The pronouns *ceci* (this) and *cela* (that / it) have similar meanings but are used differently, as the subject or object of a sentence. *Cela* is just the formal way to say *ça* (that / it).

Ceci est plus important que cela / ça. **This** is more important than **that.**

LINK ⚛

The agreement patterns for *tout* (all) are on page 123.

Retrieval

Answer the questions below. Cover the answers column with a piece of paper and write down as many answers as you can. Check and repeat.

Questions

Answers

1 Translate the following phrases into French: a chatty boy, a sporty girl, some vegetarian meals, some dangerous activities.

Un garçon bavard; *une fille sportive*; *des plats végétariens*; *des activités dangereuses*

2 Give all five possible forms of the French adjective meaning 'beautiful'.

Beau (m. sing.); *bel* (m. sing. before a noun starting with a vowel or silent 'h'); *belle* (f. sing.); *beaux* (m.pl.); *belles* (f.pl.)

3 Where do the adjectives *vieux* (old) and *jeune* (young) go in a sentence?

In front of the noun they describe

4 In what way can the adjective *propre* change its meaning?

It means 'own' if placed in front of the noun and 'clean' if placed after the noun

5 What are the three different comparative structures in French?

Plus ... que (more ... than); *moins ... que* (less ... than); *aussi ... que* (as ... as)

6 Choose the correct word to complete this sentence: *Les maths sont aussi amusants / amusantes / amusante que l'histoire.*

Amusantes

7 Translate the following words into French: better than, worse than, the best, the worst.

Meilleur(e)(s) que; *pire(s) que*; *le / la / les meilleur(e)(s)*; *le / la / les pire(s)*

8 What are the three words for 'my' in French and when would you use each one?

Mon (before a m. sing. noun or a feminine noun starting with a vowel / silent 'h'); *ma* (before a f. sing. noun); *mes* (before plural nouns)

9 Translate the following phrases into French: his sister, her brother, their family.

Sa sœur; *son frère*; *leur famille*

10 What do the words *ce / cet / cette* mean and what does the word *ces* mean?

Ce / cet / cette: this / that; *ces*: these / those

11 Translate the following sentence into French: This is more important than that.

Ceci est plus important que cela / ça

12 Translate the following phrases into English: *quelques personnes, chaque jour, plusieurs fois, mes autres amis.*

Some people; every / each day; several times; my other friends

Previous questions

Use the questions below to check your knowledge from previous chapters.

Questions

Answers

1 What is a *PACS*?

A civil partnership

2 In French, name three parts of the body that are above the neck.

La tête; *l'œil / les yeux*; *les oreilles*

3 Choose the correct word to complete this sentence: *J'ai beaucoup des / de / du copains.*

De

⚙ Knowledge GRAMMAR

Adverbs

Forming and using adverbs

– Adverbs are often used with verbs to describe **how** an action is being done, for example 'slowly', 'quickly' or 'easily'. They follow the verb in a sentence: *Il court lentement.* He runs slowly.

– Regular adverbs are usually formed by adding *-ment* to the feminine, singular form of an adjective:

- *complète**ment*** = completely
- *parfaite**ment*** = perfectly
- *régulière**ment*** = regularly

– Some adverbs are formed by dropping the *-ant(e)* or *-ent(e)* ending from an adjective and adding *-amment* or *-emment* instead. For example:

- réc**ent** = recent → réc**emment** = recently
- suffis**ant** = sufficient → suffis**amment** = sufficiently

– Some adverbs are completely irregular. These do not have a *-ment* ending and may look quite different to their adjectives. For example: *bien* (well), *mal* (badly) and *vite* (quickly / fast).

Adverbs of time, frequency and place

– Adverbs are also used to describe **where** things happen, as well as **when** and **how often**.

– Adverbs of place include words like *dehors* (outside), *loin* (far) and *près* (near). They usually follow the verb in a sentence.

Vous habitez ici? Do you live here?
Regardez là-bas! Look over there!
Ils sont partout. They are everywhere.

– Adverbs of time and frequency often follow the verb:

On chante souvent dans un groupe. We often sing in a group.

However, the following adverbs usually come at the start of a sentence: *parfois* (sometimes), *normalement* (normally), *récemment* (recently), *généralement* (generally).

> **REMEMBER** ❗
>
> The prefixes **in-** and **im-** can also be used with adverbs: **in***suffisamment* (insufficiently), **im***patiemment* (impatiently).

> **REVISION TIP** ☑
>
> Memorise common adverbial phrases like *l'année dernière* (last year) and *l'année prochaine* (next year) to use in your speaking and writing.

> **LINK** 🔗
>
> See pages 7–8 for more adverbs of time and frequency.

Tu prends toujours le petit-déjeuner? *Do you always have breakfast?*

Généralement, je prends mon petit-déjeuner **assez tôt chaque jour**. Je préfère manger **lentement**. **Avant**, je prenais **souvent** du lait mais **maintenant** je bois **tout le temps** du café. **Parfois**, je dois partir **vite** le matin, mais je peux **toujours** acheter quelque chose **plus tard**.

Generally, I have my breakfast quite early every day. I prefer to eat slowly. Before, I often used to have milk but now I drink coffee all the time. Sometimes, I have to leave quickly in the mornings, but I can always buy something later.

> **EXAM TIP** 🎯
>
> Try to include a range of different adverbs in your own speaking and writing to add variety and complexity.

Comparative and superlative adverbs

Comparative adverbs

- Adverbs can be used with the comparative phrases:
  - *plus … que* = more … than
  - *moins … que* = less … than
  - *aussi … que* = as … as

  Je lis plus vite que mes amis. I read more quickly than my friends.
  Ils font leurs devoirs moins souvent que moi.
  They do their homework less often than me.
  Nous nageons aussi régulièrement que possible.
  We swim as regularly as possible.

- Unlike comparative adjectives, no agreements are needed as adverbs describe the verb rather than the noun.

- The irregular comparative form *mieux* (better) can also be used as an adverb:

  Vous chantez mieux que votre copine.
  You sing better than your girlfriend.

Superlative adverbs

- Adverbs can be used with the superlative phrases *le plus…* (the most) and *le moins…* (the least).

  C'est lui qui parle le plus rapidement. He is the one who speaks the fastest.
  Elle joue au foot le moins souvent. She plays football the least often.

- Use *le mieux* (the best) or *le moins bien* (the least well) to describe how well (or badly) someone does something:

  C'est elle qui se souvient le mieux de ce jour.
  She is the one who remembers that day the best.
  C'est moi qui travaille le moins bien.
  I am the one who works the least well.

LINK

To revise comparative and superlative adjectives, go to page 125.

REMEMBER

Superlative adverbs always start with the masculine singular *le* (the), unlike superlative adjectives.

La concurrence parmi des amies *Competition among friends*

Mes copines et moi, nous sommes très sportives – et extrêmement compétitives! C'est moi qui joue au foot **le moins bien** mais c'est mon équipe qui gagne **le plus régulièrement**. C'est ma meilleure copine qui court **le plus vite** parmi nous mais c'est moi qui nage **le mieux**. Chacune de nous veut toujours gagner – mais c'est moi qui bats **le plus souvent** les autres en sport!

My friends and I are very sporty – and extremely competitive! I am the one who plays football the least well but it's my team who wins the most regularly. It's my best friend who runs the fastest among us but I am the one who swims the best. Each one of us always wants to win – but I am the one who beats the others in sport the most often!

REVISION TIP

Try reading the French text on the left out loud to practise your pronunciation skills.

Answer the questions below. Cover the answers column with a piece of paper and write down as many answers as you can. Check and repeat.

Questions	Answers
1 True or false? The following words are all adverbs: *récemment, parfois, tôt*.	True (recently; sometimes; early)
2 How do you usually form regular adverbs in French?	By adding the ending -*ment* to the feminine, singular form of an adjective
3 Translate the following adverbs into French: completely, perfectly, regularly.	*Complètement*; *parfaitement*; *régulièrement*
4 Translate the following adverbs into English: *bien, mal, vite*.	Well; badly; quickly / fast
5 List as many adverbs of place in French as possible.	Possible answers include: *dehors* (outside); *loin* (far); *près* (near); *ici* (here); *là-bas* (over there)
6 Answer this question in French: *Tu chantes souvent?*	Possible answer: *Oui, je chante souvent dans un groupe*
7 Translate the phrases 'last year' and 'next year' into French.	*L'année dernière*; *l'année prochaine*
8 Answer this question in French: *Tu prends toujours le petit-déjeuner?*	Possible answer: *Oui, je prends toujours le petit-déjeuner*
9 True or false: You can use adverbs with comparative phrases.	True
10 Choose the correct word to complete the sentence: *Vous chantez bon / bien / mieux que moi.*	*Mieux*
11 Correct the mistake in this sentence: *C'est elle qui parle la plus vite.*	*C'est elle qui parle <u>le</u> plus vite*
12 Translate this sentence into English: *C'est moi qui bats le plus souvent les autres en sport.*	I am the one who beats the others in sport the most often

Put paper here *Put paper here* *Put paper here* *Put paper here* *Put paper here*

Previous questions

Use the questions below to check your knowledge from previous chapters.

Questions	Answers
1 Answer these questions in French: *Quelle est ta matière préférée? Pourquoi?*	Possible answer: *Ma matière préférée, c'est (l'anglais) parce que c'est (plus intéressant que le français)*
2 How do you say in French: 'I want to' and 'I would like to'?	*Je veux*; *je voudrais / j'aimerais*
3 Translate the following words into French: better than, worse than, the best, the worst.	*Meilleur(e)(s) que*; *pire(s) que*; *le / la / les meilleur(e)(s)*; *le / la / les pire(s)*

Put paper here

Pronouns

Subject and emphatic pronouns

Subject pronouns

– Subject pronouns are words like 'I', 'you' and 'they'. They replace a name or another noun that is the subject of the sentence (the person or thing doing the action):

Elles *regardent la télé.* They are watching TV.

– Learn the French subject pronouns in this order, as this will help you later, when memorising verbs:

je (I)   *nous* (we)

tu (you – informal, singular)   *vous* (you – formal / plural)

il / elle / on (he / she / we)   *ils / elles* (they)

– If you wish to use gender neutral pronouns, you can use *iel* instead of *il / elle* and *iels* instead of *ils / elles*.

Indefinite and negative pronouns

– Indefinite pronouns like *quelqu'un* (someone), *tout le monde* (everyone), *chacun(e)* (each one / person) and *quelque chose* (something) can be used as the subject of a sentence:

Quelqu'un écoute de la musique. Someone is listening to music.

– The negative pronouns *personne ne…* (nobody) and *rien ne…* (nothing) can also be used as the subject of a sentence or clause:

Personne ne mange et rien ne se passe. Nobody is eating and nothing is happening.

Emphatic pronouns

– Emphatic pronouns like *moi* (me) and *toi* (you) are used to stress who you are referring to.

Moi, je pense que c'est super. I think that it's great.

– They are also used to refer to people after certain prepositions, like *avec* (with):

Elle vient avec toi? Is she coming with you?

– Make sure you learn all these emphatic pronouns.

moi (me)   *nous* (us)

toi (you – informal, singular)   *vous* (you – formal / plural)

lui / elle (him / her)   *eux / elles* (them)

– Emphatic pronouns can be combined with the word *même*: *moi-même* (myself), *toi-même* (yourself), *lui-même* (himself), *elle-même* (herself), etc.

REMEMBER (!)

There are two ways to say 'you' in French. Use *tu* to talk to one friend or family member (and in role play tasks). *Vous* is used to address a group of people or as a polite form to talk to one person more formally.

REMEMBER (!)

There are two ways to say 'we' in French *(on* and *nous)* and there are masculine and feminine versions of 'they' *(ils / elles).*

REVISION TIP 📝

Practise making French phrases by combining these prepositions with different emphatic pronouns: *avant* (before), *après* (after), *pour* (for), *derrière* (behind), *devant* (in front of) and *selon* (according to).

⚙ Knowledge `GRAMMAR`

Pronouns

Direct and indirect object pronouns

Direct object pronouns

– The **direct object** of a sentence usually follows the verb and is the person or thing that the action is being done to:

*Je lis **un roman**.* I am reading **a novel**.

– Direct object pronouns replace the direct object in a sentence to avoid repetition:

*Je **le** lis.* I am reading **it**.

– Learn all these direct object pronouns.

me (me)	*nous* (us)
te (you – informal, singular)	*vous* (you – formal / plural)
le / la (him / her / it)	*les* (them)

> **REMEMBER** ❗
>
> In front of a vowel or silent 'h', shorten *me*, *te* and *le / la* to *m'*, *t'* and *l'*.

– In most tenses, direct object pronouns go in front of the verb:

*Il **m'**aimera toujours.* He will always love **me**.

– In the perfect tense, direct object pronouns go in front of the auxiliary verb (the first verb):

*Vous **l'**avez vu?* Did you see **him**?

– In a sentence that contains an infinitive, the direct object pronoun goes in front of the infinitive:

*Je voudrais **te** voir.* I would like to see **you**.

– In a negative sentence, direct object pronouns still go before the verb (after the *ne / n'*):

*Nous ne **les** connaissons pas.* We don't know **them**.

Indirect object pronouns

– The **indirect object** of a sentence usually follows a verb plus a preposition (such as *à* or *pour*):

*J'achète un cadeau pour **mon frère**.* I am buying a present for **my brother**.

– Indirect object pronouns replace the indirect object in a sentence to avoid repetition:

*Je **lui** achète un cadeau.* I am buying **him** a present.

– These are the indirect object pronouns.

me (to) me	*nous* (to) us
te (to) you – informal, singular	*vous* (to) you – formal / plural
lui (to) him / her / it	*leur* (to) them

– The position of indirect object pronouns in a sentence follows the same rules as for direct object pronouns (see above).

> **REVISION TIP** ☑
>
> Indirect object pronouns are often used with verbs followed by *à*, such as *donner à* (to give to), *parler à* (to talk to) or *demander à* (to ask).

> **LINK** 🔗
>
> Go to page 136 to find out more about verbs followed by *à*.

> **REVISION TIP** ☑
>
> Indirect object pronouns look similar to direct object pronouns. *Lui* (to him / her / it) and *leur* (to them) are the ones that are different.

Relative pronouns and extended sentences

The relative pronouns *qui* and *que*

– Relative pronouns are used in front of a relative clause to give us more information. A relative clause is a phrase that can't stand alone as a sentence. For example, in the sentence 'Look at the clothes that I bought', the relative clause 'that I bought' isn't a full sentence on its own.

Using *qui*

– You may be familiar with *qui* as a question word (who). However, *qui* can also be used as a relative pronoun to extend a sentence, with the meaning of 'who', 'which' or 'that'. *Qui* goes before a verb and relates to the **subject** of the sentence:

*Nous avons un chien **qui** s'appelle Astérix.*
We have a dog **that** / **who** is called Asterix.
*Je voudrais un emploi **qui** m'offre plus de flexibilité.*
I would like a job **which** offers me more flexibility.

Using *que*

– As well as being a question word meaning 'what', *que* can also be used as a relative pronoun. It can translate as 'who', 'which' or 'that'. *Que* goes before a noun or pronoun in a relative clause and relates to the **object** of the sentence:

*Voilà le chanteur **que** mes amis adorent.*
There's the singer **that** / **who** my friends love.

Extended sentences using *quand* and *où*

– You may know *quand* (when) and *où* (where) as question words but they can also be used to join two clauses:

*On aime faire du camping **quand** il fait beau.*
We like camping **when** the weather is nice.
*La plage est l'endroit **où** je peux me relaxer.*
The beach is the place **where** I can relax.

LINK

To revise question words and question formation, go to page 12.

REVISION TIP

You can also extend your sentences using words like *parce que* (because), *mais* (but) and *puis* (then).

⚙ Knowledge GRAMMAR

Pronouns

The pronouns *y* and *en*

The pronoun *y*

– The pronoun *y* is used to mean 'there' when replacing the name of a place in a sentence. It is placed in front of the verb:

*Elles sont chez leur père et elles **y** mangent ce soir.*
They are at their father's house and they are eating **there** tonight.

– You can also use *y* to mean 'it' or 'them' when it replaces an object introduced by the preposition *à*:

*Tu fais attention à cette situation? Oui, j'**y** fais attention.*
Are you paying attention to this situation? Yes, I'm paying attention to **it**.
*Vous pensez toujours à vos problèmes? Oui, j'**y** pense tout le temps.*
Are you still thinking about your problems? Yes, I'm thinking about **them** all the time.

> **LINK** 🔗
> To revise verbs that are followed by *à*, go to page 136.

The pronoun *en*

– The pronoun *en* is used to replace a noun in an expression of quantity. It is often used to replace a quantity introduced by a number or by *de, du, de la, de l'* or *des*. Its meaning isn't always translated into English but it conveys 'of it' or 'of them'.

*Tu bois du café? Non, je n'**en** bois pas.* Do you drink coffee? No, I don't drink any.
*As-tu un chien? Oui, j'**en** ai deux.* Have you got a dog? Yes, I have two (of them).

– *En* is also used with verbs that take the preposition *de*, to replace the object that follows *de*. This may translate in different ways according to the context.

*Elle fait de la natation. Elle **en** fait le samedi.* She does swimming. She does **it** on Saturdays.
*Qu'est-ce que tu **en** penses?* What do you think **about it**?

> **LINK** 🔗
> To revise verbs that are followed by *de*, go to page 136.

Y and *en* used together

– The pronouns *y* and *en* can be used together. Make sure you know these phrases:

Il y en a. There is / are some (of it / them).
Il y en avait. There was / were some (of it / them).
Il y en aura. There will be some (of it / them).

Answer the questions below. Cover the answers column with a piece of paper and write down as many answers as you can. Check and repeat.

Questions

Answers

#	Question	Answer
1	List the nine subject pronouns in French (e.g. I, you, he / she / we, etc.)	*Je; tu; il; elle; on; nous; vous; ils; elles*
2	Translate the following sentence into English: *Rien ne se passe.*	Nothing is happening
3	Choose the correct word to complete the question: *Elle vient avec tu / toi / ton?*	*Toi*
4	Translate the following sentence into French: I would like to see him.	*Je voudrais le voir*
5	Translate the following sentence into English: *Ils nous achètent un cadeau.*	They are buying us a present
6	Choose the correct word to complete the sentence: *J'ai un emploi que / quand / qui est intéressant.*	*Qui*
7	Complete this sentence in French: *La plage est un endroit où…*	Possible answers include: *je peux me relaxer / on va en été*
8	What does the pronoun *y* mean when it replaces the name of a place?	There
9	What type of verb could *y* also be used with?	Verbs that are followed by *à*
10	Use the pronoun *en* to answer this question: *Tu bois beaucoup de café?*	*Oui; j'en bois (beaucoup / trop) / Non; je n'en bois pas*
11	Translate this question into French: What do you think about it?	*Qu'est-ce que tu en penses?*
12	Put these words into the correct order to make a sentence: *en a y il*	*Il y en a* (there is / are some of it / them)

Put paper here

Previous questions

Use the questions below to check your knowledge from previous chapters.

Questions

Answers

#	Question	Answer
1	Translate this sentence into French: I make music because it's my passion.	*Je fais de la musique car c'est ma passion*
2	Which verb is the odd one out and why? *diffuser, enregistrer, rire*	*Rire* (to laugh) as *diffuser* (to broadcast) and *enregistrer* (to record) are both things you can do with a programme
3	List as many adverbs of place in French as possible.	Possible answers include: *dehors* (outside); *loin* (far); *près* (near); *ici* (here); *là-bas* (over there)

Put paper here

Prepositions

The prepositions *à*, *de* and *en*

The preposition *à*

- The preposition *à* can mean 'to', 'at' or 'in'. It is always used before names of towns or cities:

  *Il habite **à** Londres mais il veut aller **à** Paris.* He lives **in** London but he wants to go **to** Paris.

- When *à* is followed by *le, la / l'* and *les* it becomes *au, à la / l'* and *aux*.

  *Samedi, on va aller **au** cinéma, **à la** piscine et **aux** magasins.*
  On Saturday, we are going to go to the cinema, to the swimming pool and to the shops.

- Some verbs are followed by *à* + a noun, for example:

  - *jouer à* = to play (a game)
  - *s'intéresser à* = to be interested in

- Some verbs can be followed by *à* + an infinitive, for example:

  - *commencer à* = to start to
  - *apprendre à* = to learn to

REVISION TIP ☑

Try explaining key grammar points to a friend or family member to help them stick in your memory.

The preposition *de*

- The preposition *de / d'* can mean 'of' and is used with expressions of quantity and possession:

  *Elle boit un verre **de** vin avec beaucoup **d'**eau.*
  She's drinking a glass of wine with a lot of water.
  *Demain, c'est l'anniversaire **de** ma mère.*
  It's the birthday of my mother (my mother's birthday) tomorrow.

- *De / d'* can also mean 'from'. When *de* is followed by *le, la / l'* and *les* it becomes *du, de la / l'* and *des*.

  *Nous rentrons **du** collège à 4 heures.* We get back from school at 4:00pm.

- Some verbs are followed by *de* + a noun, for example:

  avoir besoin de (to need)

- Some verbs can be followed by *de* + an infinitive, for example:

  - *essayer de* = to try to
  - *décider de* = to decide to

The preposition *en*

- The preposition *en* can mean 'in' or 'to', according to the context. For example, it is used in front of feminine countries:

  *Ma famille va rester **en** Angleterre mais moi, je vais aller **en** France.*
  My family is going to stay **in** England but I am going to go **to** France.

- *En* can be used in front of months and seasons or to say how long something takes to do:

  *Les examens sont **en** été, **en** juin.* The exams are **in** the summer, **in** June.
  *J'ai fait mes devoirs **en** dix minutes.* I did my homework **in** ten minutes.

- *En* can also be used to say what something is made of:

  - *un sac **en** plastique* = a plastic bag
  - *un jeu **en** bois* = a wooden game

LINK 🔗

To find out how *en* is used as a pronoun, go to page 134.

Prepositions of time and place

Prepositions of time

- Prepositions of time tell us when something takes place or for how long. They include words like:
  - *dès* = from, as soon as
  - *jusque* = until
  - *pour* = for (+ time in the future)
  - *pendant* = during (or 'for' + times in the past or present)
- The prepositions *avant* (before) and *après* (after) can also be used in these structures:
  - *avant de* (+ infinitive) = before (doing)
  - *après avoir* (+ past participle) = after (doing)

*Je prends un sac **avant d'aller** aux magasins.*
I take a bag **before going** to the shops.
***Après avoir fini** les courses, je range la nourriture.*
After finishing the shopping, I put the food away.

Prepositions of place

- Prepositions of place tell us where things are exactly and include words like:

  - *dans* = in
  - *sur* = on
  - *sous* = under
  - *devant* = in front (of)
  - *derrière* = behind
  - *entre* = between

LINK

For more information on forming past participles, see page 150.

REMEMBER

The preposition *chez* means 'to / at the place of' and is used to refer to where people live.

*Tu vas **chez ton père** ce week-end?* Are you going **to your dad's place** this weekend?

Un séjour en France *A stay in France*

L'année dernière, j'ai logé* **chez** une famille **en** France **pendant** une semaine. **Avant de** partir, j'ai téléchargé une appli **sur** mon portable qui traduit **entre** le français et l'anglais. C'était super et je voudrais y retourner **pour** deux semaines l'année prochaine.

Last year, I stayed with a family in France for a week. Before leaving, I downloaded an app on my mobile phone that translates between French and English. It was great and I would like to go back there for two weeks next year.

*****loger** = to stay

REVISION TIP

Use prepositions in your speaking and writing to give more detailed information.

Retrieval

GRAMMAR

Answer the questions below. Cover the answers column with a piece of paper and write down as many answers as you can. Check and repeat.

Questions

Answers

	Questions	Answers
1	Give three possible meanings of the preposition *à* in English.	To; at; in
2	What are the missing words in the following sentence? *Je vais … cinéma, … piscine et … magasins.*	*Au; à la; aux*
3	Give an example of a verb that is followed by *à* + noun.	Possible answers: *s'intéresser à* (to be interested in); *jouer à* (to play)
4	Translate the following sentence into French: I would like to learn to speak Spanish.	*Je voudrais apprendre à parler espagnol*
5	Choose the correct word to complete this sentence: *J'essaie de boire beaucoup d' / de / de l' eau.*	*D'*
6	How does *de* change when it is followed by *le* or *les*?	It becomes *du* or *des*
7	Give an example of a verb that is followed by *de* + infinitive.	Possible answers: *essayer de* (to try to); *décider de* (to decide to)
8	Which two-letter word is used in front of feminine countries to mean 'in' or 'to'?	*En*
9	Translate the following sentence into French: I did my homework in ten minutes.	*J'ai fait mes devoirs <u>en</u> dix minutes*
10	What is the opposite, in French, of each of these words? *avant, sur, devant*	*Après; sous; derrière*
11	Translate the following phrase into English: *avant d'aller aux magasins.*	Before going to the shops
12	Choose the correct word to complete this phrase: *chez / dans / en ma maison.*	*Dans*

Put paper here

Previous questions

Use the questions below to check your knowledge from previous chapters.

Questions

Answers

	Questions	Answers
1	List four places of worship in French.	*La mosquée; l'église; le temple; la synagogue*
2	Answer this question in French: *Qui est ta célébrité préférée et pourquoi?*	Possible answer: *Ma célébrité préférée s'appelle … et je l'adore car il / elle est drôle*
3	Translate the following sentence into English: *Rien ne se passe.*	Nothing is happening

Put paper here

⚙ Knowledge **GRAMMAR**

Infinitives, imperatives and the present participle

Infinitives and infinitive structures

What is an infinitive?

– Infinitives are the basic form of a verb, for example 'to do' in English. This is the form of the verb that you will find if you look it up in a dictionary.

– There are three groups of regular verbs in French, which all follow set patterns. They are grouped by the endings of the infinitives: *-er* verbs, *-ir* verbs and *-re* verbs. Here are some examples in each group:

-er verbs	-ir verbs	-re verbs
regard**er** = to watch jou**er** = to play écout**er** = to listen	fin**ir** = to finish chois**ir** = to choose réuss**ir** = to succeed	vend**re** = to sell attend**re** = to wait (for), expect perd**re** = to lose

– Many other French verbs are irregular and don't follow any set pattern. Here are the infinitives of some common irregular verbs:

- *avoir* = to have
- *être* = to be
- *faire* = to make / do
- *aller* = to go
- *mettre* = to put / put on
- *boire* = to drink
- *suivre* = to follow
- *rire* = to laugh

> **LINK**
> *Avoir* and *être* are important verbs to know as they are used to form the perfect tense. Find out more about the perfect tense on pages 150–151.

Other uses of the infinitive

– Infinitives can be used on their own. In this case, they act as the subject of the sentence and translate as '-ing' in English:

Manger beaucoup de fruits est bon pour la santé. **Eating** a lot of fruit is good for your health.

– Infinitives can follow other verbs. They are useful when giving positive and negative opinions in any tense. For example:

J'adore **dessiner**. I love **drawing.**
Il n'aimait pas **être** seul. He didn't use to like **being** alone.

> **REMEMBER**
> When using negatives, like *ne … pas*, make sure you put these around the first verb rather than the infinitive.

– Use the infinitive after *pour* to mean 'in order to' do something:

Je vais à Paris **pour améliorer** mon français. I'm going to Paris **(in order) to improve** my French.

– Use the infinitive after *sans* to mean 'without doing' something:

Je ne sors jamais **sans prendre** mon portable.
I never go out **without taking** my mobile phone (with me).

Infinitive use with expressions

– Infinitives are used after some impersonal expressions, such as *il faut* (it is necessary / one must), *il vaut mieux* + infinitive (it's better to do) and *ça vaut la peine de* + infinitive (it is worth doing):

Il faut **arriver** à neuf heures. One must **arrive** at nine o'clock.
Il vaut mieux **marcher.** It's better **to walk**.
Ça vaut la peine de **recycler**. It's worth **recycling**.

> **LINK**
> Find out more about impersonal verbs on page 161.

⚙ Knowledge GRAMMAR

Infinitives, imperatives and the present participle

Infinitives and infinitive structures

- The expression *être en train de* + infinitive means 'to be in the middle of doing' something. It is useful when describing what people are doing in a photograph, for example:

  *Ils sont **en train de manger**.* They are **in the middle of eating**.
  *Elle est **en train de faire** ses devoirs.* She is **in the middle of doing** her homework.

- The expression *venir de* + infinitive translates into English as 'to have just done' something:

  ***Je viens de poster** un commentaire.* **I have just posted** a comment.
  ***L'artiste vient de finir** son tableau.* **The artist has just finished** his painting.

REVISION TIP 📋

Summarise everything you know about using infinitives on a revision card or separate piece of paper.

Qu'est-ce que tu fais pour te relaxer? *What do you do to relax?*

Pour **me relaxer,** j'aime **faire** des activités pratiques avec mon grand-père. Par exemple, nous venons de **faire** un petit bateau en bois. Maintenant, je suis en train de **construire** un lit pour mon chien. Pour moi, **travailler** avec mes mains est le meilleur passe-temps qui existe. Il vaut mieux **créer** quelque chose d'unique, sans **copier** les autres.

I like doing practical activities with my grandfather to relax. For example, we have just made a little wooden boat. Now, I'm in the middle of making a bed for my dog. For me, working with my hands is the best hobby in the world. It's better to create something unique, without copying others.

EXAM TIP 🎯

Look at the infinitives in bold in this text. Notice the different ways that they have been used here to add complexity to this answer.

Imperatives

The imperative

- Imperatives are used to give orders, advice and instructions, or to make suggestions. Here are some examples:

  Regarde! = Look!   **Mangez!** = Eat!   **Sortons!** = Let's go out!

- The imperative is formed from the present tense of the *tu*, *vous* and *nous* forms of regular verbs. Notice how the *nous* form of the imperative means 'let's…'

Present tense	Imperative examples
Tu finis (you finish)	**Finis** *ton travail.* – Finish your work.
Vous finissez (you finish)	**Finissez** *les légumes.* – Finish the vegetables.
Nous finissons (we finish)	**Finissons** *le jeu.* – Let's finish the game.

- When forming the imperative of regular *-er* verbs, drop the final *-s* from the *tu* form: *Tu clique***s** (you click) – **Clique** *ici.* (Click here.)

- To make an imperative negative, place the negatives around the imperative as you would with other forms of the verb:

  Ne pars pas! = Don't leave!
  Ne fumez jamais ici. = Never smoke here.
  Ne parlons plus de cette situation. = Let's not talk about this situation any more.

Forming the imperative with *faire* and *aller*

- Make sure you know the *tu*, *vous* and *nous* forms of the irregular verbs *faire* and *aller* so that you can form the imperative.

Present tense of faire	Imperative examples
Tu fais (you make / do)	**Fais** *de ton mieux.* – Do your best.
Vous faites (you make / do)	**Faites** *un effort.* – Make an effort.
Nous faisons (we make / do)	**Faisons** *un gâteau.* – Let's make a cake.

Present tense of aller	Imperative examples
Tu vas (you go)	**Vas**-*y maintenant!* – Go now!
Vous allez (you go)	**Allez** *plus vite.* – Go faster.
Nous allons (we go)	**Allons**-*y ensemble.* – Let's go there together.

Forming the imperative with *être*

- The imperative forms for the verb *être* are an exception – they are not formed from the present tense of the verb and have to be learned separately.

Present tense	Imperative examples
Tu es (you are)	**Sois** *fort.* – Be strong.
Vous êtes (you are)	**Soyez** *patient.* – Be patient.
Nous sommes (we are)	**Soyons** *gentils.* – Let's be kind.

⚙ Knowledge

GRAMMAR

Infinitives, imperatives and the present participle

The present participle

What is the present participle?

- The present participle in English ends in '-ing'. It can be used as a verb (e.g. play**ing**) or an adjective (e.g. annoy**ing**).

- In French, the present participle ends in '-*ant*' and can also be used as a verb (e.g. *jouant*) or an adjective (e.g. *embêt**ant***).

- In French, the present participle is often used after *en* to mean 'while' doing or 'by' doing something.

  *Je cours **en écoutant** de la musique.* I run **while listening** to music.
  *Nous aidons **en donnant** de notre temps.* We help **by giving** our time.

Forming the present participle

- To form the present participle of most verbs, follow these three steps:

  2. Take the *nous* form of the present tense verb, e.g. *nous regardons*

  3. Remove the pronoun *nous* and the *-ons* ending to leave the stem: *regard-*

  4. Add the ending *-ant*: *regardant* (watching).

- Here are some more examples, using regular *-ir* and *-re* verbs:

Infinitive	*Nous* form of present tense	Present participle
choisir (to choose)	*nous choisissons* (we choose)	*choisissant* (choosing)
entendre (to hear)	*nous entendons* (we hear)	*entendant* (hearing)

- The verbs *être* (to be) and *avoir* (to have) do not follow this pattern. Their present participles are *étant* (being) and *ayant* (having).

> **REMEMBER** ❗
>
> Make sure you **always** start with the *nous* form and **not** the infinitive to get the correct stem – especially with irregular verbs. For example: *faisant* (doing).

Je sais faire plusieurs choses à la fois! *I can do several things at once!*

En organisant mon temps, je peux être beaucoup plus efficace. Le matin, je mange **en finissant** mes devoirs. Si j'ai un contrôle, j'apprends tout dans le bus, **en allant** au collège. Le soir, je fais de l'exercice **en regardant** la télé et je lis **en prenant** un bain. Je m'occupe toujours!

*By organising my time, I can be a lot more efficient. In the morning, I eat **while finishing** my homework. If I have a test, I learn everything on the bus, **while going** to school. In the evening, I exercise **while watching** TV and I read **while taking** a bath. I always keep busy!*

> **EXAM TIP** 🎯
>
> Look out for this structure in translation tasks, where it may well be tested.

Retrieval

Answer the questions below. Cover the answers column with a piece of paper and write down as many answers as you can. Check and repeat.

Questions

Answers

	Questions		Answers
1	What is an infinitive?	*Put paper here*	An infinitive is the basic form of a verb
2	What are the three groups of regular infinitives in French?		*-er*, *-ir* and *-re* verbs
3	What are the French infinitives for 'to be', 'to have', 'to go' and 'to do'?		*Être, avoir, aller, faire*
4	Translate the following sentence into English: *Apprendre une langue est très utile.*		Learning a language is very useful
5	What does the phrase *être en train de* + infinitive mean?		To be in the middle of (doing)
6	Translate the following sentence into French: I have just finished.	*Put paper here*	*Je viens de finir*
7	What are imperatives used for?		To give orders, advice, instructions or to make suggestions
8	How is the imperative formed?		The imperative is formed from the present tense of the *tu*, *vous* and *nous* forms of the verb
9	What do you need to remember when forming the *tu* form of the imperative of regular *-er* verbs?	*Put paper here*	Drop the final *-s*
10	What are the three imperative forms of the verb *être*?		*Sois; soyez; soyons*
11	Explain how to form the present participle of a regular verb in three steps.	*Put paper here*	Take the *nous* form of the present tense. Remove the pronoun *nous* and the *-ons* ending. Add *-ant*
12	Translate these irregular present participles into English: *en ayant, en étant.*		While / by having; while / by being

Previous questions

Use the questions below to check your knowledge from previous chapters.

Questions

Answers

	Questions		Answers
1	List as many countries as possible in French.	*Put paper here*	*La Belgique; la France; le Maroc;* etc. See page 84 for more ideas
2	In French, give one reason why the internet can be dangerous.		Possible answer: *On risque d' être victime d'un crime*
3	What are the missing words in the following sentence? *Je vais … cinéma, … piscine et … magasins.*		*Au, à la, aux*

The present tense

The present tense of regular verbs

Using the present tense

– The present tense in French is used to talk about actions that happen regularly or that are happening now:

je regarde la télé. I watch **or** I am watching TV.

– As in English, the present tense can also be used to talk about future events:

Demain, nous regardons un film en classe.
Tomorrow, we are watching a film in class.

– The present tense can also be used with *depuis* to mean 'have been -ing' for a period of time:

Elle habite ici depuis trois ans. She has been living here for three years.

Forming the present tense of regular verbs

– Regular verbs follow a set pattern and can be divided into three groups, according to their infinitive endings:

- *-er* verbs (e.g. *jouer*)
- *-ir* verbs (e.g. *finir*)
- *-re* verbs (e.g. *attendre*)

– To form the present tense, remove the infinitive ending to form the 'stem'. Then add the correct ending for each subject pronoun. Most regular verbs follow these patterns:

Jouer (to play)	*Finir* (to finish)	*Attendre* (to wait)
Je joue	*Je finis*	*J'attends*
Tu joues	*Tu finis*	*Tu attends*
Il / Elle / On joue	*Il / Elle / On finit*	*Il / Elle / On attend*
Nous jouons	*Nous finissons*	*Nous attendons*
Vous jouez	*Vous finissez*	*Vous attendez*
Ils / Elles jouent	*Ils / Elles finissent*	*Ils / Elles attendent*

> **REMEMBER** ❗
>
> Some verbs need an extra *-e* or a cedilla accent before the **-ons** ending, to soften the sound. For example, *nous mangeons* (we eat), *nous commençons* (we start).

Other regular patterns in the present tense

Verbs that follow different patterns

- Some verbs follow a different regular pattern.
- Some *-ir* verbs follow one of these patterns:

Partir (to leave)	*Venir* (to come)	*Ouvrir* (to open)
Je pars	Je viens	J'ouvre
Tu pars	Tu viens	Tu ouvres
Il / Elle / On part	Il / Elle / On vient	Il / Elle / On ouvre
Nous partons	Nous venons	Nous ouvrons
Vous partez	Vous venez	Vous ouvrez
Ils / Elles partent	Ils / Elles viennent	Ils / Elles ouvrent

REVISION TIP

Think about which verbs and parts of the verb might be most useful to you for speaking and writing tasks. For example, you could prioritise learning *je* and *on / nous* forms of common verbs.

Dormir (to sleep) follows the pattern in the first column above, *devenir* (to become) follows the second pattern and *découvrir* (to discover) follows the last pattern.

- Some *-re* verbs follow one of these patterns:

Prendre (to take)	*Traduire* (to translate)
Je prends	Je traduis
Tu prends	Tu traduis
Il / Elle / On prend	Il / Elle / On traduit
Nous prenons	Nous traduisons
Vous prenez	Vous traduisez
Ils / Elles prennent	Ils / Elles traduisent

Comprendre (to understand) follows the pattern of prendre. Some other verbs follow the pattern of *traduire*, for example *construire* (to build) and *réduire* (to reduce).

Les jours fériés, que fais-tu normalement?
What do you normally do on bank holidays?

Normalement, je dors jusqu'à midi et puis je regarde la télé avec mes frères ou nous jouons sur notre ordinateur. Parfois, mes grands-parents viennent chez nous et puis on sort ensemble. Ils prennent des photos et je les partage avec la famille.

Normally, I sleep until noon and then I watch TV with my brothers or we play on our computer. Sometimes my grandparents come to our house and then we go out together. They take photos and I share them with the family.

⚙ Knowledge   GRAMMAR

The present tense

The present tense of irregular verbs

Avoir (to have) and *être* (to be)

– Make sure you learn the key irregular verbs *avoir* (to have) and *être* (to be) in the present tense.

Avoir (to have)	*Être* (to be)
J'ai	Je suis
Tu as	Tu es
Il / Elle / On a	Il / Elle / On est
Nous avons	Nous sommes
Vous avez	Vous êtes
Ils / Elles ont	Ils / Elles sont

J'ai un demi-frère et il est sympa. I have a half-brother and he is nice.

Aller (to go) and *faire* (to do)

– *Aller* (to go) and *faire* (to make / do) are also key irregular verbs in the present tense.

Aller (to go)	*Faire* (to make / do)
Je vais	Je fais
Tu vas	Tu fais
Il / Elle / On va	Il / Elle / On fait
Nous allons	Nous faisons
Vous allez	Vous faites
Ils / Elles vont	Ils / Elles font

Je vais souvent au centre sportif où je prends des cours de natation.
I often go to the sports centre, where I have swimming lessons.

LINK 🔗

Avoir and *être* are also used to help form the perfect tense. See pages 150–151.

REMEMBER ❗

The verb *avoir* is used in French to give ages and with certain expressions:

Elle a 15 ans.
She is 15 years old.

Nous avons froid.
We are cold.

LINK 🔗

Aller is also used to help form the near future tense. See page 154.

REVISION TIP 📝

Notice the patterns in the *ils / elles* (they) forms of the four irregular verbs on this page: *ont* (have), *sont* (are), *vont* (go), *font* (make / do).

More irregular verbs in the present tense

Mettre (to put), connaître (to know) and écrire (to write)

– You are also expected to know the following irregular present tense verbs:

Mettre (to put)	Connaître (to know)	Écrire (to write)
Je mets	Je connais	J'écris
Tu mets	Tu connais	Tu écris
Il / Elle / On met	Il / Elle / On connaît	Il / Elle / On écrit
Nous mettons	Nous connaissons	Nous écrivons
Vous mettez	Vous connaissez	Vous écrivez
Ils / Elles mettent	Ils / Elles connaissent	Ils / Elles écrivent

> **REMEMBER !**
>
> *Mettre* can mean 'to put' and also 'to put on': *Je mets mon uniforme scolaire.* I'm putting on my school uniform.

Useful verbs in the singular

– You are expected to know the following irregular verbs in their singular forms only (the *je*, *tu*, *il / elle / on* forms).

Boire (to drink)	Courir (to run)	Croire (to believe)
Je bois	Je cours	Je crois
Tu bois	Tu cours	Tu crois
Il / Elle / On boit	Il / Elle / On court	Il / Elle / On croit

Recevoir (to receive)	Rire (to laugh)	Suivre (to follow)
Je reçois	Je ris	Je suis
Tu reçois	Tu ris	Tu suis
Il / Elle / On reçoit	Il / Elle / On rit	Il / Elle / On suit

Voir (to see)
Je vois
Tu vois
Il / Elle / On voit

> **REVISION TIP**
>
> Notice the pattern of **-s**, **-s**, **-t** endings with these verbs.

> **REMEMBER !**
>
> *Je suis* can mean 'I follow' as well as 'I am'.

The present tense

The present tense of modal verbs

Pouvoir, vouloir and devoir

- *Pouvoir* (to be able to / can), *vouloir* (to want / want to) and *devoir* (to have to / must) are called 'modal verbs'. Here they are in the present tense:

Pouvoir (to be able to / can)	Vouloir (to want / want to)	Devoir (to have to / must)
Je peux	Je veux	Je dois
Tu peux	Tu veux	Tu dois
Il / Elle / On peut	Il / Elle / On veut	Il / Elle / On doit
Nous pouvons	Nous voulons	Nous devons
Vous pouvez	Vous voulez	Vous devez
Ils / Elles peuvent	Ils / Elles veulent	Ils / Elles doivent

> **REMEMBER** ❗
>
> Notice how the *nous* and *vous* forms of these verbs look more like their infinitives than the other forms.

- Modal verbs are often followed by another verb in the **infinitive** form:

  *Je peux **organiser** ta fête.* I can organise your party.

  *Nous voulons **sortir** en ville.* We want to go out in town.

  *Elles doivent **travailler** ce soir.* They must work tonight.

- *Vouloir* can also be followed by a noun: *Je veux un billet.* (I want a ticket.)

Savoir

- The verb *savoir* means 'to know' (something) and can be used on its own, for example:

  Je sais / Je ne sais pas. I know / I don't know.

> **REMEMBER** ❗
>
> The verb *connaître* also means 'to know' but refers to knowing (of) a person or a place.

- It can also be used with an infinitive, with the sense of knowing 'how to' do something:

  Il sait parler allemand. He knows how to (can) speak German.

Savoir (to know)
Je sais
Tu sais
Il / Elle / On sait
Nous savons
Vous savez
Ils / Elles savent

Answer the questions below. Cover the answers column with a piece of paper and write down as many answers as you can. Check and repeat.

Questions | Answers

	Questions	Answers
1	Give two possible English translations for the French verb *je regarde*.	I watch / I am watching
2	Translate this sentence into French: She has been living here for three years.	*Elle habite ici depuis trois ans*
3	What are the three groups of regular verbs in French?	*-er*, *-ir* and *-re* verbs
4	In French, list all the parts of the verb 'to play' in the present tense.	*Jouer* (to play): *je joue; tu joues; il / elle / on joue; nous jouons; vous jouez; ils / elles jouent*
5	True or false? The verb *dormir* (to sleep) follows the same pattern as *partir* (to leave) in the present tense.	True
6	Translate the following phrase into French: they reduce.	*Ils / Elles réduisent*
7	Choose the correct present tense verb: *nous comprennent / comprenons / comprendront*.	*Comprenons*
8	Which two irregular verbs are used in the present tense to help form the perfect tense in French?	*Avoir* (to have) and *être* (to be)
9	In French, list all parts of the verb 'to go' in the present tense.	*Aller* (to go): *je vais; tu vas; il / elle / on va; nous allons; vous allez; ils / elles vont*
10	Choose the correct translation of 'they do': *ils sont / ont / font / vont*.	*Ils font*
11	What do the following verbs mean in English? *Pouvoir, vouloir, devoir*	To be able to / can; to want (to); to have to / must
12	Which two French verbs both mean 'to know'?	*Connaître* (to know (of) a person or place) and *savoir* (to know a fact or how to do something)

Put paper here

Previous questions

Use the questions below to check your knowledge from previous chapters.

Questions | Answers

	Questions	Answers
1	Give an environmental problem that affects your area.	Possible answer: *Il y a trop de circulation*
2	Give an alternative expression that you could use with a countable noun instead of *beaucoup de*.	*De nombreux / de nombreuses* (many)
3	Translate the following sentence into French: I have just finished.	*Je viens de finir*

Put paper here

⚙ Knowledge GRAMMAR

The perfect and imperfect tenses

The perfect tense with *avoir*

The perfect tense of regular verbs

- The perfect tense is used to talk about an action that happened or that has happened in the past, to describe completed actions or events.

  J'ai regardé la télé. I watched / I have watched TV.

- For most verbs, it is formed from the present tense of the verb *avoir* (the auxiliary verb) plus a past participle.

- The past participles of regular verbs are formed by removing the *-er*, *-ir* or *-re* ending from the infinitive and then adding *-é* (for *-er* verbs), *-i* (for *-ir* verbs) or *-u* (for *-re* verbs). For example:

Infinitive	jou**er**	fin**ir**	entend**re**
Past participle	jou**é**	fin**i**	entend**u**

  Nous avons joué. We played / we have played.
  Ils ont fini. They finished / they have finished.
  Tu as entendu. You heard / you have heard.

Irregular past participles

- Many common verbs have irregular past participles, for example:

  J'ai vu… I saw / I have seen…
  Nous avons bu… We drank / We have drunk…

- Here are some other irregular past participles to learn:

Infinitive	Irregular past participle	Infinitive	Irregular past participle
avoir (to have)	*eu* (had)	*mettre* (to put)	*mis* (put)
découvrir (to discover)	*découvert* (discovered)	*ouvrir* (to open)	*ouvert* (opened)
devoir (to have to / must)	*dû* (had to)	*pouvoir* (to be able to / can)	*pu* (was able to / could)
dire (to say / tell)	*dit* (said / told)	*prendre* (to take)	*pris* (took / taken)
être (to be)	*été* (was / been)	*savoir* (to know)	*su* (knew / known)
faire (to make / do)	*fait* (made / did)	*traduire* (to translate)	*traduit* (translated)
lire (to read)	*lu* (read)	*vouloir* (to want to)	*voulu* (wanted to)

Après avoir + past participle

- You can also use the past participles of verbs that take *avoir* in the perfect tense in the structure *après avoir* + past participle. This means 'after having' done.

  Après avoir mangé, nous avons fini nos devoirs.
  After having eaten, we finished our homework.

LINK 🔗

To revise the verb *avoir* (to have) in the present tense, see page 146.

REMEMBER ❗

Remember, you can use names or other nouns instead of subject pronouns:

Mon copain et moi avons fini. – My friend and I have finished.

Mes frères ont joué hier. – My brothers played yesterday.

REVISION TIP ☑

Start by learning all the part participles that end in *-u*, e.g. *lu, bu, vu, eu…*

REMEMBER ❗

The past participle of *devoir* is *dû* (had to) and the circumflex accent is important to differentiate it from *du* (some).

The perfect tense with *être*

Forming the perfect tense with *être*

– The perfect tense of some verbs is formed from the present tense of the verb *être* (the auxiliary verb) and a past participle. For example:

Il est allé… He went / has been…

– Add an **-e** to the past participle if the subject of the sentence is feminine:

*Ma sœur est allé**e**…* My sister went / has been…

– Add an **-s** to the past participle if the subject of the sentence is masculine and plural:

*Mes parents sont allé**s**…* My parents went / have been…

– Add **-es** to the past participle if the subject of the sentence is feminine and plural:

*Elles sont allé**es**…* They (a group of girls / women) went…

Verbs that take *être* in the perfect tense

– The mnemonic 'DR & MRS VAN DER TRAMP' can help you remember these 16 verbs that all take *être* in the perfect tense:

Infinitive	Past participle
Devenir (to become)	devenu(e)(s)
Revenir (to come back)	revenu(e)(s)
Monter (to go up, to climb)	monté(e)(s)
Rester (to stay)	resté(e)(s)
Sortir (to go out)	sorti(e)(s)
Venir (to come)	venu(e)(s)
Aller (to go)	allé(e)(s)
Naître (to be born)	né(e)(s)
Descendre (to go down)	descendu(e)(s)
Entrer (to go in, to enter)	entré(e)(s)
Rentrer (to go back in / home)	rentré(e)(s)
Tomber (to fall)	tombé(e)(s)
Retourner (to return)	retourné(e)(s)
Arriver (to arrive)	arrivé(e)(s)
Mourir (to die)	mort(e)(s)
Partir (to leave)	parti(e)(s)

LINK

To revise the verb *être* (to be) in the present tense, see page 146.

EXAM TIP

Always check for agreements when using the perfect tense with *être*. In a mixed gender group, the ending is always masculine and plural.

REMEMBER

You can also try learning these verbs in pairs, for example *venir* (to come) and *aller* (to go).

LINK

Reflexive verbs also take *être* in the perfect tense, for example *je me suis levé(e)* (I got up). See page 160.

The perfect and imperfect tenses

The imperfect tense

Uses of the imperfect tense

- The imperfect tense is a past tense used for habitual actions in the past. It is often translated in English as 'used to'.

  Je quittais la maison à huit heures tous les jours. I used to leave home at 8:00am every day.

- It is also used for continuous actions in the past (what **was happening** or what people **were doing**).

  J'écoutais de la musique dans ma chambre. I was listening to music in my room.

- The imperfect tense can be combined with the perfect tense to say what **was happening** when something else took place.

  ***Nous mangions** quand nos amis sont arrivés.* We were eating when our friends arrived.

- The imperfect tense is often used for opinions and descriptions in the past.

  Il faisait chaud et l'hôtel était excellent. It was hot and the hotel was excellent.

> **LINK** 🔗
>
> See pages 150–151 to revise the perfect tense.

> **REVISION TIP** ☑
>
> Two very useful imperfect expressions are *c'était* (it was) and *il y avait* (there was / were).

Forming the imperfect tense

- To form the imperfect tense, follow these three steps:

  1. Take the *nous* form of the present tense verb, e.g. *nous regardons*
  2. Remove the pronoun *nous* and the *-ons* ending to leave the stem: *regard-*
  3. Add the imperfect tense endings:

Je	regard**ais**	I used to watch / I was watching
Tu	regard**ais**	You used to watch / You were watching
Il / Elle / On	regard**ait**	He / She / We used to watch, He / She was / We were watching
Nous	regard**ions**	We used to watch / We were watching
Vous	regard**iez**	You used to watch / You were watching
Ils / Elles	regard**aient**	They used to watch / They were watching

- Make sure you always use the *nous* form of the present tense to form the stem, not the infinitive. For example, with the verb *choisir* (to choose):

  1. *nous choisissons* (we choose)
  2. *choisiss-* (verb stem for the imperfect)
  3. *je choisissais* (I used to choose)

- The only irregular verb in the imperfect tense is *être* (to be). The endings follow the same pattern but the stem is *ét-*. For example:

  Quand j'étais petit … When I was little …

> **REMEMBER** ❗
>
> Some verbs need an extra 'e' or a 'ç' (cedilla) accent before the imperfect endings that start with 'a', to soften the pronunciation. For example: *je mang**e**ais* (I used to eat), *ils commen**ç**aient* (they used to start).

Answer the questions below. Cover the answers column with a piece of paper and write down as many answers as you can. Check and repeat.

Questions | Answers

#	Question	Answer
1	What is the perfect tense used for in French?	An action that happened or that has happened in the past
2	What are the past participle endings for regular -er, -ir and -re verbs?	-é; -i; -u
3	Translate this phrase into French: we watched.	*Nous avons regardé*
4	What are the irregular past participles for the verbs *voir*, *lire* and *boire*?	*Vu; lu; bu*
5	Choose the correct word to complete the sentence: *J'ai du / dû / dois rentrer tôt* (I had to go home early).	*Dû*
6	Which French structure translates as 'after having' done?	*Après avoir* + past participle
7	What are the possible agreements needed when forming the perfect tense with *être*?	Add ending to the past participle: -e for feminine subject, -s for plural, -es for feminine plural
8	List as many French verbs that take *être* in the perfect tense as you can, with the help of the mnemonic DR & MRS VAN DER TRAMP.	*Devenir; revenir; monter; rester; sortir; venir; aller; naître; descendre; entrer; rentrer; tomber; retourner; arriver; mourir; partir*
9	Give three uses of the imperfect tense.	Habitual actions in the past; continuous actions in the past; opinions / descriptions in the past
10	Explain how to form the imperfect tense.	Take the *nous* form of the present tense verb, remove *nous* and -ons, and add the imperfect ending
11	Which is the only irregular verb in the imperfect tense?	*Être* (to be)
12	Translate this sentence into French: It was hot and the hotel was excellent.	*Il faisait chaud et l'hôtel était excellent*

(Put paper here)

Previous questions

Use the questions below to check your knowledge from previous chapters.

Questions | Answers

#	Question	Answer
1	What is the French pronoun that means 'there'?	*Y* (pronounced 'ee')
2	Translate the following sentence into French: I have never done (any) sport.	*Je n'ai jamais fait <u>de</u> sport*
3	What do the following verbs mean in English? *Pouvoir, vouloir, devoir*	To be able to / can; to want (to); to have to / must

(Put paper here)

Future tenses and the conditional

Future tenses

The near future tense

– One way to talk about future events is to use the present tense of the verb *aller* (to go) plus an infinitive. This translates in English as 'going to' do something:

Je vais	*jouer*	I am going to play
Tu vas	*aller*	You are going to go
Il / Elle / On va	*voir*	He / She is / We are going to see
Nous allons	*sortir*	We are going to go out
Vous allez	*continuer*	You are going to continue
Ils / Elles vont	*faire*	They are going to do

> **REVISION TIP** ☑
>
> The present tense can also be used with a future time phrase to talk about the future: *Demain soir, on reste à la maison.* We're staying at home tomorrow evening.

The simple future tense

– The simple future tense in French translates as 'I will + verb' in English: *Je travaillerai* (I will work).

– To form this tense with regular *-er* verbs, take the infinitive (for example, *manger*) and add the correct future tense ending:

Je	*manger**ai***	I will eat
Tu	*manger**as***	You will eat
Il / Elle / On	*manger**a***	He / She / We will eat
Nous	*manger**ons***	We will eat
Vous	*manger**ez***	You will eat
Ils / Elles	*manger**ont***	They will eat

– You are also expected to know the following irregular future tense verbs in these singular forms only:

Aller (to go)	*Avoir* (to have)	*Être* (to be)	*Faire* (to make / do)
J'irai	*J'aurai*	*Je serai*	*Je ferai*
Tu iras	*Tu auras*	*Tu seras*	*Tu feras*
Il / Elle / On ira	*Il / Elle / On aura*	*Il / Elle / On sera*	*Il / Elle / On fera*

The conditional

Using and forming the conditional

- The conditional is used to express what 'would' happen or what someone 'would' do.
- The verb *vouloir* (to want to) is often used in the conditional to mean 'would like':
  - *Je voudrais* = I would like
  - *Tu voudrais* = You would like
  - *Il / Elle / On voudrait* = He / She / We would like
- To form the conditional of regular *-er* verbs, take the infinitive (for example, *manger*) and add the correct conditional ending:

Je	manger**ais**	I would eat
Tu	manger**ais**	You would eat
Il / Elle / On	manger**ait**	He / She / We would eat
Nous	manger**ions**	We would eat
Vous	manger**iez**	You would eat
Ils / Elles	manger**aient**	They would eat

> **REVISION TIP**
>
> If you forget the conditional ending for *je*, remember that *je voudr**ais*** means 'I would like' so the *je* ending is *-**ais***.

- You are also expected to know the following irregular conditional verbs in these singular forms only:

Aller (to go)	*Avoir* (to have)	*Être* (to be)	*Faire* (to make / do)
J'irais	J'aurais	Je serais	Je ferais
Tu irais	Tu aurais	Tu serais	Tu ferais
Il / Elle / On irait	Il / Elle / On aurait	Il / Elle / On serait	Il / Elle / On ferai

> **REVISION TIP**
>
> To give an opinion in the conditional, use *ce serait* (it would be) plus an adjective.

Using the conditional in 'if' sentences

- The conditional is often used with the imperfect tense in 'if' sentences, using the structure *Si* (if) + imperfect tense, conditional.

  Si c'était possible, j'habiterais en France.
  If it were possible, I would live in France.
  The two clauses of the sentence could also be switched around:
  J'habiterais en France si c'était possible.
  I would live in France if it were possible.

Retrieval

GRAMMAR

Answer the questions below. Cover the answers column with a piece of paper and write down as many answers as you can. Check and repeat.

	Questions	Answers
1	True or false? The present tense can be used to talk about future events.	True (with a future time phrase)
2	Explain how to form the near future tense.	Use the present tense of the verb *aller* (to go) plus an infinitive
3	Translate the following phrase into French: they are going to go.	*Ils / Elles vont aller*
4	Translate the following verb into English: *je travaillerai.*	I will work
5	Explain how to form the simple future tense with regular *-er* verbs.	Take the infinitive and add the correct future endings
6	What are the simple future tense endings for each subject pronoun?	*-ai*; *-as*; *-a*; *-ons*; *-ez*; *-ont*
7	Which four irregular verbs do you need to know in the simple future tense?	*Aller* (to go); *avoir* (to have); *être* (to be); *faire* (to make / do)
8	Choose the correct verb to complete the sentence: *Un jour, j'irai / je serai / j'aurai* trois enfants.	*J'aurai* (I will have)
9	Translate the following verbs into French: I would like, you would like, he / she / we would like.	*Je voudrais*; *tu voudrais*; *il / elle / on voudrait*
10	What is the missing conditional ending here for 'we would eat'? *nous manger____*	*-ions*
11	Translate the following conditional verbs into English: *j'irais, j'aurais, je serais, je ferais.*	I would go; I would have; I would be; I would do
12	Explain how to form an 'if' sentence, using the conditional and one other tense.	Possible answer: *Si* (if) + imperfect tense, conditional

Put paper here

Previous questions

Use the questions below to check your knowledge from previous chapters.

	Questions	Answers
1	In what way can the adjective *propre* change its meaning?	It means 'own' if placed in front of the noun and 'clean' if placed after the noun
2	Answer this question in French: *Tu prends toujours le petit-déjeuner?*	Possible answer: *Oui, je prends toujours le petit-déjeuner*
3	What are the past participle endings for regular *-er*, *-ir* and *-re* verbs?	*-é*; *-i*; *-u*

Put paper here

⚙ Knowledge   GRAMMAR

Negatives and the passive voice

Negatives

Negative structures in the present tense

- In the present tense, negative sentences are formed by placing negative structures around the verb:

  *Nous **ne** faisons **pas** de sport.* We don't do any sport.

- *Ne* becomes *n'* in front of a verb that begins with a vowel or silent *h*:

  *Je **n'**aime **pas** les maths.* I don't like maths.

- When a verb is followed by an infinitive, the negative wraps around the first verb:

  *Elle **ne** veut **pas** fumer.* She doesn't want to smoke.

- Here are some key negative structures, with examples in the present tense.

ne … pas (not)	Je ne parle pas chinois. (I don't speak Chinese.)
ne … jamais (never / not ever)	Tu ne manges jamais de viande. (You never eat meat.)
ne … rien (nothing / not anything)	Elle ne fait rien. (She does nothing. She is not doing anything.)
ne … personne (nobody / not anyone)	Il n'y a personne ici. (There is nobody here.)
ne … que (only)	Nous n'avons qu'un stylo. (We only have one pen).
ne … plus (no longer / not any more)	Vous ne jouez plus au foot. (You no longer play football.)
ne … aucun(e) (no / not one / not any)	Il n'y a aucun problème. (There isn't any problem).
ne … ni … ni … (neither … nor…)	Elles n'aiment ni les fruits ni les légumes. (They like neither fruit nor vegetables.)

Using negatives with other tenses

- As in the present tense, in the imperfect, simple future and conditional, negatives are placed around the verb:

  *Tu **n'**utilisais **jamais** de portable.* You never used to use a mobile phone.
  *Elle **ne** mangera **plus** de poisson.* She will no longer eat fish.
  *Je **ne** voudrais **rien** changer.* I wouldn't like to change anything.

- In the perfect tense, the negatives wrap around the auxiliary verb. In the near future tense, the negatives are placed around the first verb (the conjugated form of *aller*).

- *Ne … pas encore* is another negative structure. It means 'not yet' and tends to be used in the perfect tense.

  *On **n'a pas encore** fini.* We haven't finished yet.
  *Ils **ne** vont **pas** venir.* They are not going to come.

Questions using negatives

- To use negatives in a question, form your sentence as usual and either use upward intonation, or add *est-ce que…* (with a question word if necessary):

  Tu ne vapotes plus? Do you no longer vape?
  Pourquoi est-ce que vous n'aidez jamais? Why do you never help?

LINK

To revise the use of the negative subject pronouns *rien ne* (nothing) and *personne ne* (nobody), see page 131.

REMEMBER !

The negative expression *ne … aucun* takes an -e when followed by a feminine noun, e.g., **aucune** plainte (not one complaint).

LINK

Remember that *du, de la, de l'* and *des* become *de* or *d'* after most negative expressions. See page 121.

⚙ Knowledge

GRAMMAR

Negatives and the passive voice

The passive voice

The passive voice in the present

– The passive voice is used to indicate that something is being done to a subject by an agent. To form it, use the present tense of the verb *être* (to be), plus a past participle.

Ce livre est emprunté. This book is borrowed.
Je suis invité. I am invited.

– The past participle must agree with the noun being described. Add an *-e* for a feminine noun, an *-s* for a masculine plural noun and *-es* for a feminine plural noun.

– To give information about who or what is doing the action, add *par* (by) and a second noun.

*Cette actrice est interview**é**e par les médias.*
This actress is interviewed by the media.
Le rôle principal est joué par un chanteur célèbre.
The main role is played by a famous singer.

Forming past participles

– The past participles of regular verbs are formed by removing the *-er*, *-ir-* or *-re* ending from the infinitive and then adding *-é* (for *-er* verbs), *-i* (for *-ir* verbs) or *-u* (for *-re* verbs). For example:

Infinitive	*jou**er***	*fin**ir***	*entend**re***
Past participle	*jou**é***	*fin**i***	*entend**u***

– There are many irregular past participles, which need to be learned separately. Some of these are featured on page 150. Here are some of the other irregular past participles that you need to know.

Infinitive	Past participle
boire (to drink)	*bu* (drunk)
conduire (to drive)	*conduit* (driven)
courir (to run)	*couru* (run)
croire (to believe)	*cru* (believed)
décevoir (to disappoint)	*déçu* (disappointed)
écrire (to write)	*écrit* (written)
recevoir (to receive)	*reçu* (received)
voir (to see)	*vu* (seen)

> **REVISION TIP** ☑
>
> Past participles are also used to form the perfect tense. See pages 150–151.

> **REVISION TIP** ☑
>
> Look at this list of past participles as well as the lists on pages 150–151. Prioritise learning the ones you are most likely to use in speaking and writing tasks.

Answer the questions below. Cover the answers column with a piece of paper and write down as many answers as you can. Check and repeat.

Questions | Answers

1 List the following negative structures in French: not, never, nothing, nobody.

Ne … pas; ne … jamais; ne … rien; ne … personne

2 Translate the following negative structures into English: *ne … que, ne … plus.*

Only; no longer / not any more

3 Where do you place negative structures in a present tense sentence?

Around the (first) verb

4 Translate the following sentence into French: They like neither fruit nor vegetables.

Ils / Elles n'aiment ni les fruits ni les légumes

5 Translate the following sentence into English: *Ils n'ont pas encore commencé.*

They have not yet started / They haven't started yet

6 Where do you place negative structures in the perfect tense?

Around the auxiliary (the first) verb

7 Use a negative to change the meaning of this sentence: *Ils vont venir.*

Ils ne vont pas venir / Ils ne vont jamais venir / Ils ne vont plus venir

8 How do you form a negative question?

Form your negative sentences as usual and use upward intonation, or add *est-ce que*

9 True or false? The passive voice is used to say what someone is doing.

False. The passive voice is used to indicate that something is being done to a subject by an agent

10 Explain how to form the passive voice in the present tense.

Use the present tense of the verb *être* (to be), plus a past participle

11 Choose the correct word to complete this sentence: *Les chanteuses sont connu / connue / connus / connues.*

Connues

12 What is the missing word in this sentence in the passive? *Le livre est lu … des célébrités.*

Par (by)

Put paper here

Previous questions

Use the questions below to check your knowledge from previous chapters.

Questions | Answers

1 Translate the following sentence into English: *Ils nous achètent un cadeau.*

They are buying us a present

2 Translate the following sentence into French: I would like to learn to speak Spanish.

Je voudrais apprendre à parler espagnol

3 What are the simple future tense endings for each subject pronoun?

-ai; -as; -a; -ons; -ez; -ont

Put paper here

⚙ Knowledge GRAMMAR

Reflexive and impersonal verbs

Reflexive verbs

Reflexive verbs and pronouns

– Reflexive verbs often describe an action that you do to yourself, or an action that reflects back on the person doing it in some way. They include a reflexive pronoun. With an infinitive, the reflexive pronoun is *se* (or *s'* before a vowel or silent *h*):

- *se laver* = to wash (yourself)
- *s'organiser* = to organise (yourself) / to get organised

– Reflexive verbs are conjugated in the same way as other verbs except for the additional reflexive pronoun in front of the verb, which changes according to who is doing the action.

Je **me** *lave*	I wash (myself)
Tu **te** *laves*	You wash (yourself)
Il **se** *lave*	He washes (himself)
Elle **se** *lave*	She washes (herself)
On **se** *lave*	We wash (ourselves)
Nous **nous** *lavons*	We wash (ourselves)
Vous **vous** *lavez*	You wash (yourself / yourselves)
Ils / Elles **se** *lavent*	They wash (themselves)

REVISION TIP ☑

Je m'appelle (my name is) comes from the reflexive verb *s'appeler* (to be called / to call yourself).

– *Me*, *te* and *se* are shortened to *m'*, *t'* and *s'* in front of a vowel or silent *h*.

– Here are some other useful reflexive verbs:

- *se coucher* = to go to bed
- *se demander* = to wonder
- *s'entendre avec* = to get on with
- *se lever* = to get up
- *se passer* = to happen
- *se marier* = to get married
- *se perdre* = to get lost
- *se préparer* = to get ready
- *se relaxer* = to relax

Reflexive verbs with reciprocal meanings

– Reflexive pronouns can also be used with any verb to give a reciprocal meaning of doing the action 'to each other'.

Pour l'Aïd, nous nous donnons des cadeaux. We give each other presents for Eid.
Ils se parlent tous les jours. They talk to each other every day.

Position of reflexive pronouns

– Reflexive pronouns always go in front of a verb, even in negative sentences.

Ils ne **se** *parlent plus.* They no longer talk to each other.

– In the perfect tense, they go in front of the auxiliary verb (which is *être* for all reflexive verbs):

Je **me** *suis demandé pourquoi.* I wondered why.

– In the near future tense, the reflexive pronoun goes in front of the infinitive but still needs to change according to who is doing the action:

Nous allons **nous** *changer.* We are going to get changed.

Impersonal verbs

What are impersonal verbs?

– Impersonal verbs are verbs that are only used in the third person singular, with the pronoun *il* or **cela**.

– Rather than describing what someone is doing, they are used to talk about things in general, for example, the time.

Il est huit heures. It is eight o'clock.

– Impersonal verbs are also used in certain expressions, for example:
il y a (there is / are).

– Impersonal verbs and expressions can be used in different tenses but always with the pronoun *il,* for example: *il y avait* (there was / were), *il y aura* (there will be).

Impersonal verbs with weather expressions

– Impersonal verbs are used to describe the weather, in any time frame.

Il fait beau. It is fine.	*Il faisait froid.* It was cold.
Il y a du soleil. It is sunny.	*Il y avait du vent.* It was windy.
Il pleut. It is raining.	*Il fera chaud.* It will be hot.

Impersonal expressions with infinitives

– *Il faut* is an impersonal expression meaning 'it is necessary'. It is followed by an infinitive:

Il faut écouter maintenant. It is necessary **to listen** now.

It often translates better in English as 'you must' do something:
Il faut suivre les règles. You must **follow** the rules.

– *Il vaut mieux* (it is better to) and *ça vaut la peine de* (it is worth) are also impersonal expressions that are followed by infinitives.

Il vaut mieux arrêter cette habitude. It is better to stop this habit.
Ça vaut la peine de voir ce film. It's worth **seeing** this film.

– You only need to know how to use these impersonal expressions with infinitives in the present tense.

Il est + adjective + *de*

– The impersonal expression *il est* can be followed by an adjective + *de* followed by a verb in the infinitive.

Il est interdit de fumer ici. It is forbidden to smoke here.
Il est impossible de le comprendre. It is impossible to understand it.

Il manque + noun

– The impersonal expression *il manque* means that something 'is missing' and is always followed by a noun.

Il manque un couteau sur la table. A knife is missing on the table.

> **REMEMBER** !
> Notice how the English translations of the infinitives can vary in these example sentences (**to listen**, **follow**, **seeing**).

> **REVISION TIP** ☑
> Don't mix this up with the noun *un manque* (a lack) and the verb *manquer* (to miss or to fail to catch).

Retrieval

GRAMMAR

Answer the questions below. Cover the answers column with a piece of paper and write down as many answers as you can. Check and repeat.

Questions | ## Answers

1 Give three reflexive verbs in French and English (in the infinitive forms).

Possible answers include: *se laver* (to wash); *se coucher* (to go to bed); *s'entendre avec* (to get on with)

2 What are the reflexive pronouns for *je*, *tu* and *il / elle / on*?

Me, te and *se*

3 What are the reflexive pronouns for *nous*, *vous* and *ils / elles*?

Nous, vous and *se*

4 Translate this sentence into English: *Je me suis demandé pourquoi.*

I wondered why

5 Translate this sentence into French: They talk to each other.

Ils / Elles se parlent

6 Choose the correct word to complete the sentence: *Nous allons nous / se / nos changer.*

Nous

7 What is an impersonal verb?

A verb only used in the third person singular / with the pronoun *il* or *cela*

8 How do you say 'it is eight o'clock' in French?

Il est huit / vingt heures

9 Translate the following phrase into French: there will be.

Il y aura

10 Give three weather expressions in French, in the present tense.

Possible answers include: *il fait beau; il y a du soleil; il pleut*

11 What type of word follows the impersonal expressions *il faut, il vaut mieux* and *ça vaut la peine de*?

The infinitive

12 Choose the correct word to complete the sentence: *Il est interdit se / de / pour fumer ici.*

De

Put paper here

Previous questions

Use the questions below to check your knowledge from previous chapters.

Questions | ## Answers

1 What does the phrase *être en train de* + infinitive mean?

To be in the middle of (doing)

2 Translate this sentence into French: She has been living here for three years.

Elle habite ici depuis trois ans

3 List the following negative structures in French: not, never, nothing, nobody.

Ne … pas; ne … jamais; ne … rien; ne … personne

Put paper here

Word formation

Recognising prefixes and suffixes

You are expected to be able to recognise how certain prefixes and suffixes can change the meaning of core vocabulary from AQA's set word list. These grammar rules are only required for the Reading exam.

For example, if you know that the French prefixes *in-* or *im-* change the meaning of a word to its opposite, you should be able to work out the meaning of **in**égalité (**in**equality), **in**juste (**un**fair) or **im**parfait (**im**perfect).

Make sure you also understand the following suffixes:

Adding *-ième*

Adding the suffix *-ième* to a French number changes its meaning:

trois (three) → *trois**ième*** (third)

French numbers ending in *-e* drop this final letter before adding the suffix:

trente (thirty) → *trent**ième*** (thirtieth)

Cinq (five) takes a *-**u*** before adding the suffix: *cinq**uième*** (fifth).

Adding *-able* or *-eable*

An adjective can be created by adding *-able* or *-eable* to a verb stem:

casser (to break) → *cass**able*** (breakable)

manger (to eat) → *mang**eable*** (edible)

Adding *-ion* or *-ation*

A noun can be created by adding *-ion* or *-ation* to a verb stem:

préparer (to prepare) → *prépar**ation*** (preparation)

Adding *-eur* or *-ateur*

A noun can also be created by adding *-eur* or *-ateur* to a verb stem:

créer (to create) → *cré**ateur*** (creator)

Adding *-ment* or *-amment*

Adverbs can be formed by adding *-ment* to the feminine form of adjectives:

traditionnelle (traditional) → *traditionnelle**ment*** (traditionally)

If the adjective ends in *-ante* or *-ente*, remove these endings and add *-amment* or *-emment*:

indépendante (independent) → *indépend**amment*** (independently)

patiente (patient) → *pati**emment*** (patiently)

⚙ Knowledge

Paper 1 Listening

What to expect in the Listening exam

This exam knowledge section will help you understand the structure of the Listening exam and how to tackle some of the types of questions that may come up.

Try covering up the tips and having a go at the tasks before checking the answers in the transcripts.

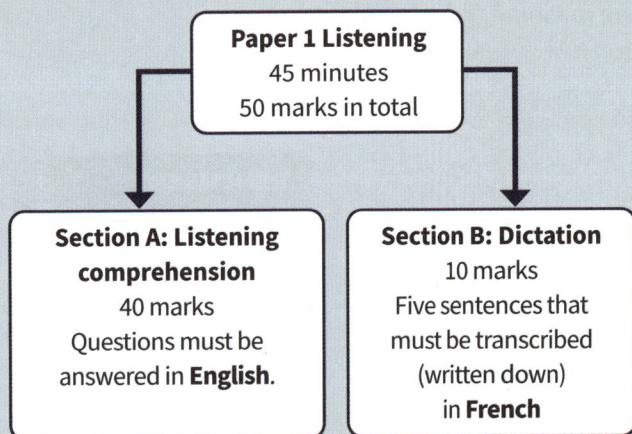

```
        ┌─────────────────────┐
        │  Paper 1 Listening  │
        │     45 minutes      │
        │  50 marks in total  │
        └─────────────────────┘
         │                    │
         ▼                    ▼
```

Section A: Listening comprehension
40 marks
Questions must be answered in **English**.

Section B: Dictation
10 marks
Five sentences that must be transcribed (written down) in **French**

Paper 1 Listening	Timings	Marks
Reading through the paper	5 minutes	–
Section A: Listening comprehension	38 minutes	40
Section B: Dictation		10
Checking your answers	2 minutes	–

EXAM TIP 🎯

Use the 5 minutes' reading time at the start to read through **Section A** to familiarise yourself with the topics, instructions and question types.

Section A: Listening comprehension

In Section A:

- You might hear a range of audio items, such as a conversation, an interview, an advert, a news story or a podcast.
- Most of the questions will be multiple choice – you might have to write the correct letter or letters from the answer options provided.
- Some of the questions will require you to complete sentences or answer questions in English to show your understanding.
- Each item will be heard twice, with pauses built in for you to read and then answer each question. There will be a bleep before each question starts.

EXAM TIP 🎯

You can make notes at any time – for example, jotting down any key words in French that you might expect to hear in a particular question.

Sample listening comprehension questions

Listen to this example of a multiple-choice question.

Part-time work

You hear some young people talking about their jobs.

What is the opinion of the students on the following aspects?

Write **P** for a **positive** opinion.

N for a **negative** opinion.

P+N for a **positive** and **negative** opinion.

1	Workplace		[1 mark]
2	Hours		[1 mark]
3	Pay		[1 mark]
4	Colleagues		[1 mark]

Scan the QR code to listen to the sample listening comprehension question.

EXAM TIP

Write your answers neatly in the boxes provided. Do not leave any answers blank. If you are not sure of the answer, make an intelligent guess.

Here is a copy of the transcript for this question:

1. J'ai de la chance de travailler dehors. Par contre, il fait plutôt froid en hiver!

2. Malheureusement, il faut travailler tard donc je suis toujours fatigué le lendemain.

3. Le salaire n'est pas du tout mal pour un jeune de mon âge. Je gagne plus que mes amis.

4. Je m'entends bien avec la plupart de mes collègues. D'autres sont moins gentils.

The phrase *par contre* (on the other hand) is a clue that this answer contains both positive and negative statements.

The word *malheureusement* (unfortunately) is a clue that a negative statement will follow.

Don't assume that a 'not' statement means the opinion is negative. Here, the salary is described as 'not bad at all' – which is positive!

This person gets on well with **most** of their colleagues. However, **others** are less kind so this answer is both positive and negative.

EXAM TIP

There will be a mixture of low, medium and high demand questions appearing at different points throughout the paper, so don't panic if you get stuck on one question as the next one might be easier.

Paper 1 Listening

Sample listening comprehension questions

Listen to this example comprehension question – there are two questions about this extract rather than separate audio items for each.

Scan the QR code to listen to the sample listening comprehension question.

A podcast

You hear this podcast from Sara, a French influencer and celebrity. Answer the questions in English. Answer both parts of question 5.

5.1 How did Sara become famous?   **[1 mark]**

....

5.2 What does she enjoy about being an influencer?   **[1 mark]**

....

The marks for each question are shown in brackets. There is one mark for each piece of information required. You don't need to write complete sentences to get the mark.

Here is a copy of the transcript for this question:

Les gens disent que je suis devenue célèbre parce que ma maman est star quand, en réalité, j'ai dû travailler dur. Il y a beaucoup de concurrence.

Le bonheur pour moi, c'est soutenir les autres. Partager mes images en ligne me fait peur car il y a toujours des plaintes.

Listen to the **whole** of the first section carefully. The answer to the first question is in the middle of this section: 'by working hard'. Ignore the two things mentioned that are **not** reasons for her fame (her famous mum and the amount of competition).

The clue here is the sentence starter, 'Happiness for me is…' The key information (supporting others) follows this. The final sentence is about things she does **not** like to do (sharing pictures and getting complaints).

EXAM TIP 🎯

Once you have had a go at a practice listening task, look at the transcript and translate anything you missed. You can use an online dictionary or translation tool to help you.

In Section B:

- You will hear five short sentences dictated to you and you must write them down in French.

- The sentences are marked as a whole – there are five marks for communication and five marks for accuracy.

- You will hear each sentence three times: first as a full sentence, then in short sections and finally as a full sentence again.

Sample dictation sentences

Listen to these example dictation sentences. In the answer booklet, you will have two blank lines to write each sentence.

> Listen carefully and using your knowledge of French sounds, write down in **French** exactly what you hear for each sentence.
>
> You will hear each sentence **three** times: the first time as a full sentence, the second time in short sections and the third time again as a full sentence.
>
> Use your knowledge of French sounds and grammar to make sure that what you have written makes sense. Check carefully that your spelling is accurate.
>
> **[10 marks]**

Scan the QR code to listen to the sample dictation sentences.

Here is an example of how the dictation sentences appear in the transcript. They are divided into short sections for the second time of listening and this has been indicated using a /.

Sentence 1	Ma famille / est grande.
Sentence 2	L'équipe a gagné / ce match.
Sentence 3	Il vaut mieux / pratiquer / une langue étrangère.
Sentence 4	Elle va essayer / de **baisser** / la musique.
Sentence 5	Nous avons / vraiment apprécié / votre **compagnie**.

The sentences will gradually increase in demand from low to high.

There will always be two words that are not on AQA's set vocabulary list that will be unfamiliar to you. You will need to use your knowledge of French sounds and grammar to write what you hear.

EXAM TIP

Use the two minutes' checking time at the end of the paper to make sure that what you have written makes sense, is grammatically accurate and is spelled correctly.

Retrieval EXAM

Answer the questions below. Cover the answers column with a piece of paper and write down as many answers as you can. Check and repeat.

Questions | Answers

#	Question	Answer
1	What is the difference between the types of question in Section A and Section B for Paper 1: Listening?	Section A contains comprehension questions and Section B is the dictation task
2	How many marks are there for Section A of Paper 1: Listening?	40 marks
3	How many marks are there for Section B of Paper 1: Listening?	10 marks
4	How long do you have to read through the Listening paper before the test begins?	5 minutes
5	How many times will you hear each item in Section A of Paper 1: Listening?	Twice
6	How many times will you hear each dictation sentence in Section B of Paper 1: Listening?	Three times
7	Does the Listening paper only contain vocabulary from AQA's set vocabulary list?	No – there will be two words in Section B that are not on the set vocabulary list
8	Are you allowed to make notes during the Listening paper?	Yes – you can make notes at any time
9	How will you know that the next question in the Listening paper is about to start?	You will hear a bleep
10	What should you do if you are unsure of an answer in the Listening paper?	Make an intelligent guess – do not leave any blank answers
11	What would be a good way to use the two minutes' checking time at the end of the Listening paper?	To check the grammar, spelling and sense of the sentences in Section B

Put paper here

Previous questions

Use the questions below to check your knowledge from previous chapters.

Questions | Answers

#	Question	Answer
1	In French, list five ways of watching something at home using a different technology.	Any five from: *en ligne / sur internet / en streaming / à la télé / sur un portable / sur un ordinateur / sur une appli*
2	Translate the following sentence into English: *Apprendre une langue est très utile.*	Learning a language is very useful
3	How is the imperative formed?	The imperative is formed from the present tense of the *tu, vous* and *nous* forms of the verb

Put paper here

Practice

EXAM

Section A: Listening comprehension

Careers advice

You hear some advice from a career adviser on a podcast.

Write   **A** if only statement **A** is correct.

            B if only statement **B** is correct.

            A+B if both statements **A** and **B** are correct.

Answer both parts of question 1.

1.1   To find the right career, you must firstly…   **[1 mark]**

A	understand your skills.
B	listen to your friends.

> **EXAM TIP**
>
> Where there are two-part questions (e.g. 1.1, 1.2), you will hear **one** passage that will contain **both** answers.

1.2   Make the most of every chance to…   **[1 mark]**

A	take part in school activities.
B	try something new.

2.   Get some experience by doing…   **[1 mark]**

A	a work placement.
B	a summer job.

An interview about hobbies

You listen to two people being interviewed about their free time.

They are talking about why they do particular leisure activities.

A	To make some money
B	To meet new people
C	To make music
D	To be creative
E	To spend time outside
F	To get in shape

What **two** reasons does each person give?

Write the correct letters in the boxes.

3. ☐ ☐   **[2 marks]**

4. ☐ ☐   **[2 marks]**

Practice

Paper 1 Listening

Weather reports

You hear these weather reports for different regions.

5.

			[2 marks]
A	The weather is unusually hot.		
B	There have been fires in the forests.		
C	The advice is to keep all windows open.		
D	Rain is on the way.		

Chose the **two** correct statements. Write the correct letters in the boxes.

6.

			[2 marks]
A	A road accident took place last night.		
B	The police blame the weather conditions.		
C	You should avoid car journeys if possible.		
D	The weather will clear up later tonight.		

Chose the **two** correct statements. Write the correct letters in the boxes.

> **EXAM TIP**
> Read each of the options carefully before the audio starts.

Section B: Dictation

You will now hear 5 short sentences. Listen carefully and using your knowledge of French sounds, write down in **French** exactly what you hear for each sentence.

[10 marks]

> **EXAM TIP**
> Think about the meaning of the sentences as you listen.

Sentence 1

....

....

Sentence 2

....

....

Sentence 3

....

....

Sentence 4

....

....

Sentence 5

....

....

Paper 2 Speaking

What to expect in the Speaking exam

This exam knowledge section will help you understand the structure of the Speaking exam and how to tackle each task.

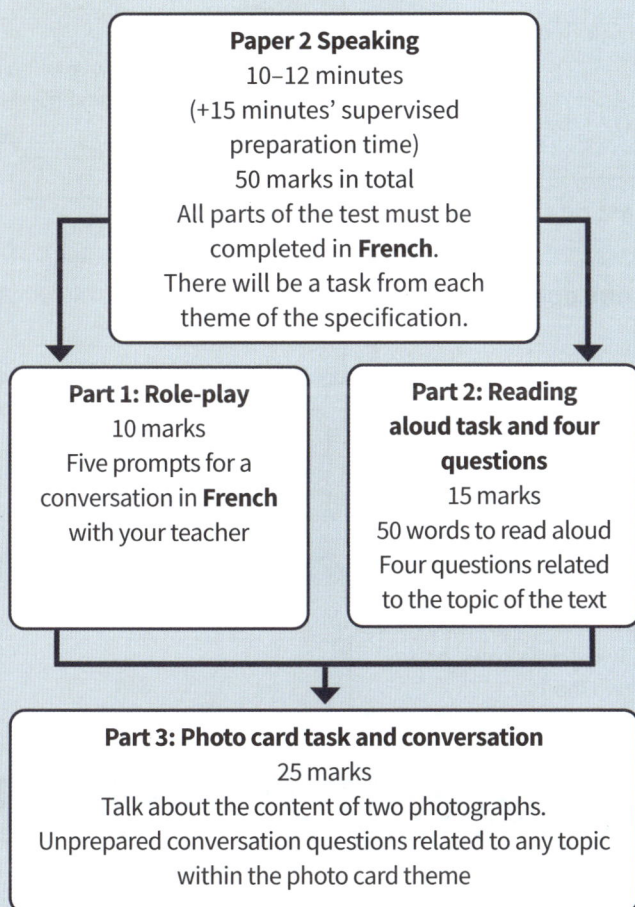

Paper 2 Speaking
10–12 minutes
(+15 minutes' supervised preparation time)
50 marks in total
All parts of the test must be completed in **French**.
There will be a task from each theme of the specification.

Part 1: Role-play
10 marks
Five prompts for a conversation in **French** with your teacher

Part 2: Reading aloud task and four questions
15 marks
50 words to read aloud
Four questions related to the topic of the text

Part 3: Photo card task and conversation
25 marks
Talk about the content of two photographs.
Unprepared conversation questions related to any topic within the photo card theme

Paper 2 Speaking	Timings	Marks
Supervised preparation time	15 minutes	–
Part 1: Role-play	1–1.5 minutes	10
Part 2: Reading aloud task and four questions	3–3.5 minutes	15
Part 3: Photo card task and conversation	1.5 minutes responding to the photos 4.5–5.5 minutes unprepared conversation	25

EXAM TIP 🎯

During the 15 minutes' supervised preparation time, you will have time to look at the role-play card, reading aloud task and photo card. You are allowed to make notes in French on the answer sheet provided by your teacher to refer to during the test.

Part 1: Role-play

For the role-play:

- The scenario will be a conversation with a friend so remember to use the *tu* form when asking questions.
- The five role-play prompts are in English and will direct you about what to say in French.
- You will need to ask one question. This will be shown with a '**?**' symbol next to the prompt.
- Instructions on how many details are required for each prompt are given in brackets.

Paper 2 Speaking

Sample role-play card

Read the sample role-play card and annotations.

You are talking to your Swiss friend.

Your teacher will play the part of your friend and will speak first.

You should address your friend as *tu*.

When you see this – **?** – you will have to ask a question.

In order to score full marks, you must include at least one verb in your response to each task.

1.   Say what you think about sport and why. (Give **one** opinion and **one** reason.)

2.   Say when you did some exercise recently. (Give **two** details.)

3.   Give **one** advantage of healthy eating.

4.   Describe your favourite meal. (Give **two** details.)

?5.   Ask your friend a question about what they drink.

> **EXAM TIP** 🎯
>
> For the role-play task, there are two marks per prompt. Say only what is required for each prompt and no more.

The easiest way to give an opinion is to use the structure 'I like / love / hate … because it's…'.

Two details would be what you do and who with or where.

You could use the sentence starter: *Un avantage, c'est…*

A simple way to ask a question is to ask: *Tu aimes…?*

Two details could be any two foods.

Sample role-play card notes and script

Here is a sample of some notes that have been written for the role-play task:

1.   J'adore le sport parce que c'est amusant.

2.   Le week-end dernier, j'ai joué au foot avec mes copains.

3.   Un avantage, c'est avoir plus d'énergie.

4.   Mon plat préféré, c'est du poisson et des frites.

5.   Quelle est ta boisson préférée?

> **EXAM TIP** 🎯
>
> Use around five minutes of the supervised preparation time before the test begins to write down what you want to say for each prompt on the answer sheet provided. Keep it simple and use French you know.

Here is a sample teacher's script for this task:

Introductory text: Tu parles avec ton ami(e) suisse. Moi, je suis ton ami(e).

1.   Qu'est-ce que tu penses du sport? Pourquoi?

2.   Quand est-ce que tu as fait de l'exercice récemment?

3.   Dis-moi un avantage de manger sain.

4.   Quel est ton plat préféré?

5.   Allow the candidate to ask you a question and give an appropriate response e.g. *J'aime le café.*

🔊 Scan the QR code to listen to the sample role-play in full.

Part 2: Reading aloud task and four questions

For the reading aloud task:

- You should read out the sentences in French using your best pronunciation and intonation.

- The sentences will include some of the sound-spelling links that are required by the AQA specification.

- Your teacher will then ask you four questions related to the topic of the text. You should answer all four questions as fully as you can.

- There are five marks for the reading aloud task and ten marks for the responses to the four questions.

LINK

Make sure you can recognise and say all the sounds required for this part of the text. A full list is provided on page 196.

EXAM TIP

Your last attempt at the reading aloud task will be the one that is marked so you can stop and start again if you need to, as long as you don't go over the allotted time for the task.

Sample reading aloud task

When your teacher asks you, read aloud the following text in **French**.

Mon influenceur preféré est chef. ←

Il est chinois et il partage ses recettes originales en ligne. ←

J'adore regarder ses vidéos parce que la cuisine m'intéresse beaucoup.

Récemment, il a participé à un concours à la télé et il était très populaire. ←

J'aimerais manger dans son restaurant.

Cependant, ça serait assez cher!

You might note this down phonetically as 'pray-fair-ay'.

You could write this phonetically as 'sheen-wah'.

Use the punctuation to add pauses and give yourself time to think about what you are going to say next.

EXAM TIP

Use a couple of minutes of the supervised preparation time to read through the text in your head. Notice any words that you find tricky to say and practise them quietly. You could also write them down phonetically on the answer sheet provided.

Scan the QR code to listen to the sentences being read aloud and practise repeating them to improve your pronunciation.

A short conversation follows the reading aloud task. You will not be able to prepare answers to the four questions ahead of time but you could use some of the preparation time to anticipate the kind of questions you might be asked.

> You will then be asked four questions **in French** that relate to the topic of **Celebrity culture**.
>
> In order to score the highest marks, you must try to **answer all four questions as fully as you can**.

Here is an example of the kind of questions you might anticipate on celebrity culture:

- Who is your favourite celebrity?
- Which celebrity would you like to meet?
- Describe a celebrity you like.
- Tell me about your favourite influencer.
- What do you think of influencers online?
- What sort of videos / programmes do you watch?
- What are the advantages / disadvantages of being famous?

REVISION TIP

Try recording your answers to these questions in French.

Here are four questions in French that you could be asked:

1. *Parle-moi d'une célébrité que tu aimes.*
2. *Qu'est-ce que tu penses de suivre des célébrités en ligne?*
3. *Quelle personne célèbre voudrais-tu rencontrer?*
4. *Quelles sont les avantages d'être célèbre?*

EXAM TIP

An extended response to each question would contain at least three bits of information, each with a suitable verb.

An example of a fully developed answer to question 1 would be: *J'adore l'acteur Ryan Reynolds parce qu'il est très drôle. Il aime le foot aussi!*

For the photo card task:

- You must talk about the content of two photos for about 1.5 minutes and say at least one thing about each photo.
- After you have described the photos, your teacher will then ask you questions related to any of the topics within the theme of the photo card.
- You should try to develop your answers to the conversation questions during the 4.5–5.5 minutes that this part of the test lasts.
- There are five marks for the photo descriptions and twenty marks for the unprepared conversation.

174   Paper 2 Speaking

Sample photo card task

During your preparation time, look at the two photos. You may make as many notes as you wish on an Additional Answer Sheet and use these notes during the test.

Your teacher will ask you to talk about the content of these photos. The recommended time is approximately **one and a half minutes**. **You must say at least one thing about each photo**.

After you have spoken about the content of the photos, your teacher will then ask you questions related to **any** of the topics within the theme of **Communication and the world around us**.

Photo 1

Photo 2

EXAM TIP

The photos in the paper will be black and white but that doesn't mean you can't mention colours in your description if you want to.

REVISION TIP

Have a go at the photo card task before you check the sample description on page 176.

EXAM

Paper 2 Speaking

Sample photo card task

Here is a sample description that a student might make about the photos:

> **Sur la première photo**, **il y a** un jeune couple. Ils sont des touristes et **je pense qu'ils sont** un mari et une femme. La femme est petite avec les cheveux longs et l'homme est plus grand avec les cheveux courts. Il porte un sac et il tient son portable.
>
> **Ils semblent** contents car ils sourient. Ils décident où ils vont aller et quels sites ils vont visiter. Ils sont dehors, en ville. **Derrière** eux, **je vois** des arbres et des batîments intéressants – peut-être un temple ou une église. Je pense qu'ils sont en vacances mais il fait un peu gris.
>
> **Sur la deuxième photo**, **il y a** quatre **personnes** dans un musée d'art. Il y a un garçon qui est adolescent. Il a **environ** treize **ans**, **à mon avis**. Il regarde un objet d'art et il écoute de la musique. Il a les cheveux courts et il porte un sac. **Il semble** triste ou malade et il est seul.
>
> Derrière lui, il y a une femme avec deux filles qui parlent et regardent un tableau. La femme est **peut-être** leur mère **ou** leur prof.

EXAM TIP

Learn some standard phrases, like the ones in bold here, that you can use or adapt to describe any photo.

After the photo description, you will be asked questions related to any topics within the theme of that card. Spend a minute of your preparation time thinking about what these questions might cover.

Here are some possible question starters:

- *Parle-moi de…*
- *Décris-moi…*
- *Quels sont les avantages de…?*
- *Quels sont les problèmes pour…?*
- *Qu'est-ce que tu penses de…?*

EXAM TIP

Listen carefully to each question that you are asked to understand how to respond. You can often adapt the verb in the question to give your answer. For example:

*Qu'est-ce que tu **penses** de…?*
*Je **pense** que c'est…*

EXAM TIP

To get the best marks, make sure you develop each response, with at least **three** bits of information, including a suitable verb. Use a variety of vocabulary and structures. For example: *Qu'est-ce que tu penses de voyager? Je pense que ça serait intéressant et j'aimerais aller à l'étranger. Je n'ai jamais visité la France, par exemple.*

Retrieval

EXAM

Answer the questions below. Cover the answers column with a piece of paper and write down as many answers as you can. Check and repeat.

Questions

Answers

1. What do the three different parts of the Speaking paper consist of?

Role-play; reading aloud task; photo card task

2. How long will you have to prepare the exam materials before the Speaking paper starts?

15 minutes' supervised preparation time

3. Which part of the Speaking paper carries the most marks?

The photo card task: 25 marks (five marks for the photo descriptions and 20 marks for the unprepared conversation)

4. Is this statement true or false: You should give as much information as possible for each role-play prompt?

False. You should say only what is required for each prompt and no more

5. In which part of the Speaking paper will you have to ask a question?

In the role-play

6. How many questions will you be asked after the reading aloud text?

Four

7. How many photos will you have to talk about during the photo card discussion?

Two

8. Is this statement true or false: You must use a verb in every answer for the Speaking paper?

True. To get the best marks you will need to use full sentences throughout, including suitable verbs

9. What should an extended answer in the Speaking paper include?

At least three bits of information, with suitable verbs

10. Can you refer to your notes during the Speaking paper?

Yes. You can look at your notes on the additional answer sheet at any time

Put paper here

Previous questions

Use the questions below to check your knowledge from previous chapters.

Questions

Answers

1. What are the three imperative forms of the verb *être*?

Sois / Soyez / Soyons

2. What is the difference between the types of question in Section A and Section B for Paper 1: Listening?

Section A contains comprehension questions and Section B is the dictation task

3. What would be a good way to use the two minutes' checking time at the end of the Listening paper?

To check the grammar, spelling and sense of the sentences in Section B

Put paper here

Paper 2 Speaking

Part 1: Role-play

Prepare the following role-play task. Then listen to the teacher's prompts and respond.

You are talking to your friend from Quebec.

Your teacher will play the part of your friend and will speak first.

You should address your friend as *tu*.

When you see this – **?** – you will have to ask a question.

> **In order to score full marks, you must include at least one verb in your response to each task.**
>
> 1. What is your favourite subject? Why? (Give **two** details.)
>
> 2. What is the advantage of your school? (Give **one** opinion and **one** reason.)
>
> 3. Describe one of your teachers.
>
> **? 4.** Ask your friend what they think of their favourite subject. (Give **one** detail.)
>
> 5. What did you do at school last week? (Give **two** details.)

> **EXAM TIP** 🎯
>
> Keep your answers for the role play task simple and accurate.

Part 2: Reading aloud task

Read aloud the following text in **French**.

> Dans la société actuelle, Internet est devenu indispensable.
>
> Il faut l'utiliser pour réserver des billets, par exemple.
>
> Certains employés peuvent travailler de chez eux s'ils ont un ordinateur.
>
> Pour les jeunes, faire des achats en ligne, c'est courant.
>
> Dans le passé, il n'y avait pas d'Internet et la vie quotidienne était très différente.

> **EXAM TIP** 🎯
>
> Take care to pronounce accented letters correctly.

Then listen and respond to the four questions on the topic of **Media and technology**.

In order to score the highest marks, you must try to **answer all four questions as fully as you can**.

Part 3: Photo card task

- Prepare a description of these two photos. You may make as many notes as you wish and use these notes during the test.

- Then record yourself talking about the content of these photos for approximately **one and a half minutes. You must say at least one thing about each photo**.

- After you have spoken about the content of the photos, you will be asked questions related to **any** of the topics within the theme of **Popular culture**. Listen to and respond to the example questions.

EXAM TIP

Practise preparing photo tasks within a time limit as you get closer to your speaking test.

Photo 1

Photo 2

EXAM TIP

People in photos are often smiling or laughing so make sure you know the French verbs *sourire* (to smile) and *rire* (to laugh) as well as how to describe people as *heureux / heureuse(s)* (happy).

Paper 3 Reading

What to expect in the Reading exam

This exam knowledge section will help you understand the structure of the Reading exam and how to tackle some of the types of questions that may come up.

Try covering up the tips and having a go at the tasks before checking the answers.

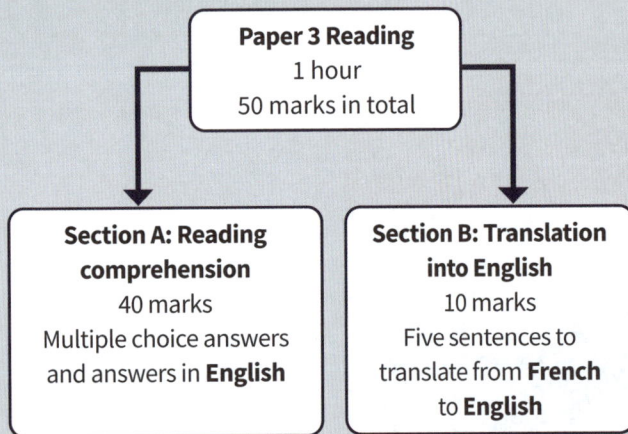

Paper 3 Reading
1 hour
50 marks in total

Section A: Reading comprehension
40 marks
Multiple choice answers and answers in **English**

Section B: Translation into English
10 marks
Five sentences to translate from **French** to **English**

Paper 3 Reading	Timings	Marks
Section A: Reading comprehension	Approximately 45 minutes	40
Section B: Translation into English	Approximately 12 minutes	10
Checking your answers	Approximately 3 minutes	–

EXAM TIP 🎯

Leave a few minutes to check your translations and review any comprehension answers you were not sure about. Do not leave any answers blank.

Section A: Reading comprehension

In Section A:

- You will read a variety of different text types in French, such as adverts, headlines, articles, emails and website content.
- The texts will vary in length, from short sentences up to about 160 words.
- Most of the questions will be multiple choice – you might have to write the correct letter or letters from the answer options provided.
- Some of the questions will require you to answer questions in English to show your understanding.
- There will be a few words that are not on AQA's set vocabulary list that you will need to work out from the context. There might also be some cognates (French words that look very similar to English and that have the same meaning).

Sample reading comprehension questions

Read the sample reading comprehension questions and annotations.

Environmental tips

You read this online forum.

People are giving tips on being more environmentally friendly.

Ahmed

Je garde des feuilles de mes vieux cahiers si j'ai seulement écrit sur un côté. Je les utilse pour noter mes listes de courses avant d'aller au supermarché. J'y vais à pied, naturellement!

Benjamin

Dans ma ville, il y a un magasin 'vert' où on peut apporter ses propres boîtes en plastique pour les remplir avec des produits. J'ai aussi des sacs en papier pour **emballer*** mes déjeuners.

Clara

Après avoir nettoyé le sol de la cuisine, l'eau peut être recyclée pour laver la voiture. N'allumez pas les lumières pendant la journée et ne quittez pas la maison sans fermer toutes les fenêtres.

*emballer = to wrap

> If you see an unfamiliar word marked with * in a sentence, it means that the English meaning is provided below the text.

> **REMEMBER**
>
> Remember that *journée* means 'day' – not journey!

Who gives tips that relate to the following points?

Write   **A** for Ahmed

         B for Benjamin

         C for Clara

Write the correct letter in each box.

1. Saving electricity   ☐   [1 mark] ←

2. Choosing environmentally friendly packaging   ☐   [1 mark] ←

3. Reducing water use   ☐   [1 mark] ←

4. Reusing paper   ☐   [1 mark] ←

5. Walking to the shops   ☐   [1 mark]

> Clara talks about not switching on the lights in the day – which would save electricity.

> Benjamin mentions taking plastic boxes to fill up at the 'green' shop and using paper bags to make his packed lunches.

> Clara suggests cleaning the kitchen floor and then using the same water to wash the car.

> Although Benjamin mentions a shop, it's Ahmed who talks about going to the supermarket on foot.

> Ahmed keeps sheets of paper from his old exercise books to use as shopping lists.

Paper 3 Reading

Sample reading comprehension questions

Studying choices

You see an article by Alex, a teenager who is thinking about which subjects to carry on studying.

> Je dois choisir mes matières pour le bac. Ce n'est pas un choix évident. Il y a plusieurs avantages de continuer avec les sciences. Je m'entends bien avec le prof de physique. En plus, on travaillerait dans le nouveau batîment d'informatique.
>
> Cependant, il y a des inconvénients aussi. Il est difficile d'obtenir les meilleures notes, même si on est intelligent. J'aime rire avec mes amis en cours mais tous mes copains veulent faire du théâtre.
>
> Quand je vais au lycée, mes parents vont me donner **une mallette** pour protéger mon ordinateur portable en voyageant en métro.

Alex mentions getting on well with the physics teacher and working in the new computer building (question 6).

The word *inconvénients* helps you find the paragraph where the two disadvantages are mentioned: it's hard to get the best marks and all their friends want to do drama (question 7).

You need to work out the most likely meaning of *une mallette* from the context. We know from the rest of the sentence that it is something you would use to protect your laptop when travelling on the tube. This helps you decide that option B (carry it) is the correct option (question 8).

6. According to Alex, what are **two** advantages of choosing sciences?

    [2 marks]

    ....

    ....

7. What **two** disadvantages do they mention? **[2 marks]**

    ....

    ....

8. Read the last sentence again. What would you do with *une mallette*? Write the correct letter in the box. **[1 mark]**

    | A | Eat it. |
    | B | Carry it. |
    | C | Read it. |

EXAM TIP

Don't panic if you get stuck on a question – make an intelligent guess and move on to the next question, which might be easier.

EXAM TIP

You are not expected to know that *une mallette* means 'briefcase' as this word is not on AQA's set vocabulary list. This is an example of a question where you have to infer what kind of object it might be.

Section B: Translation into English

In Section B:

- You will translate five sentences from French to English.
- The sentences will include different tenses and grammatical structures.
- All of the vocabulary will be taken from AQA's set vocabulary list, covering a range of different topics.

EXAM TIP ⊙

Each sentence is broken into two parts for marking, with one mark for each clause.

↓

Sample translation into English

Read the sample sentences for translation into English and the annotations. Try translating the sentences before you look at the answers on the next page.

EXAM TIP ⊙

Start by identifying the verbs and tenses.

Translate these sentences into **English**.

Nous habitons au deuxième étage depuis six mois.   **[2 marks]**

....

....

Pendant leur enfance, mes grand-parents étaient extrêmement pauvres.   **[2 marks]**

....

....

Il faut aller directement à l'accueil au début de votre séjour.   **[2 marks]**

....

....

Je serai très heureux la semaine prochaine si le ministre est élu.   **[2 marks]**

....

....

Après avoir fini ses études de droit, ma mère est devenue avocate.   **[2 marks]**

....

....

REMEMBER ⊙

Remember that *depuis* with the present tense verb *nous habitons* translates in English as 'we have been living … for…'.

This could be translated as either 'were' or 'used to be' in this sentence.

You could translate *il faut* as 'you must', 'you have to', or 'it is necessary to'.

This is the simple future tense – 'I will be'.

This is the perfect tense, meaning 'became'.

Paper 3 Reading

Sample translation answers

Each sentence is divided into two for marking. Here is an example of how the sentences are divided and the answers that would be accepted.

French	English translation	Alternative translation	Mark
Nous habitons … depuis six mois.	We have been living … for six months.	We have lived … for six months.	1
…au deuxième étage…	on the second floor		1
Pendant leur enfance,	During their childhood,		1
mes grand-parents étaient extrêmement pauvres.	my grandparents were extremely poor.	my grandparents used to be extremely poor.	1
Il faut aller directement à l'accueil	You must go straight to reception	You have to / it is necessary to go directly / straight to reception	1
au début de votre séjour.	at the beginning of your stay.	at the start of your stay.	1
Je serai très heureux la semaine prochaine	I will be very happy next week		1
si le ministre est élu.	if the minister is elected.		1
Après avoir fini ses études de droit,	Having finished her law studies,	Having finished studying law,	1
ma mère est devenue avocate.	my mother became a lawyer.	my mum became a lawyer.	1

REMEMBER ❗

There is no article before the job word in French but remember to add one in your English translation.

EXAM TIP 🎯

There is often more than one way to translate a sentence correctly and the mark scheme allows for this.

Retrieval

Answer the questions below. Cover the answers column with a piece of paper and write down as many answers as you can. Check and repeat.

Questions | ## Answers

#	Question	Answer
1	What is the difference between the types of question in Section A and Section B for Paper 3: Reading?	Section A contains comprehension questions and Section B is the translation into English
2	How many marks are there for Section A in Paper 3: Reading?	40 marks
3	How many marks are there for Section B in Paper 3: Reading?	10 marks
4	How long does the Reading paper last?	1 hour
5	What language should you use to write your answers in the Reading paper?	English
6	What is the length of the longest text you will have to read in the Reading paper?	Approximately 160 words
7	Is this statement about the Reading paper true or false: Section A will only contain vocabulary from AQA's set vocabulary list?	False – there will be some words in Section A that are not on the set vocabulary list (cognates and words you have to work out from the context)
8	Is this statement about the Reading paper true or false: There may be more than one possible correct answer for the translation sentences in Section B?	True
9	In the Reading paper, if you see a word marked with * in a text, what does it mean?	It means that the English meaning is provided below the text
10	If you have a few minutes at the end of the Reading paper, what should you do?	Check your answers

Put paper here

Previous questions

Use the questions below to check your knowledge from previous chapters.

Questions | ## Answers

#	Question	Answer
1	Translate this question into English: *Comment utilises-tu ton portable?*	How do you use your mobile phone?
2	Translate the following sentence into French: I have just finished.	*Je viens de finir*
3	How long do you have to read through the Listening paper before the test begins?	5 minutes

Put paper here

Paper 3 Reading

Section A: Reading comprehension

Carnival in the city of Nice

You see a travel website about different carnivals around the world.

Le Carnaval de **Nice*** est une fête française traditionnelle. Un des meilleurs moments de l'événement, c'est la bataille de fleurs, quand les participants jettent des milliers de fleurs au public! L'autre, c'est le défilé de nuit, un spectacle extraordinaire!

Le carnaval est moins populaire parmi certains habitants. Selon eux, il y a maintenant trop de visiteurs pendant ce festival. Les commerçants apprécient mais les touristes laissent beaucoup de déchets dans les rues qu'il faut nettoyer après.

Si vous y allez, n'oubliez pas de mettre **un déguisement** pour profiter de l'entrée gratuite!

*Nice = a city in the south of France

Answer the following questions in **English**.

1. According to the article, what are the **two** best moments of the carnival? **[2 marks]**

    1 ....

    2 ....

2. What **two** things make the carnival less popular with some locals? **[2 marks]**

    1 ....

    2 ....

3. Read the last sentence again. What would you do with **un déguisement**?

    Write the correct letter in the box.

A	Eat it.
B	Wear it.
C	Throw it.

    [1 mark]

    EXAM TIP

    For question 3, look for any key words in the last sentence of the text that give you clues about the meaning of the unfamiliar word in bold.

A business article

You read an article about two friends.

Zoé et Rachid sont deux amis avec un seul but: avoir leur propre entreprise et devenir riches avant l'âge de trente ans. Leur chemin vers cet objectif a commencé tôt.

À l'école primaire, Rachid vendait déjà des gâteaux pendant la récré même si c'était interdit par le règlement. Alors, quand le petit garçon a eu des problèmes avec l'école, c'est Zoé qui a persuadé la directrice de permettre à son copain de continuer.

Rachid a ensuite demandé à son amie de devenir son associé. Quelques années plus tard, l'adolescente a eu l'idée géniale de poster des photos de leurs produits sur les réseaux sociaux.

Aujourd'hui, à vingt ans, Rachid reste un jeune homme timide qui laisse à sa copine le rôle du visage public de leur commerce. Contrairement à elle, il préfère travailler en cuisine pour développer de nouveaux goûts.

Who do the statements on the right refer to?

Write   **R** for **Rachid**

          Z for **Zoé**

          R+Z for **Rachid** and **Zoé**.

Write the correct letter(s) in each box.

4. Who wanted to have their own business?   [1 mark]

5. Who broke the rules to get started?   [1 mark]

6. Who promoted their products on the internet?   [1 mark]

7. Who is responsible for representing their company today?   [1 mark]

Friends of the Earth

You read some information online about a French environmental organisation.

L'association Les Amis de la Terre existe en France depuis 1970. Ses membres luttent pour protéger l'environnement.

Leur but est de transformer la société pour créer un monde en harmonie avec la nature. Ils se battent aussi pour l'égalité et une culture de paix où on partage des ressources. Récemment, ils ont organisé une manifestation contre l'énergie nucléaire et un tour de vélo contre le réchauffement de la planète.

Si vous souhaitez découvrir tous leurs moyens d'action, vous pouvez vous inscrire à un de leurs groupes dans votre région, ou bien créer un nouveau groupe dans votre ville. Les membres essaient d'aider les citoyens à devenir plus conscients des problèmes de notre planète. Vous pouvez également soutenir leur travail de chez vous, en donnant un peu d'argent chaque mois.

8. What has this organisation done recently? Give **two** details.   [2 marks]

    1 ....

    2 ....

9. What do members of their local groups try to do?   [1 mark]

    ....

Paper 3 Reading

Adverts

You see some newspaper adverts describing different products.

A	Des vins français de la meilleure qualité
B	Des sièges de jardin faits (à la) main
C	Le chapeau parfait pour chaque événement
D	Des valises et des sacs de marques célèbres
E	Un grand choix de tableaux et d'affiches à vendre

Which description matches each type of product?

Write the correct letter in each box.

10. Luggage   [1 mark]

11. Artwork   [1 mark]

12. Drinks   [1 mark]

Section B: Translation into English

13. Translate these sentences into **English**.

Je ne vais jamais vapoter parce que ce n'est pas sain!   [2 marks]

....

....

Rien n'est aussi intéressant que l'informatique, selon mon prof.   [2 marks]

....

....

Nos voisins nous ont invités à assister à leur mariage au printemps.   [2 marks]

....

....

L'année prochaine, ils passeront deux semaines en Belgique.   [2 marks]

....

....

Il vaut mieux réagir maintenant pour trouver de bonnes solutions
à la crise.   [2 marks]

....

....

EXAM TIP

Always re-read your translations to check they make sense and are written in natural-sounding English.

Paper 4 Writing

What to expect in the Writing exam

This exam knowledge section will help you understand the structure of the Writing exam and how to tackle each task.

Have a go at each task before checking the sample answers.

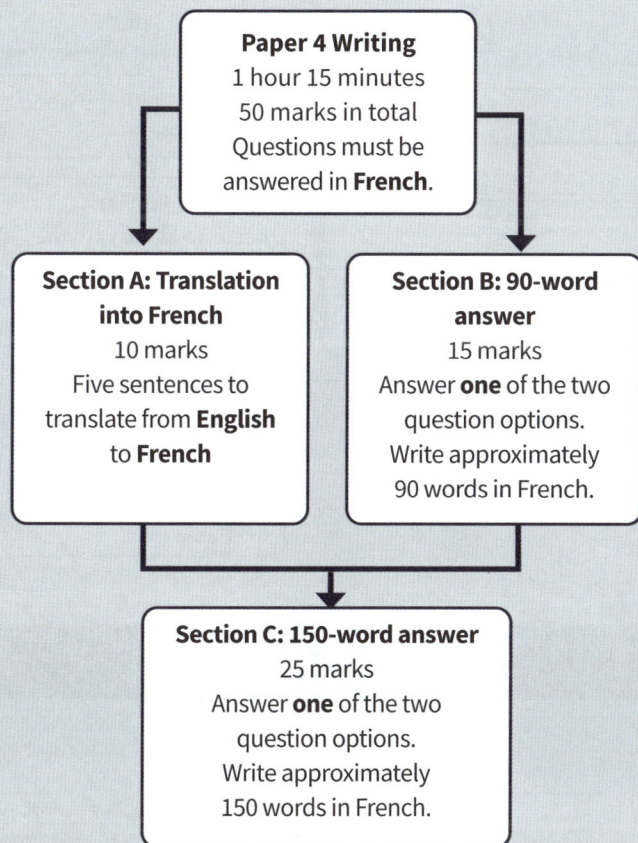

Paper 4 Writing
1 hour 15 minutes
50 marks in total
Questions must be answered in **French**.

Section A: Translation into French
10 marks
Five sentences to translate from **English** to **French**

Section B: 90-word answer
15 marks
Answer **one** of the two question options.
Write approximately 90 words in French.

Section C: 150-word answer
25 marks
Answer **one** of the two question options.
Write approximately 150 words in French.

Paper 4 Writing	Timings	Marks
Section A: Translation into French	Approximately 15 minutes	10
Section B: 90-word answer	Approximately 20 minutes	15
Section C: 150-word answer	Approximately 35 minutes	25
Checking your answers	5 minutes	–

EXAM TIP

Remember you only need to write **one** answer for Section B and **one** for Section C. Take a minute to read the two question options for each section carefully to choose the topic you feel most confident to write about.

Section A: Translation into French

In Section A:

- You will translate five sentences from English to French.
- The sentences will include different tenses and grammatical structures.
- All of the vocabulary will be taken from AQA's set vocabulary list, covering a range of different topics.

EXAM TIP

All five sentences will be marked as one set, with five marks for getting the meaning across and five marks for vocabulary knowledge and grammatical accuracy overall.

Paper 4 Writing

Sample translation into French

Read the sample sentences for translation into French and the annotations. Cover the bottom half of this page and try translating the sentences before you check the sample answers.

> Translate the following sentences into **French**.   [10 marks]
>
> I want to tell you a very funny joke. ←
>
> We have noticed a change in her behaviour recently. ←
>
> I have just won a prize at school for my work. ←
>
> → It is not necessary to charge your new phone every day.
>
> Young people are going to fight against this problem by protesting.

EXAM TIP ✔
Think about translating chunks of language or phrases rather than individual words.

Be careful with the word order here.

The word for 'her' needs to agree with the masculine noun that follows it.

Remember to translate the negative here.

Use *en* + the present participle to translate the phrase 'by protesting'.

Don't try to translate this word for word. Use the structure *venir de* + infinitive (to have just done) in the present tense in French.

Sample translation answers

Here are possible translations for each of the sentences:

> Je veux te raconter une blague très amusante / drôle.
>
> Nous avons remarqué un changement dans son comportement récemment.
>
> Je viens de gagner un prix au collège pour mon travail.
>
> Il n'est pas nécessaire de recharger ton / votre nouveau portable tous les jours / chaque jour.
>
> Les jeunes vont / La jeunesse va lutter contre ce problème en manifestant.

EXAM TIP ✔
There is often more than one correct way to translate something into French.

Five marks are awarded for getting the meaning across. The mark scheme for this is applied by breaking the sentences down into fifteen elements (around three for each sentence) and awarding a tick for each. If you get 13–15 ticks, you are awarded the full five marks.

A further five marks are awarded for knowledge of vocabulary and grammar. This mark is based on all five sentences as a whole. Your vocabulary and grammar doesn't have to be perfect to be awarded the full five marks, but there should only be minor errors.

Section B: 90-word answer

In Section B:

- You will have a choice of tasks and should answer **either** question 2.1 **or** question 2.2.
- You must write something about each of the three bullet point prompts in your chosen task.
- You will need to use verbs in different time frames and give opinions.
- You should aim to write about 90 words.
- There are 10 marks for communication and development of ideas.
- There are 5 marks for variety of language and grammatical complexity.

EXAM TIP

You don't need to spend time in the exam counting every word you write as everything you write will be marked. Aim to answer the question fully, to the best of your ability, in the time you have allocated to Section B.

LINK

To practise 90-word tasks, go to pages 55, 79 and 118.

Section C: 150-word answer

In Section C:

- You will have a choice of tasks and should answer **either** question 3.1 **or** question 3.2.
- You must write something about both bullet point prompts in your chosen task.
- You will need to use a variety of language, including some more complex structures.
- You should aim to write about 150 words.
- There are 15 marks for communication and development of ideas.
- There are 10 marks for variety of language and grammatical complexity.

EXAM TIP

Spend a few minutes planning your answer, noting some French vocabulary and grammatical structures for each bullet point.

Sample 150-word task

You are writing an article about relationships with others.

Your article is for a French well-being website.

Write approximately **150** words in **French**.

You must write something about both bullet points.

Describe:

- the importance of good relationships
- how you will create a positive social life in the future. **[25 marks]**

EXAM TIP

To help organise your writing, you could write three paragraphs of about 50 words each. This answer has two paragraphs for bullet point 1 and one paragraph for bullet point 2.

Paper 4 Writing

Sample 150-word answer

Read the sample answer to the 150-word task and the annotations on it.
This answer would score the full 25 marks.

EXAM TIP 🎯

You don't have to just use French words that are on AQA's set vocabulary list for your answer. If you use words that aren't on the set vocabulary list, you won't be awarded more marks.

This paragraph uses a variety of vocabulary, for example different words for friends and for relationships.

Try and include a negative structure.

Using *en envoyant* (by sending) helps to extend the sentence.

Use connectives like *mais* and *donc* to develop your ideas.

Using *après avoir* + a past participle as a sentence starter is one way to develop a more complex sentence.

The time phrase *À l'avenir* and the simple future tense (*il sera*) make it clear that this relates to the second bullet point of this task.

Avoir un bon rapport avec les autres est très important dans la vie. Pour les jeunes, les relations entre amis sont une partie essentielle de la vie quotidienne. Même si tu ne t'entends pas toujours bien avec ta famille, tes copains sont toujours là pour toi.

J'apprécie beaucoup ma meilleure copine, qui est très sympa et sensible. Nous sommes amies depuis trois ans. Je sais qu'elle ne me blesserait jamais et je peux lui parler de tout. Après avoir passé du temps avec elle, je me sens toujours mieux. Il n'y a jamais de conflit entre nous.

À l'avenir, je pense qu'il sera important de faire un effort pour garder mes amis d'école. Nous pouvons rester en contact en nous envoyant des messages mais rien ne peut remplacer une longue conversation. J'aimerais aussi rencontrer de nouveaux amis donc je vais m'inscrire à un club sportif.

Here is a translation of the answer:

Having a good relationship with others is very important in life. For young people, relationships between friends are an essential part of daily life. Even if you don't always get on well with your family, your friends are always there for you.

I really appreciate my best friend, who is very kind and sensitive. We have been friends for three years. I know that she would never hurt me and I can talk to her about everything. After having spent time with her, I always feel better. There is never any conflict between us.

In the future, I think that it will be important to make an effort to keep my school friends. We can stay in contact by sending each other messages but nothing can replace a long conversation. I would also like to meet new friends, so I am going to join a sports club.

Retrieval

Answer the questions below. Cover the answers column with a piece of paper and write down as many answers as you can. Check and repeat.

Questions

Answers

1 What do the three different sections of the Writing paper consist of?

Translation into French; 90-word answer; 150-word answer

2 Which section of the Writing paper should you spend most time on and why?

Section C because it is worth 25 marks out of 50 for the whole paper

3 Do you have to answer every question in the Writing paper?

No – there is a choice of question options for sections B and C

4 How long does the Writing paper last?

1 hour 15 minutes

5 Is this statement true or false: There is only one correct way to translate the sentences in section A of the Writing paper?

False – there may be more than one way to correctly translate certain words or phrases

6 How many bullet point prompts will there be for the 90-word task?

Three

7 How many bullet point prompts will there be for the 150-word task?

Two

8 Is this statement true or false: You can get full marks without responding to all the bullet points in the Writing paper?

False

9 Will you lose marks for writing fewer words or more words than recommended in the Writing paper?

No. However, very short answers may not contain enough content and over-long answers may contain more mistakes

10 Will you get more marks for using French words that are not on AQA's set vocabulary list?

No but you can use other words (where appropriate) if you wish to

Put paper here

Previous questions

Use the questions below to check your knowledge from previous chapters.

Questions

Answers

1 Translate into French: Let's go there.

On y va

2 How long will you have to prepare the exam materials before the Speaking paper starts?

15 minutes' supervised preparation time

3 What language should you use to write your answers in the Reading paper?

English

Put paper here

Practice EXAM

Paper 4 Writing

Section A: Translation into French

1. Translate the following sentences into **French**. [10 marks]

My parents' bedroom is bigger than our lounge.

....

I am going to travel to a foreign country in order to study.

....

When he was little, my brother used to hate green vegetables.

....

I have never wanted to be famous because I am shy.

....

In my opinion, you cannot succeed without working hard.

....

EXAM TIP

Underline all the verbs and identify which tense is needed in the context of each sentence.

Section B

Answer **either** Question 2.1 **or** Question 2.2

Either

Question 2.1

You are writing a blog about healthy living.

Write approximately **90** words in **French**.

You must write something about each bullet point.

Describe:

* what you like to eat and drink
* a recent activity you did to relax
* what you are going to do to improve your health in the future. [15 marks]

Or

Question 2.2

You are writing an article about places to visit.

Write approximately **90** words in **French**.

You must write something about each bullet point.

Describe:

* activities for tourists in your area
* a recent event in your area
* an interesting place that you will visit in the future. [15 marks]

EXAM TIP

You don't have to write the same amount about each bullet point, as long as you cover everything required by the task.

EXAM TIP

You can give opinions in different tenses and in different ways to add variety to your writing.

EXAM TIP

Use some other forms of the verb as well as *je* forms.

Section C

Answer **either** Question 3.1 **or** Question 3.2

Either

Question 3.1

You are writing an article for a French website.

Your article is about holidays.

Write approximately **150** words in **French**.

You must write something about both bullet points.

Describe:

- the importance of holidays
- where you would like to travel in the future.

[25 marks]

Or

Question 3.2

You are writing a blog about traditional celebrations.

Your post is designed for people who are not familiar with local traditions.

Write approximately **150** words in **French**.

You must write something about both bullet points.

Describe:

- the positive aspects of celebrating a traditional festival or event
- how you have celebrated a special event or tradition in the past.

[25 marks]

> **EXAM TIP** ⊙
>
> When writing about the importance of holidays, you don't have to mention going away. You can also write about the school holidays or a break from work.

> **EXAM TIP** ⊙
>
> Try to organise your ideas logically, using sequencers like *d'abord* (firstly), *ensuite* (next) and *enfin* (finally).

⚙ Knowledge

Sound-spelling links

Here is a list of the sound-spelling links included within the specification. You need to learn these to be able to complete the dictation task (Paper 1: Listening) and the reading aloud task (Paper 2: Speaking).

Scan the QR code to listen to and practise the example words provided for each sound.

Sound	Examples
silent final consonant	nou**s** somme**s**, effor**t**
a	**a**rriver, **a**vec, **a**nimal
i / y	ph**y**sique, publ**i**c, il **y** a
eu	d**eu**x, un p**eu**, danger**eu**x
e	l**e**, d**e**, m**e**
au / eau / closed o / ô	s**au**f, b**eau**, n**o**s, c**ô**te
ou	v**ou**s, t**ou**j**ou**rs, s**ou**vent
u	t**u**, d**u**r, conn**u**
silent final e	drôl**e**, jeun**e**, chaqu**e**
é (-er, -ez)	**é**té, all**er**, mang**ez**
en / an / em / am	excell**en**t, gr**an**d, **em**bêt**an**t, j**am**be
on / om	m**on**, n**on**, t**om**ber, c**om**bien
ain / in / aim / im	dem**ain**, **in**telligent, f**aim**, **im**portant
è / ê / ai	m**è**re, t**ê**te, m**ai**s
oi / oy	t**oi**, p**oi**sson, v**oy**age, m**oy**en
ch	**ch**er, mar**ch**é, pro**ch**ain
ç (and soft 'c')	fran**ç**ais, le**ç**on, **c**ette, **ci**toyen
qu	**qu**el, musi**qu**e, puis**qu**e
j	**j**e, **j**ouer, **j**eune
-tion	pollu**tion**, situa**tion**
-ien	b**ien**, canad**ien**, végétar**ien**
s-liaison	le**s** animaux, no**s** amis
t-liaison	peti**t** hôtel, hui**t** ans
n-liaison	u**n** ami, bo**n** achat
x-liaison	di**x** heures, deu**x** actions
h	**h**omme, **h**ôpital, **h**abitant
un	br**un**, l**un**di, empr**un**ter
-gn-	monta**gn**e, ga**gn**er, campa**gn**e
r	**r**ouge, **r**ester, comp**r**end**r**e
open eu / œu	s**œu**r, c**œu**r, l**eu**r, n**eu**f
open o	al**o**rs, p**o**rte, s**o**rtir
-s-	télévi**s**ion, mai**s**on
th	**th**é, bibli**oth**èque, ma**th**s
-ill- / -ille	fam**ill**e, b**ill**et, f**ill**e
-aill- / ail	trav**ail**, t**aill**e, **ail**leurs

Notes

Notes

Notes

OXFORD
UNIVERSITY PRESS

Great Clarendon Street, Oxford, OX2 6DP, United Kingdom

Oxford University Press is a department of the University of Oxford.
It furthers the University's objective of excellence in research, scholarship,
and education by publishing worldwide. Oxford is a registered trade mark
of Oxford University Press in the UK and in certain other countries.

Written by Sheena Newland
The moral rights of the author has been asserted

First published in 2025

British Library Cataloguing in Publication Data
Data available

978-1-38-207019-5
978-1-38-207018-8 (eBook)

10 9 8 7 6 5 4 3 2 1

The manufacturing process conforms to the environmental regulations
of the country of origin.

Printed in the UK by Bell & Bain

The manufacturer's authorised representative in the EU for product
safety is Oxford University Press España S.A. of El Parque Empresarial
San Fernando de Henares, Avenida de Castilla, 2 – 28830 Madrid
(www.oup.es/en or product.safety@oup.com). OUP España S.A. also
acts as importer into Spain of products made by the manufacturer.

Acknowledgements

The publisher would like to thank Sheena Newland and Eve Hedley for
sharing their expertise and feedback in the development of this resource.

Photos: p22(l): imtmphoto / Shutterstock; **p22(r)**: Lomb / Shutterstock;
p52(t): popcorner / Shutterstock; **p52(b)**: Gorodenkoff / Shutterstock;
p76(t): gorodenkoff / iStock / Getty Images; **p76(b)**: Studio Romantic /
Shutterstock; **p115(t)**: Ground Picture / Shutterstock; **p115(b)**: BJ Day
Stock / Shutterstock; **p175(t)**: Hananeko_Studio / Shutterstock; **p175(b)**:
SeventyFour / Shutterstock; **p179(t)**: KOTOIMAGES / Shutterstock;
p179(b): RossHelen / Shutterstock.

Artwork by QBS Learning

Every effort has been made to contact copyright holders of material
reproduced in this book. Any omissions will be rectified in subsequent
printings if notice is given to the publisher.

MIX
Paper | Supporting
responsible forestry
FSC
www.fsc.org   FSC® C007785